It is a hot summer evening. I am sitting on the steps in front of the house on Miller Drive. I am alone. I have played hard all day. I'm dirty all over and my mouth is sticky with dried Popsicle. I'm wearing nothing but a pair of underpants. In the house behind me, I feel a sense of unease.

Somehow, I was aware as a small child that people in that house loved me, but that things were not right. Things could easily spin out of control. I knew it had something to do with my mother...

MY MOTHER'S KEEPER is a daughter's wrenching story of growing up with a schizophrenic mother, with haunting memories of a woman who drifted in and out of her life like a fading fairy princess. By the time Tara Holley turned seventeen, she had become her mother's guardian, bent on rescuing the shambling street person her mother had become and turning her back into the beautiful, lively woman Tara remembered.

In this dramatic and inspiring memoir, Tara recounts her struggle over the years: reckoning with the pain and denial that has permeated three generations of her family, pursuing the elusive hope of a cure, and surviving the days of despair, joy, rage and love. MY MOTHER'S KEEPER is a deeply moving exploration of the mother-daughter bond—of how Tara learned to balance her mother's needs with her own, and of how she finally came to terms with her family legacy after the birth of her own child. Here is a towering testament to the power of love to transcend tragedy.

A Selection of the Literary Guild®

My Mother's Keeper

A DAUGHTER'S MEMOIR
OF GROWING UP IN THE
SHADOW OF SCHIZOPHRENIA

TARA ELGIN HOLLEY
WITH JOE HOLLEY

AN AVON BOOK

Some of the names in this book have been changed. Each of these pseudonyms appears for the first time in the text with an asterisk.

Permissions constituting a continuation of the copyright page appear on page 368.

AVON BOOKS, INC.
1350 Avenue of the Americas
New York, New York 10019

Published in hardcover by William Morrow and Company, Inc.; for information address Permissions Department, William Morrow and Company, Inc., 1350 Avenue of the Americas, New York, New York 10019.

The William Morrow edition contains the following Library of Congress Cataloging in Publication Data:
Holley, Tara Elgin, 1951-
    My mother's keeper : a daughter's memoir of growing up in the shadow of schizophrenia / Tara Elgin Holley, with Joe Holley.
    p.   cm.
    1. Elgin, Dawn.   2. Schizophrenics—United States—Biography.   3. Holley, Tara Elgin, 1951-   .   4. Schizophrenics—United States—Family relationships.   I. Holley, Joe, 1946-   II. Title.
RC514.H595   1997
616.89´82´0092—dc20   96-32114
[B]   CIP

First Bard Printing: July 1998

BARD TRADEMARK REG. U.S. PAT. OFF. AND IN OTHER COUNTRIES, MARCA REGISTRADA, HECHO EN U.S.A.

Printed in the U.S.A.

OPM 10 9 8 7 6 5 4 3 2 1

For Dawn

Acknowledgments

I wish to thank my family, teachers, friends, and the professionals who sustained me through a forty-year history of living with and growing toward an understanding of what it means to have a deeply loved and always desired—no matter how inaccessible—mother with a devastating mental illness.

Thanks to my great-great-aunt Elsa, for the books, the music, the images, and the gardens that filled me up and gave me both a childhood and a place to retreat to whenever I needed it. Thank you for never seeming afraid, though you must have been. To my sweet grandparents, thank you for the hope and the dreams. To the beloved members of the Elgin family—and in particular my aunts Marian, Betty Lee, and Sally—my love and gratitude for being willing to live through the telling of this story again.

Thanks also to the close friends and supporters of this story, without whom it would never have been told: Leah and Arthur Ollman, Robert Abzug, Sherrill Tippins, and Robert Mecoy. To Jerry Frampton, Beth Covey, and Dr. Mark Longley, mental health professionals who went beyond the call of duty. Especially to Peg McCuistion who, after reading the original excerpt of Dawn's story in *Texas Monthly*, gave me back whole parts of my mother's life, affirming what I had felt was true all along. Thank you, Eddie Klonhauer! Also to Roy Flukinger, curator of the photography collection of the Harry Ransom Humanities Research Center for use of the collection.

Immediate family sustained us. As we've been working, Heather and Rachel have grown more stunning and perceptive, each in her own distinct ways. Pete and Kate have never ceased to delight and to ask difficult questions. Writing this book was an ongoing battle for my partner-in-telling. I am eternally grateful to him for the dialogue we shared about a story that often seemed too difficult to tell.

A final expression of affection goes to the lovely young woman with the resonant voice who had so much of her life taken from her but still left me the gift of imagining. This book is dedicated to you. Thank you for telling this story with us, for other families.

—Tara Elgin Holley

It was our San Diego friends Leah and Arthur Ollman who insisted that Dawn and Tara's story was one worth telling, and that literary agent Sandy Dijkstra, the best in the West, would immediately see its worth.

Arthur and Leah were right about the story and about the indefatigable Sandy, whose persistence and support made this book possible, but they couldn't have known how difficult it would be to re-create Dawn's life and Tara's—lives shaped by the most frustratingly inscrutable of illnesses, schizophrenia. More people than I can name helped us through the process of transforming letters, diaries, and the spoken word—as well as the unspoken word—into a book. I am grateful for their many kindnesses.

Thanks to Charlotte Abbott, my editor at Avon, who believed in the book. Thanks also to Greg Curtis and Katie Flato at *Texas*

Monthly and to two fine writers, John Davidson and Elizabeth Crook, who read the manuscript and made thoughtful and astute suggestions. Thanks also to Jerry Frampton, a friend and mental health professional who helped us assure accuracy about mental illness and its treatment. Any mistakes that remain, of course, are my responsibility.

I am indebted to Tara's aunts—Betty Lee, Sally, and Marian—who welcomed me into their family years ago and who were never less than patient, generous, and forthcoming in response to my frequent questionings. Sharing a life is always an act of generosity; for Tara's aunts, it was an act of courage as well. I am grateful.

I am also grateful to their beloved sister. Dawn has not only allowed us to tell her story, but she has cooperated in every way possible so that others may know the human side of the cruelest disease imaginable. I applaud her bravery, and as a son-in-law I am grateful for her love and affection.

I am also grateful to my immediate family—to Peter and Kate, who endured their parents' years-long preoccupation with "the book" and to Heather and Rachel, who helped us remember. I am grateful to my parents and to my brothers Ken and Steve, who were always encouraging.

Most of all, I am indebted to Tara, who endured my reporter's probing and my obtuseness and who would settle for nothing less than the real story in all its richness. Through the talking, the writing, the arguing, and the struggle, we've survived—together. Thanks, my love, for everything.

—Joe Holley

Acknowledgments

At most we're allowed a few months
of simply listening to the simple line
of a woman's voice singing a child
against her heart. Everything else is too soon,
too sudden, the wrenching-apart, that woman's heartbeat
heard ever after from a distance,
the loss of that ground-note echoing
whenever we are happy, or in despair.

—Adrienne Rich, "Transcendental Etude"

I see thy glory like a shooting star
Fall to the base earth
From the firmament.

—*Richard II*, II. iv. 19

O the mind, mind has mountains; cliffs
of fall
Frightful, sheer, no-man-fathomed. Hold
them cheap
May who ne'er hung there.

—Gerard Manley Hopkins (Sonnet No. 42)
["No Worst, There Is None"]

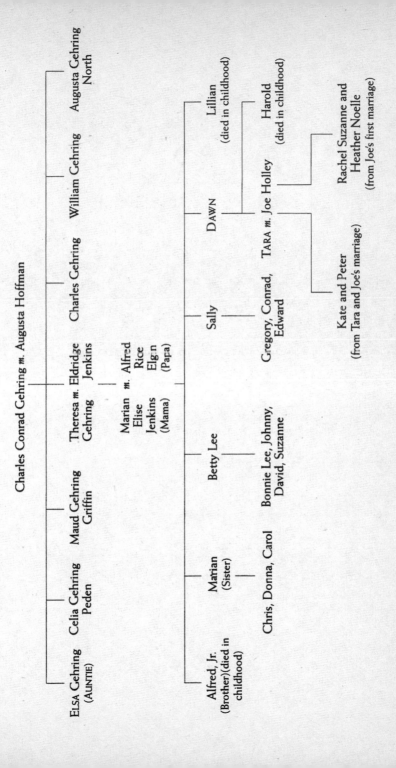

PROLOGUE

I knew Dawn before I knew her name. I knew her before I knew her story.

I knew Dawn the way you would know any stringy-haired, leathery-faced woman who sold flowers and cadged cigarettes on the street. I knew her as the bag lady who wore layer on layer of tattered, foul-smelling clothes, even when the Texas sun beat down without mercy. I knew her as the gap-toothed woman, agitated and confused, who shuffled up and down Guadalupe Street carrying on intense, animated conversations with herself.

I saw her almost every day, the way I saw other men and women who huddled in a church doorway across the street from campus or gathered in the mornings waiting for the plasma center to open so they could sell their blood. I saw her without really seeing her. Where she went at night or how she got to be the disturbed—and disturbing—person she was, I didn't know, but I knew her.

At least, I thought I did. Like most of us, I glanced at her, felt a twinge of pity, and turned away. Or tried to. With Dawn, fortunately, it was not to be that simple.

1

*   *   *

It was late summer, 1980, not long after I had left Dallas and moved to Austin with my two young daughters. Austin, I hoped, would nurture a new start for the three of us. What the girls hoped, at ages nine and ten, I wasn't really sure; they didn't talk much about the ordeal their parents had put them through.

After breakfast one sunny Sunday morning, the three of us wandered into a bookstore, a good bookstore I could tell after looking around a few minutes. A dark-haired young woman came over and asked if we needed help. She was pleasant and pretty and helped the girls find what they wanted: a book about knot tying for Heather, *Pippi Longstocking* for Rachel. I decided right then we would be regular patrons.

The next Saturday evening, the girls and I were out exploring our new city. We were drawn by the sound of music into a small outdoor amphitheater near the state capitol. It was strange music—to my ears, at least. It was like something Chaucer would have listened to.

On a natural stone stage, across a trickling stream from where we sat, three earnest-looking men and a woman were playing music on odd-looking instruments. The singer was the same young woman who had waited on us at the bookstore. She sang lilting songs in German, French, Italian, and Middle English, accompanied (I would learn) by hurdy-gurdy, gamba, and sackbut. She sang a sprightly, tongue-twisting piece in Basque about a baker hawking his wares.

The concert ended, and two sleepy girls were tugging on my hands to leave, but I looked around until I found a printed program. The singer's name, I read, was Tara Elgin.

I called on Monday. We had lunch on Tuesday. She was

raised in Houston, Tara told me, although she had been born in New York City and had lived in Hollywood until she was six. She was a classically trained musician who had been singing medieval and renaissance music for several years and was working at the bookstore to put herself through graduate school in ethnomusicology.

Her dream, Tara told me in one of our early conversations, was to sing jazz like Sarah Vaughan—or like her mother had sung.

"I never knew my father," she said, "and my mother has been in and out of institutions most of my life. I was raised by a great-great-aunt."

We were sitting on the grass outside the three-story Victorian house where Tara had an apartment. Workmen remodeling the second floor had left a hand-lettered sign on a sawhorse by the front door. ENTER AT YOUR OWN RISK, it said. I had gladly ignored it.

"Was your mother famous?" I asked. "Have I heard her sing?"

"No, she got sick before she made it big. But she was good; she was very good. I used to have some of her records."

Her mother, Tara said, was a chronic paranoid schizophrenic. Schizophrenic? I knew the word, but like most people, I thought schizophrenia had something to do with split personality—someone like Sybil, or Eve with her three faces, or Jekyll and Hyde.

"That's not what schizophrenia is," Tara informed me. I could hear the exasperation in her voice; she probably got tired of people's ignorance. The split, she explained, refers to a disintegration of personality, not a split into separate personalities. Tara didn't seem particularly eager to talk about her mother, so I didn't press her.

My own ignorance embarrassed me. I wanted to impress this attractive, accomplished woman. But I had to admit I knew little about mental illness. As a journalist who frequently wrote about social issues, I had read enough about "deinstitutionalization" to know something about the public policy debate concerning institutional care versus community care, but my experience with mental illness was limited. To tell the truth, the whole notion frightened me.

I remembered when the highway through Austin passed by the state hospital, the insane asylum we called it. As children sitting in the backseat of the car on trips to our grandmother's house in Big Foot, near San Antonio, my brothers and I would peer through the tall iron gate as we drove by. We were hoping to see a crazy person, a lunatic, gripping the barred windows and shrieking to get out.

I remembered a great-uncle, Uncle Alva, who lived in a veterans' hospital. He had been in World War I. "Shell-shocked," people would say, shaking their heads. The one time I saw him, he was quiet and withdrawn, but he wasn't noticeably disturbed.

I had much to learn—about a family, about mental illness, about a woman whose bright and shimmering mind had broken, like shattered glass, into countless pieces.

As late summer passed into fall, Heather and Rachel seemed to be adjusting well, perhaps because Tara was becoming a part of our daily lives. She helped the girls with their piano lessons and cooked exotic meals she had perfected during her years in Europe. Most everything she prepared was a welcome relief from my hapless-looking "pizza faces" and the gummy one-pan spaghetti dishes I had learned from a single-fathers cookbook someone had given me.

Most important, she was helping us put our lives back together, helping us be a family again.

One Friday evening, we pinned little name tags on the girls, gave them hugs, and handed them over to a smiling Southwest Airlines stewardess. They were looking forward to spending the weekend with their mother in Dallas. Late that night, Tara and I dropped by her apartment to pick up some of her things.

It was a warm night, a beautiful night, but as we walked across the yard and stepped onto the porch, we could tell something was wrong. Empty beer cans were scattered about, and as we started to unlock the door, we could see that it had been forced open. I could feel the hair on the back of my neck prickle and my stomach tighten. Was the burglar still inside? Did he have a gun? Should we hurry away and call the police?

As we slowly pushed open the door and peered into the darkness of the living room, I smelled the stabbing odor of urine and stale beer and an unwashed human being. In the darkness, I could barely make out someone sitting on the floor, someone mumbling incoherently.

I was scared, but Tara wasn't. She was angry and upset, not scared. She knew who had invaded her home, her well-ordered life. It was her mother waiting in the darkness. It was Dawn.

"You're going back to the hospital now," Tara told her mother, her voice near tears. "I can't have you breaking into my house like this. And I can't have you wandering around on the street. It's going to get cold, and you have to have a place to stay."

I watched as Dawn pulled away from her daughter and drifted outside into the dark.

"Should we follow her?" I asked, putting my arms around a tearful Tara. "Do we try to bring her back?"

She shook her head. "It's no use," she said. "You have no idea how often this happens. As much as I hate it, she'd rather be on the street than in a hospital."

Later that night, after Dawn had drifted off into the night to sleep God knew where, after Tara and I had cleaned up the apartment and had talked for hours about her mother's illness, I still had questions—questions that I asked myself, mostly.

My Mother's Keeper

I kept returning to the same thought: How could this be? How could the pathetic, tattered wreck of a woman standing in Tara's yard mumbling gibberish be the beautiful young woman I had seen in photographs that Tara kept in a box in her closet? How could this woman who spent her nights sleeping on flattened cardboard boxes behind a U-Tote-Em convenience store, who spent her days panhandling on street corners, be the same woman who had sung before adoring audiences in Hollywood?

What dark path had led her to the condition in which she now existed? And who, in her present condition, was she? What did she know and feel? What did she remember about those early years? Was she in pain? Could anything be done?

Lying there sleepless, my mind latched on to more immediate worries—worries about Dawn's daughter, this woman I was falling in love with, who was becoming a mother to my little girls. If Dawn was schizophrenic, could Tara—a thought too hideous to imagine—descend into madness? Could the pretty, intelligent face I had come to know melt and run into the ravaged face of her mother?

What if we eventually married and had kids of our own? Would we lose them some day to the demons that taunted Dawn?

"It's frightening to see a person in such a state," I remember saying as we did the dishes one evening after dinner. I had in mind my own mother's reaction as the two of us drove down Guadalupe one Sunday morning on the way to church. She was visiting for a few days to help with the girls.

"That's Tara's mother," I had said, nodding toward the woman selling flowers on the corner. Dawn was wearing a dirty gray man's sport coat and a Day-Glo green cap with an oversized gold pin stuck through the crown. Shifting from one foot to another, a bouquet of red rosebuds in her hand, she was grinning crazily and talking to herself.

Tara Elgin Holley with Joe Holley

6

My mother's mouth dropped open. She briefly covered her eyes with her hands, and then looked at me. "I wish you hadn't shown me," she said, and as the light turned green, she looked back at Dawn.

"It's not just me," I told Tara, handing her a plate to dry. "It's frightening to anybody."

Tara shook her head angrily. "What are you afraid of?" she asked, rubbing the plate hard with a dish towel. "People like my mother aren't going to hurt you. You don't know them. You haven't taken the time to know them."

I turned off the water and looked at her piercing brown eyes. They were shooting sparks straight at me. She *had* been around them, I knew. She had spent her weekends behind the walls of that very institution my brothers and I had stared at. She had worked as a volunteer, giving the patients baths and medication. She had helped dress and feed them. She had cleaned up after them. She had spent much of her adult life trying to reach her mother.

I looked out the kitchen window at the remnants of our summer garden, the corn stalks now yellow and bent. I tried to think of a way to explain.

"It's not the people themselves," I said, trying to choose my words carefully. "I'm not afraid they're going to come at me with an ax or something. It's the idea, the fear, of losing control. I mean, look at your mother in those pictures you have, and then look at her now. You tell me that's not frightening? That something like that could happen to you or me? To Heather or Rachel?"

Out of the corner of my eye, I saw a blond head peek around the kitchen door. Heather was supposed to be doing her homework at the dining room table, but our raised voices had disturbed her.

My Mother's Keeper

7

She too had met Dawn, just a few days earlier. Tara had taken the girls to Baskin-Robbins, and as they sat inside the store enjoying their ice cream cones, a bag lady shuffled in.

"Oh no, not you again," the young man behind the counter exclaimed. "I told you I'd call the police," he said, walking toward the phone on the wall.

Heather and Rachel watched, surprised, as Tara quickly walked over to the woman and began talking to her in a quiet voice. With her hands on the woman's shoulders, she began steering her gently toward the door. When the woman shuffled out and walked off down the street, the man thanked Tara.

"What am I supposed to do with these people?" he said, bending over the freezer for another scoop of ice cream. "They come in here, they stink up the place, they scare my customers away. I've had to call the cops twice on that ol' gal alone."

Tara began to usher the girls out the door. "They *are* human beings," she said as she walked out. The man stared after her.

"Who was that?" the girls asked after they got into the van.

"That was my mother," Tara said. She said it matter-of-factly, with no further explanation.

Heather and Rachel didn't know what to say. They looked at each other and back at Tara. She was sitting behind the wheel, staring straight ahead. She was angry, in tears.

What the girls had witnessed had happened so many times over the years. No one seemed to understand.

I have been trying to understand for more than a decade. In the years that Tara and I have been married, I've learned a lot—and I'm still learning about this cruelest of diseases. I've learned that it's not just the terrifying loss of control or the social oppro-

Tara Elgin Holley with Joe Holley

brium born of ignorance that makes it so cruel. It's the fact that schizophrenia often strikes in late adolescence or early adulthood—as with Dawn—just when a person's hopes and expectations are at their height. It shatters those expectations, and the pain and the terror are so great that sufferers often resort to suicide. Schizophrenia distorts the mind so profoundly that many victims never make their way back to reality.

I've learned that schizophrenia, the most serious mental illness, is more common than most of us realize. It strikes as many as 1 in every 100 people during their lifetimes. Some 2.5 million Americans suffer from the disease. One quarter of all the hospital beds in this country are filled by people with schizophrenia. More than half of all those discharged from Veterans Administration hospitals are diagnosed with the disease. Most studies estimate that at least 40 percent of the people we see lying on heat grates or curled up in doorways are schizophrenic.

Wandering our streets lost and alone, they are the visibly mentally ill. But, during the time that Tara and I have been writing and talking about mental illness, I've discovered that more people than I ever imagined have been touched by mental illness in their family. They are usually very reluctant to talk about it. One out of four families in America have had some experience with this disease that tears families apart, that destroys dreams and ambitions.

Tara's friend Sonia tells about her mother, who is schizophrenic. With our friend Greg, it is a brother; his aging parents still look after him. Carl, my colleague at work, tells about his schizophrenic mother; she buried eggs in the front yard when he was growing up "because someone had poisoned them." Mary's son has been schizophrenic since he was eighteen; now he's thirty-five, and she and her husband are still trying to care for him. So many people have stories, but they usually don't share them, since they are painfully aware of the stigma of mental illness.

Beyond the numbers, I've learned how devastating mental illness can be, not just to the individual but to families and friends and loved ones. I've watched Tara and her aunts ponder and scheme and plan, trying to figure out the best way to care for Dawn. She has been their charge for more than forty years; in the years I have been part of the family, I've come to understand their pain.

I've seen their frustration when they allow themselves to think now and then about how the person they knew and loved, even idolized, is somehow locked away from them. She is dead, but not dead. Dawn's life has been taken from her.

Family members also are painfully aware that schizophrenics try to kill themselves with frightening regularity. As many as half of those with schizophrenia attempt suicide, especially in the early years after diagnosis. Between 10 and 15 percent succeed.

Dawn fits the pattern. She has made two attempts to take her own life.

Family members also know something else. They know that schizophrenia, despite being a tragedy, has its moments of relief. That's hard to understand, even harder to explain without sounding deluded.

I think about a young woman named Tina whom Tara and I met in a seminar for families of schizophrenics. We were talking one night about the importance of hope to a person who has schizophrenia and how family members summon the strength to go on caring. Tina, whose brother is schizophrenic, raised her hand. Ordinarily, the slender, dark-haired woman didn't talk much in class, and she was hesitant on this night.

Tara Elgin Holley with Joe Holley
10

"I feel like my brother is a gift to me in that way," she said slowly, groping for the right words. "Because of him, the rest of us get more out of life. It's not like he tries to be sick. He's a gift."

Her voice trailed off, and I looked around at the circle of people. At the couple in their sixties whose forty-year-old son is schizophrenic. At the woman who has become mother to the eighteen-month-old daughter of her schizophrenic sister, along with her own four sons. At the woman whose father *and* son are schizophrenic. At the bright young woman whose older brother is mentally retarded and whose younger brother is schizophrenic. At the man in his thirties whose wife obeyed voices commanding her to chop off her hand.

Those people have suffered, are suffering, and yet many were nodding their heads in agreement as Tina spoke. Glancing at Tara, I caught a glint of tears and remembered what she has said about her mother's gift to her. Dawn gave her music, she says. If it hadn't been for her mother, she would never have been a singer.

Tara and the other members of the seminar were obviously moved by what Tina had said, as was I. They understood, but at that moment, I don't think I did. It was only after a member of my family came down with AIDS that I began to understand that the presence in your life of a family member who is suffering changes you, for the better. You can grieve over who they were, or who they could have been, or you can open yourself to who they are. Even as you hate the illness and what it is doing to your loved one, even as you wish with all your being that fate had dealt a different hand, you can still know that their presence in your life is, in fact, a gift.

I also thought of my gift from Dawn. The bright and engaging woman who is my wife, the mother to our children—has been integrally shaped by her experiences with her mother. This is her story, their story. It is the story of mothers and daughters.

Dawn's illness is indeed a tragedy. It's as cruel a fate as anyone can suffer. But as I have come to know Dawn and Tara and members of the family, I have come to understand that much more is involved. I know now that to tell Dawn's story is to tell of strong people—or rather people made strong by the pain and terror they have endured.

When Tara was a little girl, she fell in love with the works of George MacDonald, the nineteenth-century English author of folk and fairy tales. In *The Golden Key*, MacDonald tells of "the country whence the shadows fall." Sometimes I think that's where Tara and her mother are journeying, toward a country where shadows fall away and the light at last shines. The country is far away, and the journey is harrowing, and for Dawn, for now, it remains beyond the horizon. Perhaps it will always be, because in real life, unlike in fairy tales, good people don't always live happily ever after.

For Dawn and for her family, it's been a long journey; for others, it's just beginning. "It's a nightmare," I heard the mother of a schizophrenic young woman say not long ago. "It's just so unfair. Is this what we have to look forward to for the rest of our lives?"

It is unfair. Schizophrenia is a merciless and unrelenting foe, but more than ever there is reason to hope. Medications available today allow those who suffer from schizophrenia to live normal lives again, lives of freedom, dignity, and opportunity. People are increasingly aware that schizophrenia is a disease—that it's a medical issue and not a moral one—and that those who suffer from the disease deserve compassion and care. Today, there is reason to take hope in the continual progress of medical science.

Families dealing with schizophrenia need to know they are not alone. Many are journeying "toward the country whence the shadows fall." The journey is so very hard, but as Tara and I have learned, it's easier when we go forward together.

—Joe Holley
Austin, Texas

Great-grandparents Eldridge Jenkins and Theresa Gehring Jenkins with
daughter Marian Elise Jenkins, 1903.

CHAPTER ONE

"Put it down, Dawn." Papa is pleading in a voice so quiet I can barely hear. "Put the knife down."

I watch him half rise out of the old blue Windsor chair in the living room. His newspaper falls to the floor. I hear the old chair squeak as he stands.

"No!" I hear Mommy shout. I see her point the wooden-handled kitchen knife toward Mama, who sits in a chair near the fireplace. I see my grandmother's hands gripping the arm of the chair.

Mommy shakes her head. "I know who you are," she says in a low voice. "I know what you want!" Her eyes are open wide. She glances over her shoulder at the front door. I wonder if she will dash outside, into the darkness.

I am leaning against the hideaway bed. I want to go to my mommy, but I am afraid. I bury my head in the worn brown slipcover and close my eyes. I don't want to see.

My mother shouts, "No!" again, and when I look over my shoulder I see Papa trying to grab her arms, her shoulders.

Mommy twists out of my grandfather's grasp and runs across the room. She stumbles at Mama's feet. I see bright red blood on my grandmother's leg. My mother has run the knife down the front of Mama's leg.

Mama and Papa are kneeling on the floor with their arms around my mother. I see the knife on the floor beneath my grandmother's chair. My mother is crying, crying, crying.

I want to go to them. Instead, I hide my eyes on the bed. Then I feel my mother kneeling beside me, her head next to mine. I feel the wetness on her face.

My mother strokes my long hair. "Darling," she says. "Precious. Don't cry. It's okay. Everything's okay." She is smiling and crying at the same time.

She wants me to put my arms around her neck. I keep them tucked between the bed and my chest. I still feel afraid. I know that everything is not okay. I do not like what my mother is saying when she calls me "darling, precious." She is pretending that everything is fine. Everything is not fine.

I slept with Mama, my grandmother, that night. Mama's arms held me. Her soft, full voice lulled me to sleep, rocked me gently into a place that was soft and warm. Next morning, what had happened the night before seemed only a bad dream.

I must have been three years old. I remember wandering into the kitchen rubbing my eyes at the morning light, my long hair twisted and wild. There was Mama—that's what everyone called my grandmother—sitting at the kitchen table, her violin tucked under her chin. The tune she played, I learned, was "Alice Blue Gown."

Nothing strange about that. For all I knew, everybody's grandmother played the violin at breakfast or carried on conversations with sprites and fairies. That was Mama.

I remember crouching down and peering under the table at my grandmother's leg. Beneath the orange-brown stocking, knotted at her knee, I saw a bandage. No one mentioned what had happened the night before. I didn't ask.

Papa was standing at the kitchen stove pouring himself a cup of coffee. "Good morning to you, princess!" he said, his brown eyes twinkling. That's what he said every morning.

Papa was a big, comfortable pillow of a man, with a shiny, bald head and wisps of white hair that curled around his ears. He was the kind of grandfather a little girl could fold up into. In his arms, I felt protected.

"How's my little Tara?" he said. He lifted me onto the kitchen counter. On this morning, he was wearing his blue seersucker suit and a wide red tie. That was a good sign. It meant he was going downtown, and I would be going with him.

My mother did not come down to breakfast that morning, but her absence was not unusual. For me, my mother was more like the fairies who attended Sleeping Beauty; she drifted in and out of my life. I loved it when we were together. We sang songs, we played with dolls, we went for walks. But I never knew when she would go away for days. That's just the way it was.

Once, when I was three, she took me to MacArthur Park. It was a sunny afternoon. We were playing near the swings, when suddenly she was gone. We were playing hide-and-seek, but I didn't know where to find her. I looked behind trees. "Mommy!" I called, over and over. "Mommy. Mommy." She didn't come. I sat down on the grass and began to cry.

After a while, I saw two shiny black boots on the grass beside me, and I looked up toward the blue sky to see a police officer looking down. He knelt beside me and asked what was wrong. I told him I couldn't find my mommy. He took me by the hand, and we walked through the park, looking for my mother, calling her name. She would peer from behind a tree; I knew she would. She would be laughing and would run across the grass and scoop me into her arms. We kept searching, but she never did appear.

So the policeman put me in the front seat of his black-and-white patrol car and took me to the police station. I sat on a countertop, and policemen fed me ice cream until Papa came on the bus to pick me up. In a way, my search for Dawn, my mother, began that day and has never really ended.

I can't remember whether I knew my mother was sick when I was a little girl. I don't remember being told that she was in the hospital or going with Mama and Papa to visit her. I do remember that, more than anything, I wanted her in my life. I wanted the mommy who played the piano and sang to me, the mommy who, sometimes, would come into my room at night and hold me when I was frightened by the dark.

I learned, probably very early, that the mommy for whom I yearned might be there for me, and then again she might not. A sad mother, preoccupied and distant, might take her place. But, in a way, it didn't matter so much.

My mother was a madwoman. That's what people would have called her, had I heard them talking about her in the early stages of the illness, when young people, struck by this madness, struggle for a few short years against it, rage against it. Other ugly words might have been used: "Her mother is schizophrenic." It would be difficult to make up a word with a more jagged edge to it. Little children don't know what the big people mean when they talk that way. They do know that it feels scary and they are afraid that someone is going to take their mommy away, again. All I wanted was to be with her.

Tara Elgin Holley with Joe Holley

18

Nobody ever mentioned a father. If anyone had ever asked, I would have said that Papa was my father.

In 1951, the year I was born, Papa was in his eighties, more than twenty years older than Mama. He was retired, but from what I heard later, it seems he had always been retired. He had never held a job; he and Mama lived off their dwindling family holdings back in Houston.

I was glad, of course, that my grandfather didn't work. It meant he could spend all his time with me. He would read to me in his easy southern drawl, just as long as I was willing to sit still in his lap. He told me story after story about Davy Crockett and Jim Bowie and the old Texas Ranger Big Foot Wallace. I just naturally assumed they had been acquaintances of his.

"Ready to go, honey?" my grandfather asked after I had eaten a bit of breakfast on the morning after Mama had been hurt. Knowing Papa, he had fixed me a sugar-and-butter sandwich, on white bread, while my grandmother serenaded us on her violin.

On the back porch, I dug through the brown-paper packages of folded clothes from the laundry and found shorts and a T-shirt. Papa took his straw hat from the hat rack by the front door, and Mama gave us both a peck on the cheek. I skipped down the brick walk that switchbacked across the steeply sloping front yard while Papa followed along more slowly. I felt the warm morning sun on my face.

Mama and Papa's split-level house was perched on a steep hill that overlooked Hollywood. On our hill, it was like a tropical forest, with tall palm trees and flowers and dense foliage. I loved our neighborhood. At night we could look out the living room window and see the streaming lights of traffic on Sunset Boulevard below. Beyond Sunset, we could see the twinkling lights of Los

Angeles spread across the valley like a vast gleaming Milky Way. Maybe my grandparents, or maybe one of my aunts, told me that my mother had been a part of that life down the hill, that she sang in clubs on Sunset.

Hollywood, of course, meant nothing to me at the time. I learned later that my grandparents had purchased the house from Keenan Wynn and that illustrious neighbors lived all around us. The actor John Hodiak lived next door. The Kirk Douglas family lived up the hill. When I was older, my aunts liked to tell about the dimple-chinned actor himself strolling by with his young son Michael, the two of them on their way to a nearby park.

With Papa, the morning routine was to walk down the winding road to Sunset. We waited for the bus on the corner. It was only a short ride to Hollywood and Vine, where we got off and began our morning stroll. We walked for blocks taking in the sights, Papa leaning down to listen, occasionally responding while I chattered like a magpie. It was an uncle in Houston who later christened me Gabby; Papa would have laughed and agreed.

Papa, I would come to understand, was not the most practical of men. If a panhandler approached us on the street, Papa wouldn't think twice. He would give him whatever he could spare, even though he and Mama were practically on welfare themselves. They would eventually have to sell the house on Miller Drive. "No need to worry," he would say if anyone questioned his generosity. "God will provide."

Walking along the crowded street, we dropped in on Papa's friends and acquaintances. He knew every shopkeeper, every clerk, every waitress. He stopped to buy a newspaper at a sidewalk stand, and the man behind the counter said, "Morning, Mr. Elgin."

We stepped into a coffee shop, and the waitress greeted him with, "Good morning, Mr. Elgin! And how are you, sugar?" she said to me. I began spinning around on a red plastic counter stool.

Tara Elgin Holley with Joe Holley

Our next stop down the street was See's Candy Shop. I had to stand on tiptoe to see the dark chocolates and the pieces of heavenly white divinity candy stacked in miniature towers on plates behind the glass. It was almost impossible to decide what to have, but Papa was patient.

We had a hot dog for lunch at a little stand with picnic tables out front. I was tired and grumpy by then, and Papa had to carry me. When the bus deposited us at the foot of Miller Drive, he trudged up the steep hill with me asleep on his shoulder.

At home, we would find Mama sitting in the living room before her easel, working with her oil paints. She looked fresh and beautiful, as always. Petite, with salt-and-pepper hair cut short, she wore a flowery, see-through dress. She would turn from her easel and take her sleepy, sweaty little grandchild into her arms. Mama always smelled good.

She and Papa were devoted Christian Scientists. They regularly rode the bus to services at the Christian Science church, an imposing columned edifice on Highland Avenue. One Wednesday night, I stood on a chair in front of the congregation and gave my personal testimony about the power of prayer. I spoke loudly and clearly, with just a hint, I suspect, of a five-year-old's lisp. A front tooth had just come out, with Papa's patient, gentle help.

"My Papa was very sick," I gravely explained, looking out at the congregation. "I prayed for him every night, and God made him well."

For Mama and Papa, Christian Science, with its focus on living in a spiritual realm of absolute divine love, meshed perfectly with their devotion to the "higher things"—with art and literature and music. Though I didn't realize it as a child, my grandparents'

Christian Science ardor and their break with the extended family's more respectable Episcopalianism was an unhealed wound. It had caused a family breach as wide as the miles between Houston and Hollywood.

Respectability was not something Mama worried about. She was bright and quick and had never lost that childlike fascination with the strange and the mysterious. She said a poltergeist shared our house. He was friendly, she assured me. And harmless. All he did was move things around occasionally. Maybe he had once been a Hollywood decorator, she said. Whatever the case, Mama was glad he had found a home with us. He helped make life interesting, enchanting.

Mama believed in fairies. At night, when she tucked me into bed, she told me stories of fairy adventures. Or she quoted poetry, particularly poems that lent themselves to her dramatic flair.

I liked "The Highwayman." I waited for the part about the girl in the poem plaiting a deep red love-knot into her long black hair. I wanted to be that girl, when Mama was reading to me, I was that girl.

Sometimes Mama read poems and stories of her own. One of my favorites was a historical romance she was perennially writing about Jean Lafitte, the swashbuckling buccaneer who—as legend and Mama would have it—had left buried treasure on Galveston Island.

"The Poniard Woman" had something to do with a portrait of a beautiful woman wearing a lovely, flowing evening gown and holding a jeweled dagger (a poniard). It was Mama's version of the Dorian Gray story.

A love of music enveloped the family. Most nights in Hollywood, after the stories, after the tucking in, after the good-night kiss from Mama, music lulled me to sleep. Mama on the violin, my mother on the piano, their repertoire ranged from Gershwin's

1920s through the jazz of the 1940s, with dramatic pieces by Debussy and Rachmaninoff mingled in. Many nights I fell asleep with the sounds of their music floating into my room, washing gently around my bed.

My grandmother was wonderful, but much of the time she was in her own ethereal world. She was evasive, cloudy, and deeply devout—sometimes charmingly so, sometimes annoyingly. I imagined her floating through life, her feet hardly touching the earth. However, she drove her more practical-minded relatives to distraction. Once, one of Mama's aunts chided her for "having her head in the clouds."

"And that's where I intend to keep it," Mama answered.

Mama instilled a deep sense in me that much of what occupies our lives is trivial and evanescent.

My three aunts remind me today that their mother's behavior bordered on negligence. They knew she loved them, but their lives as children were chaotic. No one attended to the practicalities of life. It was hard on them to pick up and move across the country on a whim, which they did frequently.

My Aunt Marian, the big sister in the family—we all call her Sister—told me once, "When I got to be twenty, I realized that I was not prepared for anything. I had been given nothing in the way of skills for living. I had to discipline myself. I had to find a sense of order in myself, because we certainly weren't given that at home."

When I came along, Mama and Papa were twenty years older, their youngest daughter was ill, their granddaughter a handful. Nobody took the time and effort to fix regular meals, change the bed linens, clean the bathroom. Nobody cleaned the clutter of books and papers off the kitchen table. Nobody thought to toilet-train the wild little girl in their midst or impose a routine that a youngster might find reassuring.

My Mother's Keeper

23

A memory, as much a feeling as a memory, insinuates itself. It is a hot summer evening. I am sitting on the steps in front of the house on Miller Drive. I am alone. I have played hard all day, I'm dirty all over and my mouth is sticky with dried Popsicle. I'm wearing nothing but a pair of underpants. In the house behind me, I feel a sense of unease.

Somehow, I was aware as a small child that people in that house loved me, but that things were not right. Something about our lives had frayed, as if hardship and sadness and the fatigue of age had worn people down and threatened to overwhelm them. Things could easily spin out of control. I knew it had something to do with my mother.

Every day was unpredictable. I might wake to find that my Aunt Sally and her two little boys would be staying with us for a while. Sally and her husband Mike were having trouble. Mike was a radio announcer trying to make the big time, and he didn't have a lot of time for his family. Or maybe we would decide to take a house for the summer on the beach at Santa Monica. Papa would pile us into a car, and off we would go.

Sometimes great-grandmother Theresa, who was close in age to Papa, her son-in-law, would take the train out from Houston and stay with the family for several months. Theresa Gehring was a very proper, very Prussian woman. She would rush in like a house afire, trying to impose a bit of order on the household—preparing regular meals, making sure my clothes were clean and mended, keeping the house straight. She had been imposing order, cleaning up, fixing up for years. She still grumbled that Papa had never provided domestic help for her daughter. Proper people had help. Running the household was, of course, a Herculean task for a woman in her eighties, and Grandmother Theresa would eventually take the train back to Houston, probably in a state of exhaustion.

Tara Elgin Holley with Joe Holley

Even in their golden years, Mama and Papa acted with a teen-ager's impulse. In the summer of 1955, when I was still three, they decided that Galveston would be a nice change from Hollywood for a while. Papa said he wanted to be closer to "his girls"—Sally, who had just moved to Galveston from Hollywood, and Betty Lee and Marian, who were both married and living in Houston, an hour's drive from Galveston. He thought it might be good for my mother to be closer to her sisters.

"It'll be ten degrees cooler in Galveston than in Houston," Papa assured us. "We'll be back out here in the fall."

So the four of us—Papa and Mama, my mother and I—took the train to Texas. Papa rented us a house a couple of blocks from the beach, close enough that we could hear the waves crashing into the rocks of the seawall. My mother and I had an upstairs room with a private entrance.

That's the summer I met my great-great-aunt Elsa, the woman who would soon step in and with strong hands begin to mold my life. In later years, Aunt Elsa told me how appalled she was that at age five, I still wasn't potty-trained and that my grandparents allowed me to sit on the furniture without wearing underwear.

"You were always barefoot," Aunt Elsa grumbled, "and nobody ever bothered to comb the tangles out of your hair. First time I saw you, you had hair so long you could sit on it."

In Galveston every morning, I scampered into the foamy, slate-colored water and scoured the beach for shells and sand dollars. During the long, hot afternoons, I played by myself in the backyard under the shade of a bougainvillea, or I looked for my cat Blossom, who had given birth to kittens on a stack of mattresses in the garage. As in Hollywood, I did what I wanted. Mama and Papa prized freedom and spontaneity. Like Rousseau, they believed that to restrict a child was to extinguish the spirit.

The neighbors must have thought us strange. I remember

clinging like a monkey to the chain-link fence while chatting with the man and woman who lived next door. They were curious about the elderly couple who took walks in the evening to enjoy the Gulf breeze. They wondered about the young, reclusive woman who lived upstairs. They saw her strolling around the yard at times. She seemed to be talking to herself in an abstracted way; at other times, they could hear her singing from our upstairs room. Was that really her, they asked me, or was it the phonograph? "Gabby" was eager to tell them about her family.

Years later, my Aunt Sally shared her memory of that summer. She had left Hollywood and moved to Galveston, she said, partly to escape her parents and also to start a new life for herself and the two boys after her divorce from Mike. She was working in a bank.

As Sally told it, several afternoons a week, my mother would get me all dressed up, and the two of us would walk downtown to the bank. She wanted her favorite sister, Sally, and the women Sally worked with to see her beautiful little girl. She might have dressed me in one red sock and one yellow one, or maybe I'd be wearing clothes I'd found for playing dress-up. I was never particularly clean or tidy, Sally remembered, although my mother would have taken the time to wash and brush my long, curly hair and put ribbons in it.

Sally remembered that the women at the bank always exclaimed over me. "She's such a darling little girl, and so bright, too!" they would say. My mother and I would leave, and the women seemed to watch and wait for Sally to explain why her sister was different. Sally never explained, and the women never asked.

Sally's story affirmed my memory. I knew that my mother and I had once shared a vital connection, that we had once had a life together. Always the memories of being with my mother as a very young child tantalized me, but Sally's story confirmed what I had always sensed: that the intense feelings of connectedness with my mother were based on reality.

Those feelings had been there, buried deep inside, for a long time. Occasionally, I dare to open up to them, and moments—mementos—of those early years rush in. They are the hard-edged memories that remain, entire and brilliant. Inside those memories, I am once again a little girl with a mommy who loves me.

We are in the front yard of the house on Miller Drive. My mommy is twirling around in great swooping arcs as she clasps me to her chest. I throw my head back and giggle uncontrollably as we swirl across the grass. She wears a white dress that floats like a silken tent around her legs. The sun is shining through her golden hair. She is singing softly in my ear, and we are twirling. In slow motion . . .

We are in a variety store. I beg for a doll's baby bottle I have spotted on a rack. My mother bends down and tells me she can't buy it for me; she has no money. I start to cry. She takes me by the hand, and we hurry out the door. On the sidewalk, she hands me the little bottle. I can't figure out how she has gotten it.

My mother is driving her convertible on a busy L.A. street. I am in the backseat. She turns a corner, the door swings open, and suddenly I am sprawled on the pavement. My face and hands and knees are scraped and bleeding. My skin feels like it is on fire. I finger the little scars that still mark my nose and knee, and I remember. . . .

We are in the cool darkness of a movie theater. My mother starts talking to the giant black-and-white figures on the screen. Her voice gets louder, and people around us are saying, "Ssh." I don't understand what she is doing. A man in a uniform appears. He shines a tiny flashlight at us. He bends down to my mother and asks us to leave. Outside, the sunlight hurts my eyes. My mother is talking to herself in an angry voice. . . .

My mother left me in the park. My mother left me. . . .

The memories emerge as snapshots, as isolated moments that cohere into the young, delightful woman I knew as Mommy. The MacArthur Park memory is as clear and precise as any episode in my life. The emptiness that I felt that day, perhaps for the first time, is a void I would continue to feel for years, as does any daughter who loses a mother's love, whether from death, illness, or abandonment. In a way, my search for Dawn, for my mother, began that day, and it has never really ended.

Gradually, as the days and weeks of childhood passed into years, I understood that the mother I yearned for was like the beautiful fairy princess who lived in my grandmother's stories. As I saw less and less of my mother, I came to believe that something or someone terrible—maybe like the witch in Snow White—had spirited her away, and she could not escape. But someday, like Rapunzel or Sleeping Beauty—like Snow White herself—she would break free. The two of us would live happily ever after, together.

Later, years later, I learned to summon my memories and to put aside the child's fear. I allowed myself to imagine being Dawn, the young and beautiful woman who sang and made music and loved life.

I can, at times, almost become my mother. I can feel the terror of knowing, as the madness gestates, that my mind is failing, of knowing that the unfathomably complex circuitry we usually take for granted is shorting out. I can feel the panic that comes with knowing that the very core of your being is inexorably tearing away.

Years later, a medical report from those early days in Hollywood when Dawn was first committed to a mental hospital came into my possession. I read what my mother told the psychiatrist who examined her. Under the heading "Chief Complaint," he typed out her response: "I want my baby."

The words released years of pent-up anger and pain and frustration for me. They allowed me to share the pain and desperation that my mother, in moments when her mind was clear, must have found unbearable. I ached for what was lost, for all that could have been, for the mother I barely knew.

I realize that as time passes, I lose a little more of her, like snapshots gradually fading, but the power of those words, "I want my baby," has not dissipated. Until I read those words, I had not imagined that she had wanted me as desperately as I wanted her. I always thought it was only me, the needy child, yearning for her. Those words told me that when she went into the hospital for the first time, when she was still young and beautiful and talented, I was the focus of her life. My mother loved me.

A year after my mother's first commitment, in August of 1956, my mother and I hugged my grandparents good-bye and climbed aboard a Greyhound bus in Hollywood. With money my aunts had sent from Houston, Papa had purchased one-way tickets for us back to Texas.

For five years, Papa and Mama had tried to care for the both of us, but my aunts understood that neither of us was doing well. They insisted that we come back home to Houston. I can imagine the tears, the anguish my grandparents must have felt—because they would miss us, not because they were worried about our well-being. They still refused to acknowledge my mother's increasingly psychotic behavior. They passionately believed that God would look after all their children, despite evidence to the contrary.

I remember that Betty Lee and Sister were waiting at the Houston bus station. I can see them watching as we clambered down the stairs, my mother with a bag in one hand, gripping my hand with the other.

When I look at photographs from that time, I realize that Sister and Betty Lee must have been upset by what they saw. My mother had gained weight; her face and her body had lost shape and contour. She gazes out at the world with a lost, bewildered look in her eyes. Her face literally seems to recede into the background. It's obvious that she is gone.

It would be years before I learned what she had suffered in the previous year—the commitments to Metropolitan State Hospital, the barbaric treatment the mentally ill were forced to endure in those days, the drugs, the hours of useless psychotherapy.

The little girl getting off the bus must have been a sight as well. My curly, chestnut-colored hair fell below my waist. It was August, before buses were air-conditioned. I was hot and tired, and the front of my wrinkled plaid dress was encrusted with dried blood.

"What happened, baby?" Betty Lee asked, taking me in her arms and kissing my smudged face.

"Her nose bled on the way," my mother said. "It was a long trip."

I remember being happy the trip was finally over. In later

years, psychiatrists and counselors would probe, trying to get me to recall what it was like being five years old and traveling across the country with a mother who might not be able to feed me, who might have argued with her fellow passengers or mumbled gibberish to herself. They found it hard to believe that my grandparents entrusted me to her on such a long, arduous trip. Of course, they didn't know Mama and Papa.

It must have been traumatic, they suggested. You must have been frightened.

"Well, maybe," I would have to say with a lost feeling. Nothing ever came to mind—except for the fact, in hindsight, that it was the last time I ever really experienced my mother's comforting presence. At the station, I had no idea what was happening.

"We're in two cars," Sister said, taking my mother's bag. "Dawn, why don't you go with Betty Lee, and I'll take Tara with me."

My mother followed Betty Lee to her car. I waved and said, "Bye, Mommy," but she didn't seem to hear. I could not have imagined how long it would be before I would see my mother again. Some primordial link between my mother and me was severed that day, and in the days to come I would feel rage and sadness at the way it was done, at the suddenness and the lack of preparation I was given.

It must have been just as painful for my mother. I believe with all my heart that I was my mother's last link with reality. As long as she could hold on to me, she had a reason to battle the demons that were assaulting her, the voices that taunted and vied to dominate.

Sally told me about a letter my mother wrote at about this time. It was to a doctor she had seen in Los Angeles. "Please, Doctor," she wrote, "you have to tell me whether or not my illness is going to affect my baby."

Many years later, Betty Lee told me what happened on that hot August afternoon.

"Bennett's having the house exterminated, so we can't go home just yet," she told Dawn in a cheerful tone she didn't feel. She dreaded the ordeal she was about to face.

Instead of going home, she drove to a psychiatric clinic run by a doctor from the University of Houston. The clinic was on the edge of a quiet residential neighborhood and resembled a residence itself. Dawn was expected there. Betty Lee had almost reached the front door before my mother realized where her older sister was taking her.

"No!" she screamed. "No! Please, Betty Lee! Don't do this to me! Please! I have to be with my baby!" She started to run, but a male attendant waiting at the front door caught up with her before she could get more than a few steps. With one hand gripping her wrist tightly and one arm around her waist, the white-suited attendant gently but firmly led her back inside.

Betty Lee stood at the front desk. She was tempted to run and rescue her sister. "Surely it's for the best," she kept telling herself. "Surely it's for the best." All these years, she had tried to do what was best for her sister, or had tried to persuade her parents to do what was best. Now it was her turn. But who knew what was best? Driving home, she could not erase Dawn's desperate, accusatory look.

I remember being happy going home with Sister. I had recovered somewhat from the trip and was my usual garrulous self on the way to the house. As I heard the crunch of our tires in the oyster-shell driveway of the little white frame house on Wendell Street, I looked out the window and saw a boy and a girl about my age sitting on the front porch steps. Sister helped me out of the car, and the children ran to meet the little cousin their mother was bringing home.

Tara Elgin Holley with Joe Holley

"This is Donna," Sister said, putting her arm around the shoulders of a chubby little blond-haired girl wearing red shorts and a white blouse with puffed elastic sleeves. "She's five, just like you. And this is Chris," she said as a boy with carrot-colored hair and a riot of freckles walked out to greet us. "He's a big boy. He's six."

Sister placed her hands on my skinny little shoulders and urged me into the bathroom. She stripped off the bloodstained dress ("the blood dress," my cousins call it to this day). Opening a drawer, she took out a pair of scissors and chopped off my tangled, waist-length hair. I was stunned to see the clumps of wavy hair falling to the floor, although the attention I was getting felt good.

Sister ran hot water in the tub and plopped me in. I saw Donna and Chris peering around the bathroom door, watching their mother give the new kid a scrubbing. Chris had his hand over his mouth, trying not to giggle.

"You'll be with us for a while, honey," Sister said as she tucked me into bed that night. "Just until your mommy gets better."

A few days later, I was playing with Betty Lee's children, Suzanne and Johnny. Johnny, five years older than me, was pretending to rip apart my paper dolls.

"You'd better stop that," I said, hands on my hips, "or I'm going to tell my mommy."

Years later, Suzanne told me about the thought that flashed through her mind that day. "How's she going to do that?" she wondered. "She doesn't have a mommy."

I must have been a handful. Sister would put us all down for naps in the afternoon, and while Chris and Donna slept, I would get up and stroll out the front door. Several times, I got all the way down the street before Sister missed me. I would talk to

My Mother's Keeper
33

anyone, wander off whenever I felt like it. I was Mama and Papa's little girl.

Sister and Uncle Don were good to me, though I never really thought of them as my parents. Occasionally, I spent a few days with Sally's family or with Betty Lee's, but I lived most of the time with Sister and Don. In the fall, I started kindergarten.

I asked about my mother every day, but as time passed, I got caught up in a five-year-old's routine and didn't yearn for her as much. Once my mother even came to see me; she was on some kind of furlough from the hospital. I happily climbed into her lap and held on to her tightly. Sister was surprised that I was so easy and comfortable with her, despite her obvious disconnection from the rest of the world. I sat in her lap, and we talked and laughed and sang together. We belonged to each other.

My aunts had other plans for me. I would be part of a regular family. I shared a room with Donna, played with the neighborhood kids. I don't remember being unhappy with the arrangement, even though I missed my mother, and even though I sensed that I made the lives of Sister and Uncle Don and the children more complicated. Elsa Gehring, my old-maid great-great-aunt, had her own way of putting it. "You were treated like the fifth wheel on a wagon," she told me some years later, when I was old enough to understand.

"I didn't feel that way," I told Auntie. And I honestly didn't—until I came across a family photograph, taken at Christmas. In the black-and-white portrait, Sister is wearing a pretty dress. Curly-haired Uncle Don, in a dark double-breasted suit and a wide patterned tie, stands straight and proud with his family. He and Sister are young and smiling. Chris and Donna are cute little kids wearing their Sunday best. They are posed before a Christmas tree.

I looked at the year, written on the back: 1956. I was part of the family in 1956, but I was not in the picture. A feeling I had managed to forget welled up. They were the happy family. I didn't belong. I didn't belong anywhere.

Great-great-aunt Elsa Gertrude Katherine Gehring, "Auntie,"
age seventeen, in 1906.

CHAPTER TWO

At Auntie's as a little girl, I rescued baby birds that had fallen from the trees in our garden. I picked figs and peaches and berries. I collected glass animals. I cared for hundreds of dolls. I built cities and designed home interiors with my block collection. I drew wardrobes for my fashion models. I created a mud-pie bakery. I read all the Nancy Drew books, Little Women, Great Expectations, and all the George MacDonald fairy tales. I started writing a novel. I took care of the dogs and washed the dishes and did a hundred other chores. I sang to Auntie each night and brushed her hair. I laid my head on her chest and listened to her heart. I began growing up.

I had been living with Sister and Don for nearly a year when Elsa Gertrude Katherine Gehring took it upon herself to rescue me from what she feared would be a fate as tragic as my mother's. It was the summer of 1957.

I can imagine how it began. I see Sister's small, neatly arranged living room, Donna's and Chris's toys on the floor, their photos on the bookshelves. Sister sits on the couch. She wears a plain blue skirt and a sleeveless white blouse; her hair is pulled back from her forehead with an elastic band.

An old woman sits across from Sister in a straight-backed chair from the dining room. She is wearing a black organza dress and a wide-brimmed straw hat, black with a red grosgrain ribbon. On her wrist is a turquoise Indian bracelet; a white lace handkerchief is tucked under the bracelet.

"This child must not be wasted. I will not let it happen!" the old woman is saying. Her voice, the voice I will come to hear even in my sleep, is firm and strong and insistent. Underneath the hat, her piercing ice-blue eyes glint through gold-rim bifocals, like blue china through the glass of an old china cabinet. The glasses grip a jutting nose. She punctuates each deliberate word by poking the hardwood floor with her black, rubber-tipped walking cane.

Sister is silent. Though it is her house, she sits primly, as if she has been summoned to the principal's office. Like a hot coal next to her heart, Sister carries an old bitterness toward this imperious woman and yet she still is reluctant to assert herself. People don't cross Elsa Gehring.

"You saw what happened to her mother. And it's all because of neglect," the old woman continues. "Neglect. You know it as well as I do, Marian. Well, it's not going to happen to this little girl. Not if I have anything to say about it. There's been too much waste in this family."

Sitting stiff and erect in the hardback chair, her heavy, black Dr. Scholl's shoes planted firmly on the floor, she seems to be daring Sister to object. Sister knows it is futile to argue. Elsa Gehring always gets her way.

Actually, Sister isn't inclined to argue. Of all Mama and Papa's children, she is the most bitter about what she sometimes calls, with a sardonic laugh, her parents' "benign neglect." She left home as soon as she could, all the girls did. The older she gets, the more upset it makes her.

Perhaps Sister is thinking of the others. "Even Dawn tried to leave," she remembers. "Poor Dawn. Maybe," she thinks, "maybe it would have been better if she had died."

Mustn't think that, must never ever say it. She chases away the thought and considers Auntie's demand. If her health holds up, Auntie can probably give a needy, demanding little girl more time and attention than she receives in a busy household where she is one of three kids with a fourth coming. Maybe the old lady can save the child from wandering down Dawn's path.

"You are right, of course, Aunt Elsa. I'm not going to argue with you," Sister at last replies. "If Tara wants to go live with you, I think she should. It's probably the best thing."

Almost imperceptibly, the magisterial old woman seems to relax. The beginnings of a smile flicker across her lined and powdered face, and she nervously caresses the large rhinestone brooch at her chest. She takes her handkerchief from the bracelet. Lifting the glasses, she dabs at her eyes.

"She's lonely!" Sister suddenly realizes about this woman she has feared, perhaps even hated, her whole life. "Her mother, all those nieces and nephews she's cared for all her life; they're all gone. She has no one."

I was not quite six. It would be five years before I would see my mother again. By the time I left Sister and Don's and moved in with Auntie, my mother already had made her way back to California. Although I didn't know it at the time, she was in and out of the hospital, living with Mama and Papa between hospital commitments, her condition steadily deteriorating.

I received a couple of letters from her during my first five years at Auntie's—and dozens from my grandparents—and I may have also talked to her on the phone once or twice. Auntie was always talking on the phone *about* her with Mama and Papa, but she seems to have shielded me from those conversations, particularly in the early years.

I learned fairly early not to show that I missed my mother. Auntie didn't approve. She would be my mother *and* my father, she told me at one point. She would take care of me. At the same time, she didn't want me to forget my mother. I remember the time when I was still living at Sister's, and Auntie heard me call Sister "Mommy," echoing my cousins. "Don't let her call you that," Auntie reprimanded Sister. "She *has* a mother."

I had a mother I loved, and I did not forget her. I thought about her, dreamed about her. Every night without fail, I knelt beside my bed and prayed, "Please, God, make my mommy well."

Auntie, I would come to understand, was the family matriarch. Elsa Gertrude Katherine Gehring was born in Houston in 1882. She was one of the seven children of Charles Conrad Gehring and Augusta Hoffman, German immigrants to Houston when the town was nothing more than a muddy little malaria-ridden village on Buffalo Bayou.

Charles and Augusta Gehring's oldest child, Theresa, was my great-grandmother, the hardworking woman who came out to Hollywood occasionally to help Mama and Papa. Elsa—Auntie— was the youngest of the seven children.

Auntie was only seven years older than her niece, Marian

Elise, my grandmother. The two were very close. Although Elsa heartily disapproved of "Marian's bohemian ways"—and certainly wasn't shy about saying so—the two women stayed in touch throughout their lives. When Mama lived in California, they talked by phone at least twice weekly and wrote long, chatty letters just as often.

Elsa Gehring, who revered the past and recalled it more precisely than the present, enjoyed recalling life in her parents' house. They were prosperous, prominent members of Houston society, and their house on Main Street was alive with parties and celebrations. "A host was judged by the quality of his wine, despite the fact that he wore tough boots against the frequent mud of shaded residential avenues," one of the early German immigrants to Houston recalled many years later.

I would ask about my grandmother, and Auntie would laugh and tell me about her "antics." When she and Marian—my grandmother—were young girls, they would sneak down the stairs and hide under the grand piano. Wide-eyed, they took in the starched white linens on the long dining room table; the huge bouquet of flowers in the center; the cakes, pies, and pastries; and the hearty German fare. The house seemed to glow from all the polishing the maids had given the furniture and the woodwork.

The little girls loved watching all the people crowded into the parlor: the women so elegant in their long, beautiful gowns; the men handsome and distinguished in their dark suits, high white collars and richly patterned cravats. They loved the music, usually a chamber trio, and the dancing that made the room a candlelit swirl of light and color.

Elsa was still quite young when her parents took her on the train to St. Charles, Missouri, where they enrolled her in Sacred Heart Convent. She gave deep and earnest thought, and fervent prayer, to dedicating her life to the church. As a nun in the service of God, her life, she believed, would be endowed with meaning and purpose.

In photographs from her early years, Elsa Gehring is tall and proud, almost haughty. Her hair—fiery red, to match her temper, people said—is long and flowing. Her eyes are ice blue and direct. In a portrait that has passed down through the family to me, she is wearing a beautiful white dress with long sleeves and a high collar, a dress I remember seeing in her closet until the end of her days. She is also wearing a gold locket, which she allowed me to wear when I was a teenager. In the photograph, she is an aristocratic-looking young woman.

Like her oldest sister, Theresa, she was a proper Prussian lady. She respected tradition and custom and decorum. She nurtured family ties. At the same time, she was a thoroughly modern American. She fiercely treasured her independence. In the early years of the century, she took the train from Houston to New York and enrolled at Columbia University. Later she worked on an education degree at Berkeley.

She studied at Columbia's Teachers College, where she investigated the newfangled notions of a doctor named Freud. She listened to the lectures of the eminent philosopher John Dewey. Years afterward, she still kept a Dewey textbook, heavily underlined and notated, on a shelf in our living room. Dewey may have helped shape her fiercely held theories about the malleability of children and the importance of a sound environment to a child's upbringing.

In New York, she donned all white, held high the Stars and Stripes, and with her red hair blowing in the breeze, marched up Broadway with fellow suffragettes. When women finally got the vote more than two decades later, she was religious about using it. She was an active, outspoken Democrat her whole life.

Tara Elgin Holley with Joe Holley

For forty years, Miss Gehring was also a teacher and a principal in the Houston Independent School District. She rose each morning before daybreak and walked five miles from her house to Grady Elementary, a predominantly Mexican-American school where she was principal. Earlier, she had taught at Kincaid, an exclusive private school in Houston, but she preferred her Mexican-American children. She admired the close-knit families, the parents' devotion to their children, and she was aware of their struggle in this country. She felt a sense of noblesse oblige.

In her matriarchal, imperious way, she was devoted to "her children." Even after she retired, she kept in contact with them, and as the years passed, with their children and grandchildren.

As an old woman, she took great pride in the fact that she had forged a career, that she owned her own home, that she was financially secure. She was proud, most of all, that she had made her way in life without relying on a man.

Though she never married, her siblings over the years relied on her as a nanny for their children. She would stay for months at a time with first one relative and then another. As the years passed, it was Auntie who kept in touch with the various wings of the family, who knew the family stories, who kept up with everyone's trials and tribulations.

This was the woman who, at age seventy-five, took it upon herself to tame a little savage. Elsa Gehring had been retired for more than a decade. Except for her five dogs, she lived alone in a three-story, red-brick house in the Village, a pleasant, tree-lined neighborhood near Rice University. During that first summer and fall, in 1956, Auntie invited me over several times for weekend visits. The next summer, with Sister expecting her third child, my aunts agreed it would be better if I stayed with Auntie for a while. A month's visit became a permanent arrangement.

I loved being at Auntie's. Wandering through the big old house was like wandering through a museum with fourteen rooms, one of them all my own. I had never had a room of my own. Usually, it was the pink room, with rose curtains and a maroon silk bedspread and an antique desk. Later, after I moved in to stay, Auntie and I occasionally traded rooms, just for a change, and the blue room would be mine.

The house were built as a duplex, so there were two of everything—two living rooms, two kitchens, two dining rooms with antique dining tables. The furnishings were old and heavy and well cared for. The house had the feel and smell of a faded past.

The more recent past intruded as well. The house was a repository for family belongings. If someone in the family divorced or moved away, or if they died, their furniture, their heirlooms, and sometimes their dogs and children ended up at Auntie's. For a few months, it was my cousin Joanna, whose mother had died of cancer. David and Suzanne, two of Betty Lee's four children, occasionally stayed with Auntie for a few days at a time when their mother was busy with her graduate work.

Since Auntie went for years without renting her duplex, I could wander from room to room, dreaming, pretending, carrying on imaginary conversations. Often I wandered up to the attic. I would spend hours going through old wooden trunks reinforced with scrolled tin. In one were old photos, faded sepia-toned images of women in long dresses and men with beards. They were relatives, Auntie said. She had stories about all of them.

Another trunk contained my great-great-grandmother's quilt pieces, crewel work, and embroidery, along with Mama's exquisite china doll collection. In that same trunk, I found a stack of Mama's diaries from the 1890s and large, elaborate Valentine albums from her Houston girlhood.

The whole house was filled with days and lives passed. Poking around in an extra bedroom, I would slide out the deep drawer of a mahogany chest and find a golden locket. Opening the locket, I would come face-to-face with a handsome young man from days long ago. The grandfather clock downstairs chimed its somber, stately tones, and I imagined the young man in a carriage—a trap, I think it was called—drawn by a sleek black horse. The horse was trotting briskly down Elgin Street past the big, two-story houses with the long, shaded verandas, ornate railings, and cupolas. His quirt lightly touched the horse's shiny back. Sitting beside the man would be a tall, red-haired young woman with eyes the color of the sky. Stopping before one of the big houses, he would tie the horse to a cast-iron hitching post, help the woman from the carriage, and escort her to the veranda. Later in the evening, she would haughtily refuse his offer of marriage.

One day, I opened another trunk, and from that day on, I valued its contents more than all the others in the mysterious old house. Lifting the lid, I found the elegant dresses my mother wore when she sang in Hollywood. I had heard the stories about my mother's career from my aunts, and from Auntie, although her stories were more cautionary tales than fond memories. Nobody had to tell me whose dresses they were. Maybe I had seen them in Hollywood, maybe not, but somehow I knew. I was ecstatic. In the attic, where much was old and faded, my mother's dresses were vibrant and cheery with life.

I played with my mother's beautiful dresses every chance I got. I loved touching them, caressing them, burying my face and hands in the spangles and the bright, shiny fabric. I breathed in deeply, as if the lingering scent of my mother, inhaled from the dresses, would bring her back to me. I wrapped myself in her garments and dreamed of wrapping myself in her arms.

My all-time favorite was a shimmering red cocktail dress, with silver spangles at the low-cut neck and over the skirt. It became my own singing dress. There in the attic all alone, I would clamber into the beautiful red dress, the long skirt pooling around my feet, the collar slipping off my thin little-girl shoulders. With one hand, I would hold the dress up; with the other, I would grip my broomstick microphone. I became Dawn Elgin, the glamorous Hollywood entertainer. The dusty-gold sunlight streaming in through the narrow attic window was my spotlight, and in the shadows of the attic, I could see the beautiful men and women listening to my voice and smiling back at me. I sang the songs I had learned from my mother.

An old family friend, a woman who lived in Hollywood and knew Mama and Papa, dropped by the house one afternoon. I was sitting on the stairs listening to the conversation around the corner in one of the living rooms. That was how I found out a lot of things I knew, by being quiet and listening.

"Elsa, now listen to me," I heard the woman say. "You can't imagine the way things were for that child when she was with her crazy mother in Hollywood. What you have to do is just tell that poor little girl her mother's dead. Mark my words, she'll be better off."

The words took my breath away. I felt my hand trembling. I knew who she meant, and suddenly I hated the woman who thought she knew so much. I could feel the hot tears on my face. In my mind's eye, I could see the orange hair pulled back into a scraggly bun, the thin mouth flapping on about things she thought she knew but didn't. I held my breath to hear Auntie's reply.

I heard her characteristic "Harrumph!" She sounded as angry

as I felt. "Helen, that's ridiculous," she said. "I would never do that. Someday, that poor little girl as you call her will have the responsibility of taking care of her mother. You can't pretend she doesn't exist."

Auntie herself certainly didn't pretend. I was her project, her life's mission, and she felt an obligation to prepare me for the reality of my mother's condition.

Auntie was always loving, stern, watchful. She was with me everywhere. Even on those rare occasions when I was alone, I could still hear her voice. Good German lady that she was, she believed in regimen—for me and for herself. She knew, even without her friend Helen telling her, the chaotic, unstable life I had lived in Hollywood. There would be no such thing in her home.

During the school year, she woke me promptly at six. She had been up since five and already had taken a twenty-minute walk around the neighborhood. After she came home, she drank two glasses of warm water and lay on her right side for twenty minutes. I quickly learned not to intrude until Auntie had finished her health routine.

I would dress and run downstairs, where the breakfast table would be set, and eggs, cinnamon toast and bacon would be waiting, along with a glass of orange juice enriched with two raw eggs. The eggs, Auntie believed, helped ward off all manner of ills. (She must have been right; in twelve years, I missed only half a day of school.) The conventions of civilized living would be scrupulously observed, even when it was only the two of us at the table in the kitchen. Auntie would scrutinize everything, from fingernails to breakfast-table posture to breakfast-table conversation.

Taking care of the dogs was one of my daily chores, although Auntie doted on them as she always had. I suppose they were the children she never had. Like me, they were strays, castoffs, little creatures she had taken in. Even after I moved in, she continued to lavish a mother's attention on Buster and Spot and all the other dogs who came to be with us.

Once a week, we would drop by the butcher shop so she could buy them soup bones, and she would make beef barley soup just for the dogs. It seemed like she always had something simmering on the stove for them. "Your boarding-house lady's home," she would call to them when she came in from the butcher's.

After breakfast, Auntie would take one of her collection of canes she kept in a decorated cane holder at the foot of the stairs and walk me to Roberts Elementary. All the teachers knew I was Miss Gehring's little girl. And all the teachers knew I could sing and recite; Auntie told them. By the second grade, I was starring in all the school productions.

Auntie would be doing dishes in the evening. I would sit beside her on a red stool, repeating poems that she had recited for me. Sometimes it would be a poem, sometimes the Lord's Prayer or the Twenty-third Psalm.

In the second grade, Auntie had me memorize Henry Van Dyck's "The Real Meaning of Christmas," all ten verses. We started working on the piece in November, right after Thanksgiving. Auntie would recite the poem, verse by verse; I would say it back to her, over and over.

As soon as I had the poem memorized, I would listen while Auntie called Carrie Lou Arnold Smith, the Roberts Elementary School principal. "I would like Tara to come into your office and make a presentation," she would say.

"Why, Miss Elsa, I would love to have Tara come by," Mrs. Smith must have replied. "I'll call her out of class tomorrow."

Tara Elgin Holley with Joe Holley

48

The next day, I would hurry to the office and recite for Mrs. Smith. The principal would listen attentively, smile brightly, and clasp her hands to her well-powdered cheek. She would insist that the little performer star in the next school production.

I soon learned, however, that Auntie had her own, more exacting performance standards. In a second-grade production for PTA night, I sang a little song in my role as a dripping faucet, complete with hand motions and a bobbing head. Never was a faucet played with more fervor and panache. Never had I enjoyed myself more. I looked out at the darkened auditorium and saw the parents smiling and laughing, and I was in heaven.

"Oh, Tara, you were adorable!" Miss Witt, my teacher, bubbled afterward. "Wasn't she just adorable, Miss Elsa?"

Auntie didn't think so. She gave a "harrumph!," gripped my shoulder tightly and led me outside. "You were showing off," she said, bending down as best she could to bore into my now teary brown eyes.

Showing off? I thought I was being myself. I thought I was performing. I was in love with life, in love with myself. But that night, the admonishments Auntie constantly drilled into me came tumbling back—Beauty is only skin deep. Pretty is as pretty does.

"Other people may think you're cute, but you don't have to think so. It's not proper," Auntie hissed. We walked home in the dark. Auntie would not talk to me. Every few steps, I stared up at my aunt, but I could not see her face. In years to come, I would understand that Auntie wasn't seeing *me* on that stage. She was seeing my mother, hungry for an audience's adoration, caught up in the seductive lure of performance. She would not allow me to be seduced. I would have to be broken, disciplined.

Auntie was the one to do it. She could be as unyielding and inflexible as a bronze statue. That's one reason why I loved being at school. Not only was I usually the teacher's pet, but I was out of the range of those ice-blue eagle eyes. I could almost be the little nature child that Mama and Papa had nurtured. I could, that is, until Miss Smith mentioned something to Auntie about my high-spirited ways.

"It's just that Tara's so full of life, she can't hush up sometimes," the principal said with a smile.

Auntie wasn't smiling, and she wasn't swayed by tears the way my teachers were at times. At home that afternoon, Auntie grabbed me by the arm, pulled me out to the garden, and forced me to select the switch she would use to administer my punishment. I bent over Auntie's ample lap and cried through the stinging blows. I tried to sound as pathetic as I could, but I wasn't really pretending. Auntie was a strong old lady in those early days.

One Saturday morning when I was seven, I had the dogs out in the yard for their morning run. Inside, Tweety, the beautiful little blue canary one of my cousins had given me, was out of her cage. She was flying around while we did our Saturday-morning housecleaning. That too was part of the morning routine.

When I let the five dogs back in the house, they went dashing up the back stairs, their claws clicking loudly on the steps, and I suddenly realized I had forgotten to close the breakfast-room door at the top of the stairs. I scrambled up the steps behind the gang of panting dogs and got to Auntie's bedroom just in time to see Buster, our chow, leap onto the bed and chomp down on poor little Tweety. By the time I pulled the growling, snapping dog off the bed, Tweety was a lifeless mass of matted blue feathers.

I was horrified. I couldn't stop crying. Auntie couldn't seem to stop berating me for being so thoughtless, so irresponsible, so immature. We got a shovel from the garage and buried Tweety in the backyard.

Auntie simply stopped talking to me. She wouldn't say a word. That afternoon we rode the bus to Glenwood Cemetery to put flowers on the graves of relatives. It was a long bus ride, with several transfers, but Auntie still wouldn't talk to me. She wouldn't touch me. We visited the graves of every family member—it took at least an hour—but Auntie would not say a word to me the whole time. It felt like my funeral. When we left the cemetery and headed back to the bus stop, she wouldn't even hold my hand to cross the busy street. It shocked me. As we stepped off the curb, I reached up to take her hand the way I always did, and she jerked her hand away.

I was frightened. Did her angry silence mean she was never speaking to me again, never going to hold my hand? I felt small and scared and completely alone. I depended on Auntie for my life, and she had cut me off.

I wanted to be able to cry about Tweety, because I loved my little bird. I wanted Auntie to hold me and wipe my eyes and tell me it wasn't my fault that Tweety was dead.

As she got older, and perhaps a bit senile, these disturbing episodes became more frequent. At first, I cringed like a whimpering puppy. As I got older, I gradually came to realize I would have to take care of myself.

Life with Auntie wasn't always so bizarre. The stern old woman had her soft side. We had fun, too. Some evenings the two of us would get all dressed up, and we would venture out to theater productions and opera. She loved musicals. If it was a Wednesday, it was musical night at the Delman Theater, and the two of us would ride the bus downtown to see *Carousel, My Fair Lady, Oklahoma!*—whatever movie musical happened to be playing that week. We saw every Jeanette MacDonald–Nelson Eddy kiss ever recorded on film, heard every love song. On the bus ride home, I would go to sleep in Auntie's lap, the lush, romantic lyrics we had heard stored in my mind for safekeeping. *Carousel* also nourished a fantasy about my father. Like Bill, my father must have gotten in trouble, trying to protect me. That's why he had to go away.

Walking the dogs around the block every evening, I would rehearse the lyrics of every show tune I remembered. They became theme music to my constant longing to be with my mother, who had smiled into my eyes and sung those songs to me.

Every Saturday, after housecleaning, we rode the orange-and-white Houston city bus downtown to the stately, high-ceilinged public library, where we both checked out stacks of books. One summer, we took the bus downtown to the YWCA, where I took swimming lessons—and was banished to the side of the pool a few times for talking during class. Another summer, she took me back to the library for classes in origami.

On many Saturdays, we combined our library expeditions with shopping. Auntie believed in quality; she bought only the best at Neiman Marcus or Sakowitz or Battlesteins. The clerks knew Miss Gehring. They knew what she wanted, and they went out of their way to help her.

Every Sunday, Auntie laid out my best dress, my black Mary Janes, white lace anklets, and my white gloves. When we were dressed in our Sunday best, we rode the bus downtown again. Our first stop was the Rice Hotel coffee shop for cinnamon toast. Then we walked the two blocks to Christ Church Cathedral, the Episcopal church downtown where a bronze plaque on the wall honored my great-grandfather. Auntie made sure I noticed that the plaque had been on the wall since 1850.

Auntie was conscientious about my religious training. When I first moved in with her, she took me to the Catholic church, the Christian Science church, and to Christ Church. Even though

I was only six years old, she allowed me to choose which one we would attend regularly.

Probably she was relieved when Christ Church Cathedral became my home away from home. I was in the pew every Sunday morning, with Auntie. On Sunday afternoon, I could hardly wait for Episcopal Youth Class, and when I got a little older, I rode the bus downtown alone. Wednesday afternoons, I rode the bus downtown for choir practice. I loved the rich wood smell of the cathedral, and scampering up the stairs to the practice room with fellow choir members. On Sunday mornings, dressed like an angel in a purple robe, I loved walking in a line across the courtyard and into the dim, high-ceilinged cathedral.

Church was even better than school. At church, I was a normal kid, not a strange little girl who wore old-fashioned clothes and lived with an old woman in a big, old house. At church, as the years passed, I would find comfort and acceptance and security when the ache of my missing mother and the steadily more heavy demands of an aging aunt began to weigh me down. In years to come, I would go through my Maharishi Mahesh Yogi phase and my self-proclaimed atheism phase, but I have never forgotten that in profound ways church served and saved me.

In the summer, Auntie and I spent hour after hour outdoors. Auntie owned the vacant lot next door to the house, and over the years had transformed it into a verdant flower and vegetable garden. We started early. I rushed down the back steps as soon as I awoke every morning, hoping to get to the figs before the birds did.

Always we had planting and weeding and watering and pruning to do. Auntie, wearing a flowery voile dress, a pair of men's work shoes, and one of several wide-brimmed straw hats that hung by the back door, would be walking around the garden with her hands on her hips. She was like a plantation owner. Every few steps she bent down to pull a weed or to dig in the moist earth. She had big hands, and in the summer her nails were always dirty, even though she was always concerned about her appearance.

A neighbor walks by. It is Dr. Fenster, who teaches English at Rice. "Good morning, Miss Elsa," he calls out. "Hot enough for you?" In his bow tie and blue seersucker suit, he looks cool and dapper.

Auntie is bending down to examine a tomato plant for bugs, and when she stands up to greet Dr. Fenster, I notice that her long white hair has slipped from the tortoiseshell combs that she has worn for most of her life. As she pins up her hair, the sweat drips down her camelia-white neck and chest, down between her ample breasts. Underneath her dress, unbuttoned and askew, her silk lace Barbizon slip shows. When she is in the garden, she is totally absorbed. Nothing else matters. She is to me an earth goddess overseeing her domain. She nurtures things—plants, dogs, children. That was her life and always had been.

She talked to everyone who walked by, offered them a clipping or sweet pea seeds or a word of advice on tomato blight. "Now, where did you say you went to school, honey?" she might ask a stranger who had paused at the fence to admire the flourish of perky, pastel sweet peas growing along the garden fence or the healthy stand of tomatoes laden with rich, red fruit. And the stranger would be trapped into unraveling the story of his life.

Sometimes the fragrance of sweet peas or the tangy, earthy odor of a freshly picked tomato transports me back to that garden. We were outside most evenings until after dark. We had a redwood table and two matching chairs and, because we were always in the garden, an outside phone.

At least a couple of evenings a week, we shared our meal with Gilbert and Narcisso. Gilbert Martinez, who was Auntie's age, had worked for the Gehrings for fifty years. Narcisso Delgado had been Auntie's student in elementary school until he had to drop out and go to work.

"Narcisso was such a bright child," Auntie said. "It was a waste of a good mind when he didn't finish school. Of course, it was his wife's fault. She got pregnant and forced him to marry her." She pursed her lips and sighed. "She wasn't good enough for Narcisso."

In those early years with Auntie, when she was physically able, the two of us went downtown at Christmastime and picked out work clothes for Gilbert. We bought the same thing every Christmas: four pairs of khaki pants, four shirts, a pair of work shoes, socks, and handkerchiefs. Then we took the bus to his house and delivered the Christmas bundle.

Both men worked hard for Auntie, and she usually kept them late. They were good men, kind and gentle. I loved them both. Gilbert was eighty-five when he died. He died in Auntie's garden, planting her prize-winning sweet peas.

I was happy those first five years at Auntie's. I had a home, a yard, a place I knew was mine. I had someone who took the time and trouble to do things carefully and thoroughly. I've never known another person who had someone who rolled down their clean socks every night and draped them over their shoes, so the socks would be ready to slip into the next morning. That's the kind of attention Auntie lavished on me. With Auntie, there was ritual, a certain ordered way of doing things, and an old, wise woman always watching over.

My life with Auntie got stranger as she got older. I began to feel like a little girl living with an old woman in a musty museum. She forced me to wear odd clothes and made sure that the only children in my life were cousins or children at church. I knew it was futile to ask to have a friend from school spend the night with me or come over after school and play with dolls. She was determined to fend off evil influences. She disciplined me severely—even abused me, people would say today—for the slightest infraction.

I hated the restrictions. At times, I hated the old woman who enforced them, and yet I can't really blame Auntie. This woman from another age was doing what she thought was best for a wayward little girl with no father and with a mother who was mentally ill. I was her God-given responsibility, and she would do whatever it took to rescue me from my misfortune and to mold me into the sensible, responsible young woman she believed my mother should have been.

I also realized that in many ways I needed the discipline Auntie imposed—although perhaps not to the degree she imposed it. I needed to learn responsibility, self-reliance. I would need those qualities in the years to come, when my mother came back into my life.

The two of us, Auntie and I, needed each other. Auntie, I realized as the years passed, could not have lived on her own without my help. Her nieces and nephews would have held a family conference. "You have no choice, Aunt Elsa," my Uncle Irving would have said in his worldly-wise voice of experience. They would have forced her to sell her home and move into a rest home. As I got older, I could tell they were hovering about, just waiting.

Tara Elgin Holley with Joe Holley

56

And Auntie needed me emotionally. She had been lonely for years. As Betty Lee had predicted, I was indeed a comfort, and as our ten years together passed, she became more and more dependent on me.

"You know, it was fate that brought us together," Auntie would say late at night. I would be lying with my head on her chest; she always insisted that I listen to make sure her heart was beating regularly. "Having the same birthday just goes to confirm it. You and I were meant to be together."

I liked looking at my dark hands against the white, white skin of my aunt's soft, ample bosom. I would feel myself drifting off, and I would give a sleepy nod. Yes, I was happy.

The Christmas when I was eight, Auntie gave me a red plastic child's phonograph from World Toy and Gift Shop. In the attic some weeks later, I came across four records. I remember wiping the dust off the thick black discs and reading the name on the label: Dawn Elgin. Four records, double-sided, all recorded by my mother. I could not believe it.

I yelled to Auntie. At that moment, I didn't care about composure. I leaped and stumbled down the stairs, carrying the precious treasure in my arms. In my room, I selected one to play. "Stormy Weather," I remember it was called.

The sound was clear, with hardly any scratches. It was unmistakably the voice of my mother, the beautiful voice I had not forgotten. I played the records over and over: "Stormy Weather," "You Made Me Love You," "Embraceable You," "Stardust." Day after day, I played them. I put on my mother's bright red dress, and I sang along with her. I memorized the lyrics, and I imagined a time when we would be looking into each other's eyes and singing together.

Some days I would be singing an imaginary duet, my eyes closed, pretending I was in Hollywood, when I would feel my aunt's presence. Opening my eyes, I would find myself looking up at the grim-faced old woman standing in the door. I would feel embarrassed and guilty and a little bit afraid.

"I'm going to have to take those records away from you," Auntie would grumble. "Surely you've got something better to do than sit here and moon over that music. I don't care if it is your mother. You need to get outside and play."

Auntie was worried, I would eventually understand. Worried that I was idealizing my mother, setting myself up for bitter disappointment.

"Your mother is mentally ill," Auntie told me one evening as we sat facing each other in twin antique Stickley rockers. I was eight years old. I remember my feet didn't reach the floor. I curled them around the rung of the chair.

"Do you understand what this means?" Auntie asked.

I nodded, although I wasn't really sure. I knew I had heard Auntie talking to my grandparents on the phone plenty of times; I had heard her talking about Dawn. Sometimes I asked to talk to Mommy, but Auntie always said she wasn't home. I counted the ticks of the grandfather clock, waiting for her to continue.

"She's in a hospital," Auntie said, "and we all hope she gets better."

She paused to see how I was taking what she had to say. I waited, an anxious feeling beginning to build in my stomach. It had been so long since I had seen my mother. If Mommy wasn't going to get well, did that mean I would never see her again? My lips began to quiver and then my hands. I couldn't stop them. I was trying not to cry. I knew Auntie wouldn't like that.

"Am I going to see her?" I managed to ask.

Tara Elgin Holley with Joe Holley

"Well, of course you will see her," Auntie said. "But we have to let her get better first."

We were quiet together for a moment. "One more thing, dear," Auntie said. "No matter what happens, you don't ever have to worry. Do you understand? You always have a home here. I'm your mother *and* your father."

I understood, but I still missed my mother. I would see her again—even if it meant I had to run away to California and bring her home to Houston. Every night I walked the dogs around the block, trying to keep their leashes untangled, and every night I looked up into the night sky. "Star light, star bright," I murmured, "first star I see tonight." The insistent chatter of cicadas was the only response I heard, but I had no doubt. Someone would hear.

It was the same wish, for nearly five years. When it came true, I knew how it would be. The tall, blond, beautiful woman who held me and sang to me and swung me about in her arms would come and take her little girl away. We would live in Hollywood again. We would be like Irene and her fairy godmother in "The Princess and the Goblin," the George MacDonald story. We would live happily ever after, together.

Grandparents Marian Elise Jenkins Elgin and Alfred Rice Elgin with
Alfred, Jr. ("Brother"), age five; Marian ("Sister"), age three; and Betty Lee
Elgin, age one in 1926.

CHAPTER THREE

Auntie and I went to funerals. It didn't matter whether we knew the person who had died, as long as we knew the family. We would put on our Sunday best and take the bus to the church or the dimly lit funeral parlor. We would sit in the back, while the organ music softly played, and listen to the prayers and words of consolation. At the appropriate time, we would stand with the other mourners; Auntie would take my hand and we would file past the person lying still and composed, eyes closed and hands folded, in the silk-lined coffin. I would stand on tiptoe as I stared at the made-up face.

I know it sounds strange. I suppose it was. But to me as a little girl, it didn't seem strange or morbid. It was what we did. It was Auntie's way of marking time's passage. It was a way for her to indulge her memories.

Auntie had been reading the Houston papers from cover to cover every day, probably since O. Henry had been a popular *Houston Post* columnist in the 1890s. Coming down the stairs every morning, I often found her reading the obituaries in the *Post* or the *Chronicle*, her scanning finger pausing at a familiar name. She knew the families of the deceased, their secrets, and their successes. She loved to share them with me as I sat at the kitchen table eating breakfast.

Riding downtown on the bus, Auntie would point out where early families had lived. More often than not, their stately Victorian homes had been razed for office buildings, but in her alert mind's eye—its focus on the past more precise than on the present—Auntie saw and cherished the lovely old homes. She loved to share with anyone who would listen stories about the Elkinses, the McAtees, the Clevelands, the Cullinans, the Kirklands, the Pedens, and, of course, the Elgins—all the old families, the rooted families she had known her whole long life. Maybe one morning, I'd hear about Miss Cora Root, and her twin sister, Mary Porter Root, related to us by mariage. "They were two of the most beautiful young ladies in Houston," Auntie might say, and I would realize, years later, that the Misses Root had been young ladies in the 1890s.

The bus usually took us by the home of one of Auntie's five sisters. "That's where your mother would sit in the window and sing to any boys walking by," she would say—almost every time we passed the house. I remember how my ears perked up the first time she said it; I was about to learn a secret about my beautiful mother.

"Of course, she was only about twelve," Auntie went on, shaking her head with disapproval. "I wondered then if maybe she was a little off. But not your great-grandmother. As far as Theresa was concerned, your mother could do no wrong."

Sitting there on the bus seat, my legs stretched out in front of me, I looked at my hands in my lap and tried not to cry. I knew what she meant when she said my mother was "off." It was

Tara Elgin Holley with Joe Holley

62

a confusing, mixed message that I got from Auntie. She insisted that I honor my mother, in the abstract; I came to understand that she was preparing me for a day when my mother's welfare would be my responsibility. But she also wanted me to know that there was something willful and destructive about my mother. To Auntie's way of thinking, my mother deserved a measure of blame for her fate. I resented her remarks. No matter how often I heard them, they hurt.

At least once a month, and always on Easter and Christmas, we took the long bus ride to Glenwood Cemetery. With its beautiful, moss-laden oaks and tall, waxy-leafed magnolias, its pungent cedars, and thick St. Augustine grass, the cemetery was an enchanted forest. Majestic winged angels and soft cherubs and little lambs watched over the elaborate stone and brick mausoleums sheltering Houston's founding families. Bounded by a crumbling brick wall, it was—and still is—just outside downtown. As I strolled along the curving streets of this peaceful city of the dead, I would catch glimpses through the tall trees of downtown skyscrapers and freeway traffic, that noisy city of the living I had escaped for a little while. I loved the cemetery.

It was here that Auntie began to fill in the blanks for me about my own family. Near the caretaker's cottage, a little frame house painted sky-blue and resting on brick beams, were the graves of the Elgins, the Jenkinses, the Hoffmans, and the Gehrings. These were my relatives, Auntie wanted me to know. I had reason to be proud. After depositing our flowers at the gravestones and pulling a stray weed or two from the family plots, we would sit on a stone bench if the weather was nice, and Auntie would tell me stories about aunts and uncles and cousins, grandmothers and grandfathers, the people from a past so very dim to me and so very dear to her.

"Charles Conrad Gehring," she would say, peering through

her glasses at the gravestone of her father. "What a fine figure of a man he was! I wish you could have known him." And she would begin to tell me, not for the first time, about how he had fled the family farm in Lippe-Detmold to escape compulsory military service, and how he had booked passage on a sailing ship out of Hamburg. "He was only sixteen," she said. "His parents had died, and it was his aunt and uncle who raised him. He never saw them again."

She enjoyed telling how he washed up on Galveston Island, the sandspit gateway into the new state of Texas, United States of America. The young man who would be her father stayed in Galveston for several months. He helped tend bar at a ramshackle little place near the docks, perfected his English, and listened to tales about the wealth of opportunities in Texas. A great many immigrants, from Europe and from other parts of America, were streaming into Galveston. Many were headed fifty miles up the vine-draped Buffalo Bayou to a muddy, little town hardly a decade old. Originally called Allen's Landing, after the three New Yorkers who founded the town and laid it out, the name was soon changed to honor the hero of the Battle of San Jacinto. In 1850, Charles Gehring, Auntie's father, my great-great-grandfather, boarded a steamboat bound for Houston.

Houston, despite its swampy, subtropical location, saw itself as a city of destiny. It was a magnet for young, energetic newcomers like Charles Gehring. Already a railroad and steamboat terminus, its citizenry had begun to manufacture railcars, steam engines, cigars, and soap. It had twelve sawmills for the vast forestlands of East Texas. Auntie's father worked as a barkeeper and later opened a saloon of his own. He prospered.

A little more than a decade after his arrival in America, Charles Gehring faced the same dilemma that had driven him from the old country. Texas cast its lot with the Confederacy, and the young German immigrant, though opposed to slavery and skeptical about secession, decided to join his fellow Texans. In a small daguerreotype that has passed down through the family, he is a handsome man with a dark beard and the hint of a smile on his face.

After the war, Charles Gehring made his way back to Houston, ran several successful businesses and met a young woman who had come from Prussia with her parents in the 1850s. Her name was Augusta Hoffman. She was sixteen when she married Charles Gehring.

Charles and Augusta Gehring had seven children. The oldest, Theresa, was my great-grandmother. She was born in 1866. Elsa—Auntie—was the youngest.

All these people, all these names. To me, many of them were letters carved on mossy tombstones. They were ghosts, a dim and wavy multitude that floated in and out of minds and memories. Yet, in a way, they were almost as real to me as they were to Auntie. Every time I walked down the hall from my bedroom to the bathroom, I walked right by the photograph of Charles Conrad Gehring, my great-great-grandfather. The chairs, tables, beds, and bookshelves he and other family members had amassed over the years were the furniture we still used.

It took many visits to Glenwood Cemetery for me to sort out my relatives, but over the years I began to revere them the way Auntie did. Now, I realize that it was a rare privilege for a little girl growing up in the 1950s to be on such familiar terms with people from a century past.

Auntie was determined that I know them. It wasn't just because she dwelled in the past and liked to have someone with whom she could share her memories. Auntie was consciously trying to connect me to the city that my family had helped build. She was trying to give me a grounding, a sense of place—within my family and the community at large. She was anxious for me to know that I was not an orphan, not a waif tossed hither and thither. The rootless, careless life my grandparents had chosen was not typical of the family. I belonged to proud, distinguished people. And so did my mother.

The stories Auntie told me would be the prologue to my life. They would be stories I would live by, and as I got older, I began to do more than just listen to the tales, the family myths, from the dim past. I hungered to know about people who were still alive. I began asking questions, particularly about Mama and Papa and my three aunts and, of course, about my mother.

I loved it when my aunts got together and began reminding each other about their youth and their adventures together, when it was the four of them. Every chance I got, I looked at photos of these four smiling, beautiful young women, my mother—to my eyes, at least—the prettiest of them all.

I remember one night at Sister's house, I was probably nine. Sally had just seen a Lana Turner movie and was giggling and teasing Betty Lee about being in the Hollywood drugstore where Lana Turner was discovered. It was the first time I had heard about Schwabs' and the Lana Turner legend.

"I remember Dawn saying, 'She could have been sitting on this very stool,'" Sally said, laughing. "And she might have been. 'Course, a lot of good it did us." She turned to Betty Lee. "Do you remember what you said?" she asked.

"I most certainly do not," Betty Lee answered. "I think you're making all this up."

"You said, 'Just look at me. I've got the glossy dark hair, the peaches-and-cream complexion. Why do you think Selznick didn't audition me for Scarlett?'"

"Why, Sally, how you lie!" Betty Lee said.

Sally went on, "And then you said, 'Just listen to me. Ah've already got the southern accent.'"

"Well, I do," Betty Lee said, fluffing up her wavy, still-dark hair. "That ol' Mr. Selznick just missed a bet."

I sat on the floor and took it all in. I was in heaven, just imagining my mother sitting at the counter drinking a Coke and laughing and dreaming with her sisters.

I had so many questions. I wanted to know what they were doing in California. I wanted to know why Mama and Papa were—I would search for the word—different. Deep down, of course, I was really asking about my mother, but I learned over the years to be devious. I learned that it was easier to get Auntie—and everyone else in the family—to talk about my grandparents than to talk about my mother.

As Auntie explained it, the Jenkins family, my great-grandparents, began making trips to California early in their marriage, possibly because my great-grandfather was health-conscious. He liked to travel to Colorado to take mud bath treatments and to soak his body in hot mineral springs. He enjoyed California for the sunshine. Auntie had these sepia-toned snapshots of Eldridge and Theresa Jenkins and their only child Marian Elise (my grandmother) in the early twentieth century, standing at the foot of Pikes Peak. In another picture, they are on mules headed into the Grand Canyon.

Auntie had opinions galore about Eldridge and Theresa's only daughter Marian—her beloved niece. "They spoiled Marian rotten," she would grumble, pursing her lips and frowning. "Marian is flighty," she would say, shaking her head.

Certainly, my grandmother had had all the advantages. Her father was a prosperous Houston businessman. Her aunts and uncles on the Gehring side were prominent members of Houston society, part of the cultured class who worked to make their city something more than a provincial backwater. They were cotton buyers, steel mill owners, downtown dry-goods merchants. They supported the symphony, the opera, the newly established Rice Institute, now Rice University.

My great-grandparents resolved to rear their only child as a Renaissance woman. They sent her to the New England Conservatory in Boston and then to Rice, where she was a member of the school's first freshman class. She played the violin in Houston chamber music ensembles, and with her friend Ima Hogg, daughter of the governor, she was a founding member of the Houston Symphony. A very proper young Victorian woman, she was a Houston debutante who made her debut at the Bayou Club, a bastion of Old South tradition. But Marian Jenkins fancied herself a poet and writer, an artiste. She decided very early that art was paramount.

I loved hearing about my grandmother's life as a child. But when I got older, I pestered Auntie with questions about her. Why wasn't Mama part of Houston society; why wasn't she closer to the rest of the family; why did she and Papa live hand to mouth in California; what happened to the money? Those are the questions I was trying to ask without knowing really how to phrase them.

Auntie, always quick to judge, blamed Papa, though she conceded he was the nicest man you'd ever want to meet. Mama was in her early twenties when she met Alfred Rice Elgin, probably at church. (The family name, unlike the watch, is pronounced with a hard *g*.) Alfred was already in his mid-forties.

He came from a distinguished southern family. His great-grandfather had been George Washington's chaplain. His father, Robert Morriss Elgin, had migrated to Houston from Tennessee in the 1840s. Robert Morriss Elgin was descended on his mother's

Tara Elgin Holley with Joe Holley

side from Robert Morriss, the American revolutionary patriot who, at a critical time, saved the colonial forces from starvation and mutiny by supplying their salaries out of his own pocket when it seemed impossible to raise the money.

Robert Morriss Elgin, my great-grandfather, fought with General Zachary Taylor's army in the Mexican War. Later, Uncle Bob, as he was known all over Houston, was chief clerk in the Texas General Land Office in the years before the Civil War. Later still, he was a land commissioner for the Texas Central Railroad. He purchased rights-of-way as the railroad pushed from the Gulf Coast into the developing Texas interior, and he laid out town sites for the settlers who were sure to follow. The little town of Elgin, in central Texas, is named for him. (Early-day travelers called it Hellagin because of a gang of thieves that hung out in a thicket on the outskirts of town.)

At home in Houston, Robert Morriss Elgin was a Freemason, a member of the vestry at the oldest church in Houston, Christ Church Cathedral, and an investor in several successful Houston and Galveston businesses. He and his wife Mary Sheegog Wilson had four children, two boys and two girls. Alfred—Papa to me— was born in 1873.

Auntie would shake her head disapprovingly when she told me about Papa. "Alfred was as pampered and protected as your grandmother was," she said. "I guess they were made for each other."

He was a musician, Auntie said, a cornetist. He played at parties and church socials, but he never attempted to play full-time as a professional. Growing up in a prosperous, comfortable family, he didn't have to do anything professionally. Apparently, he didn't want to.

Once, when he was twenty-one, Alfred's father set him up in the grocery business in downtown Houston. What a mistake that must have been! Young Alfred's entrepreneurial effort was short-lived. He was such an easy touch for his customers' hard-luck tales that his father had to liquidate the store before Alfred bankrupted him.

A few years later, Robert Morriss Elgin had a stroke and was paralyzed and bedridden for several years before he died. Alfred stayed home to take care of his father.

Alfred Rice Elgin had lived forty-seven easy, uneventful years when he married Marian Elise Jenkins. My grandmother was twenty-six. As Auntie explained, the Gehrings and the Jenkinses were not pleased. "It's not that we didn't care for him," she said. "Alfred Elgin was a good man, still is. He's kind and decent and honest as the day is long. What we couldn't understand is why Marian would fall for an 'old man.'"

Pretty, talented Marian was a good catch, and she had other prospects. So did my grandfather, for that matter. According to Auntie, a Shreveport widow felt jilted when he married Marian.

But Marian was also headstrong, everyone agreed. What she wanted, she usually got. It was Alfred, the gentle, fun-loving older man whom she chose. They were soul mates, she told her friends.

Mama and Papa were married at Christ Church in 1921. The babies started coming soon after—Alfred junior, known to the family as Brother, in 1922; Marian, known as Sister, in 1923; Betty Lee in 1925; Sally in 1927; Dawn in 1929; Lillian in 1931.

The parade of new arrivals disturbed some of Auntie's sisters. It didn't bother Auntie, but her sisters found it unseemly. It was a little too earthy and sensual, although they would never have used those words. Years later, the Gehring aunts would still tut-tut about how Marian, instead of "lying in" for a week after giving birth, was invariably up and out of bed the next day. Alfred and Marian had "bohemian" tendencies, the aunts muttered.

The stories about my mother and her sisters as children made their life seem idyllic. They spent their early childhood in Houston, in a cottage on Truxillo Street surrounded by aunts and uncles and cousins from both sides of the family. They had dogs and cats in the backyard and a goat that pulled them through the leafy green neighborhood in a little green-and-red wooden cart. They packed umbrellas and picnic feasts and went on family outings to the beach at Galveston or to the San Jacinto battleground, where Texas had won its independence from Mexico. They starred in plays and musicals at church and school. To be sure, life around the Elgin home was a bit chaotic and unpredictable—just as mine would be decades later—but the children didn't complain. Not, that is, until they got older.

The children would be artists, if not bohemians, if Mama and Papa had anything to say about it. My great-grandmother, Theresa, the organist at Christ Church, gave them piano lessons. She played in a German mandolin orchestra, so she taught her grandchildren how to accompany themselves as they played the German lieder she had learned as a girl. They took dance lessons from Mr. Abel. For a certain class of Houston society, the haughty, very dignified Mr. Abel was de rigueur. Mama gave Sister and Dawn violin lessons. All of them, a neighbor told Auntie, "sang like angels."

The extended stays in California started while the girls were still young. Papa and Mama were drawn like bees to blossoms to the heady, open atmosphere of Hollywood. They told Auntie they were eager to get away from the smallish, gossipy city they called home.

They considered themselves artists, and Houston, a city of the Old South in many ways, could be stuffy and conventional.

So could their own families, they let it be known. Without completely cutting ties, they were eager to get away. Auntie and the rest of the family shook their heads and wondered.

It wasn't only Alfred and Marian's bohemianism that caused strained relations with Auntie and the rest of the family. The Gehrings, the Elgins, the Jenkinses, all stalwart members of the Houston gentry, could at least tolerate, perhaps even appreciate Mama and Papa's artistic pretensions. It was their religious inclinations that caused furrowed brows and heated family discussions.

At some point, Mama and Papa became Christian Scientists. My aunts believe it was at Papa's urging. To family members, Christian Science was little more than a bizarre cult. Back in the old country, their people had been Methodists or Lutherans, with a few Quakers sprinkled in. In Houston, they had become respectable Episcopalians; Christ Church had long functioned as a sort of ecumenical base for early upper-class Houstonians. They could not comprehend how these two intelligent people could be taken in by Christian Science's claims.

In late spring, as soon as school was out, Papa would pile children and suitcases into the big family Packard and start the long, hard trek across West Texas and the deserts of New Mexico and Arizona to California. Enduring almost hourly tire blowouts, the two-thousand-mile trip usually took four days. Mama and the other family members who preferred not being cooped up that long in the Packard took the train to Los Angeles.

Papa and Mama would find a house in Santa Monica or in Hollywood, and the family would stay for several months, sometimes a year. My great-grandmother Theresa, who had been widowed some years earlier, was with them much of the time; she assigned herself the task of managing the household.

Tara Elgin Holley with Joe Holley

72

Mama and Papa had no jobs to hold them, no routine. Whenever she and Papa needed money, they sold off a piece of Houston property. Papa was active in the church, and he had numerous friends he visited regularly. Mama dabbled at painting or wrote stories or played music. For a few years, she was captivated by the arts and crafts movement that burgeoned in southern California in the 1920s and '30s. She spent her days happily painting pottery. Sometimes, when Papa was out, she would track him down by phone. "You come home and help me with these babies!" she would demand.

In 1928, Mama and Papa and the children were living in a pleasant little house near the beach at Santa Monica. Alfred junior was six at the time. One night the little boy developed a high fever. When it lingered for several days, Mama and Papa called in a Christian Science "practitioner," a lay minister trained by the church to offer prayers and assistance to the sick. Because of their religious beliefs, they did not summon a doctor.

The practitioner's efforts could not help the child, and during the night, he died of scarlet fever. Before getting sick, he had been playing a little boy's game and had tied red ribbons to the French doors of the dining room of the Santa Monica house. After his death, Mama and Papa could not bear to let anyone remove the ribbons. They stayed on the doors, fading to a dull purple.

They took Brother to Houston for burial. At the funeral service, some family members turned their backs and refused to shake Papa's hand. They believed he had let his own child die.

Mama and Papa lost another child. Lillian, the youngest, died of pneumonia at the age of three. They almost lost Sister. She became critically ill with pneumonia, but Grandmother Theresa marched into the house, lifted the feverish little child out of bed, and got her to a doctor in time.

Their ready acceptance of God's will, as they understood it

through the tenets of Christian Science, seemed to help them accept the death of their children with an attitude approaching equanimity, but I wonder if something else was also involved. Reading about early Houston not long ago, I came across references to a scarlet fever epidemic in 1899 that killed scores of people. In 1900, the hurricane that hit nearby Galveston killed more than six thousand. In 1903, a smallpox epidemic killed a number of people. In 1918, it was the worldwide influenza epidemic. Children died in those days, and often parents were helpless, even if they were more than willing for medical help to bend "God's will."

As the Depression deepened in the early 1930s, the trips to California became less frequent. Houston property had depreciated drastically, and the family money was beginning to run out.

Grandmother Theresa, by now a widow, took a house in Los Angeles, and as my mother and her sisters got older, they occasionally spent summers with her, even when Mama and Papa stayed in Houston. Theresa had plans for her four granddaughters. She told everybody that she had the four most beautiful grandchildren in the world. She was determined to get them into the movies. It was an unlikely dream, to be sure, but not impossible. The girls were charming and pretty and talented. Maybe just as important, Grandmother Theresa had a nephew who was a Twentieth Century-Fox executive.

When the four girls got to be teenagers, Mama and Papa again began spending time in California, usually in Hollywood. They stayed long enough for the girls to be enrolled in school.

Like teenagers everywhere, my mother and her sisters had their own Hollywood dreams. At least twice a week, they sneaked into the Rialto or the Orpheum or one of the other big theaters scattered around downtown Hollywood. Every month or so, spot-lights would crisscross the night sky, and the girls would hurry over to Hollywood Boulevard and world premieres at Grauman's Chinese Theater. They would strain against the red velvet ropes as Ronald Colman and Bette Davis, Clark Gable and Carole Lom-bard, swept out of their limousines and walked through a phalanx of cheering fans into the theater.

The girls were tantalized by the notion that dreams had, in fact, come true for girls their age. When their dreams wavered, Betty Lee would remind them of the little, dark-haired girl with a big voice who was in Sister's class at Hubert Howe Bancroft Junior High. "If Judy Garland can make it, why can't we?" she asked defiantly.

During my years at Auntie's, my aunts were like surrogate mothers to me. But they were more than that. Living in the past with Auntie, I needed connections to the modern world, to the twentieth century, to the everyday concerns of normal people. My aunts provided those connections.

They had their different personalities, their designated roles to play in the extended family. I relied on each one for different things. Betty Lee, working on her doctorate in French, was the glamor girl of the family. She was smart, beautiful, and ambitious. Sally was fun-loving, but more down-to-earth than Betty Lee.

Sister was the older sister, in every way. She was practical, no-nonsense, hardworking. I knew she resented Auntie, though I didn't know why. Many years later, she told me that Auntie ac-cused her of killing her little sister Lillian. "You were supposed to be taking care of your baby sister, but you took her out in the rain, and she got pneumonia," Sister remembered Auntie telling her. "She died because of you."

Sister was deeply hurt by Auntie's cruel accusation, but after brooding about it for years, a question popped into her mind. Why, she wondered, was a nine-year-old child charged with the responsibility of caring for an infant in the first place?

I knew that Sister and Betty Lee and Sally cared about me, and I loved it when they came around, or when I spent time in their homes. I watched them as I got older, and I imagined what they were like as girls, when it was the four of them, and my mother had her dreams as well.

I needed the truth, about my mother and about me, and they were the only ones who could tell it to me. I gradually came to realize that what I heard from Auntie was tainted with her bitterness. And what I heard from Mama was just the opposite; it was too syrupy-sweet to be credible. That left my aunts as my only reliable informants. Later, I learned that their versions of the past also were selective. There were gaps in their stories—caused by silence, fear, their own pain.

On one point, however, they all agreed: It was Dawn, the youngest, who seemed to have the best chance of making her Hollywood dreams into reality. From the beginning, she was lively, precocious, and talented. It was Dawn who chatted with neighbors and greeted guests at the front door, Dawn who organized neighborhood games, who took the lead. It was my mother, as she got older, who commanded the spotlight whenever she walked into a room.

She showed a talent for music early. She could play the violin and piano almost before she could read and write. She loved to perform, and if there was a play at school, Dawn invariably landed the starring role. During the summer, she would sit in the second-floor window of the house at 110 Truxillo and sing. Neighborhood children, and sometimes their parents, would gather in the alley below to listen. (Auntie, of course, believed such behavior was not proper; people of class and refinement didn't make spectacles of themselves.)

"When she sang solos in the choir at church, it gave me goose bumps," Sally once told me. "There was something magic about her voice."

Sister had a wicker basket full of childhood photos. Whenever Auntie and I visited, I begged to look through them. I lingered over the photos of my mother, and I bothered Sister with endless questions about the vivacious little blond-haired girl who smiled back at me. It would be years before I understood the pain that those happy childhood pictures represented to Sister and Sally and Betty Lee. As a child, all I knew is that I loved learning about my mother.

Peg Orem was my mother's best friend when the Elgin girls were growing up in Houston. Peg called her friend the golden girl, because she was so talented and pretty. Dawn sang, she played tennis, she was in all the plays at school. All the boys were in love with her, but the girls liked her, too. They were never jealous, because Dawn wasn't stuck-up. That's the way Peg remembers her.

The summer of '43 was their last summer together. Although the news on the front page of the *Houston Chronicle* was often grim that summer, I can imagine three laughing teenagers—Peg; her twin sister, Ann; and their best friend, Dawn. They were fourteen, and life was fun and crazy and exciting. I can hear them giggling constantly about boys, about school, about Mr. Crane, the tall, doleful-looking general science teacher they expected to have when they began eighth grade in the fall. They called him Ichabod, of course.

"He looks like a crane," Dawn announces one hot August morning at the tennis court. She thrusts her neck in and out and prances around with her knees high and elbows akimbo, the way a long-necked crane might promenade along the shores of nearby Buffalo Bayou.

The girls can't stop laughing. They flop down in the shade of a moss-draped old live oak near the tennis courts, and plot twin tricks they can play on Mr. Crane. Suddenly, Dawn sits up.

"Oh, my God, I almost forgot!" she says, her voice breathless and excited. "Today's the day I go downtown! I gotta get home!"

"What for?" Ann asks as the three girls hurry toward their bikes.

"It's a secret," Dawn says. "I'll tell you this afternoon when I get home." Her brown eyes flash. Peg cannot imagine what the secret might be. With Dawn, you never knew. She always had big dreams, exciting plans.

They pedal up Montrose toward the Elgin house, Peg awkwardly trying to balance the three tennis rackets, Ann with Dawn perched precariously on the handlebars. Peg glances over at her curly-haired sister, her face flushed and perspiring, pumping hard with her passenger. Dawn, in her white tennis outfit, has her head thrown back, laughing her deep, full laugh. Her long, blond hair is streaming into Ann's face. Peg is in awe of Dawn; Ann, she knows, feels the same way. They are both a little bit in love with her.

In the Elgin front yard, Dawn jumped off the bike before Ann could brake to a stop. She gave Peg a hug and then Ann. "I'll call you," she said. "Wish me luck!" Tennis racket in hand, she ran up the front steps and into the house.

The phone was ringing as the girls walked through their own front door minutes later. "It's Dawn," Mrs. Orem said. She handed Peg the phone.

"Look, you gotta go with me," Dawn said. "I need moral support."

Later that afternoon, Peg, wearing a school dress, met her

Tara Elgin Holley with Joe Holley

78

friend at the bus stop. Dawn was wearing a robin's-egg-blue dress trimmed in white, with a straight skirt that came to mid-calf. She wore white heels and a pair of Betty Lee's stockings. Betty Lee would kill her if she ruined them.

"It's Betty Lee's dress, too," she said, twirling around like a model. "Like it?"

"It's heavenly," Peg said. "You look so grown up."

They caught the downtown bus. Although Dawn still hadn't said where they were going, Peg noticed she had a batch of sheet music in her hand.

They got off the bus at the Rice Hotel, the venerable hotel where the rich and famous stayed when they came to Houston. Peg had never been inside the fancy lobby with its fat, gilded columns and gleaming tile floor, black with gold patterns in the tile. On the walls were huge murals depicting scenes from Texas history. Peg looked up at the massive crystal chandelier; she had never seen anything like it.

Dawn acted as if she lived there. She walked up to a bellboy in a short maroon jacket with gold trim and a maroon pillbox hat.

"Can you tell me where Mr. Beckner is rehearsing?" Dawn asked. She smiled sweetly. The man directed them to the Empire Room, on the Travis Street side of the lobby. They walked through a draped entryway into a Hollywood-smart supper club that almost took their breath away. The tables were covered with snowy-white cloths, and the walls were silver, trimmed in dark blue and jonquil-yellow. Heavy mirrored columns and two large chandeliers made the terraced room seem to sparkle, even in the middle of the day.

The bandstand was crowded into a corner of the room, behind a square of highly polished pine dance floor. The Denny Beckner Orchestra was in rehearsal. The girls waited near the door for the band to take a break, and then Dawn, careful not to totter in her high heels, walked across the room to Beckner. A short, friendly-looking man with dark, curly hair, he wore a white shirt with the sleeves turned up and casual slacks. Peg stayed at the door. She couldn't believe her friend was so brave.

Dawn and the band leader talked for a few minutes. Peg could see him smiling. Somehow Dawn persuaded him to let her audition.

"I can do 'My Blue Heaven,' 'Embraceable You,' ' 'Deed I Do,' 'Stormy Weather,' " Peg heard Dawn tell Beckner. "These guys know them?"

"I expect they do," Beckner said, grinning. "Whaddya say, boys? 'Stormy Weather'?"

He gave the downbeat, and the band struck up a jazzy, up-tempo version. Peg, with a catch in her throat and a funny feeling in her stomach, listened to her friend's expressive, dusky voice, her casual, almost conversational way with lyrics and phrasing. She watched Beckner's face. It held the surprised and happy look of a man who knew, even after the first few bars, that the fresh-faced young woman singing with his orchestra was no starry-eyed ingenue.

As the last note faded, Beckner bowed toward Dawn and applauded. The boys in the band broke into raucous cheers. They did "My Blue Heaven" and then "Embraceable You," while Dawn remained just as confident and casual as if she were singing to neighbors in the alley at home. Beckner signed her on the spot, never knowing, apparently, that Dawn was all of fourteen.

The Empire Room had been the classiest venue for what the newspapers called Houston's café society since its grand opening in 1938. The Dorsey brothers, Freddy Martin, Paul Whiteman, Coon Sanders, Woody Herman, Vincent Lopez, Ted Weems and his young singer Perry Como—all the big bands played either the Empire Room or the Rice Roof, where you could dine and dance under the stars. (Perry Como, by the way, was making seventy-five dollars a week, I read years later; what my mother was making I don't know, although she told me that in Hollywood a few years later, she made $20 a week.)

The Denny Beckner Orchestra and other big bands played to capacity crowds at the Empire Room. Dawn sang with the orchestra for nearly a year. Thursday, Friday, Saturday, and Sunday nights, Papa would drive downtown and wait in the car for her to finish the final set at 11:00 P.M. Every Sunday night, Peg and Ann would lie in bed telling stories to keep each other awake, waiting to hear the KTRH radio announcer proclaim, "And now, live from the beautiful Empire Room of the Rice Hotel, we bring you the big band sounds of the Denny Beckner Orchestra, with the lovely Dawn Elgin on the vocals!"

Peg and Ann would tell her at school the next day how good she sounded. Their friend Ducky Musselwhite, who admired Dawn from afar, asked if the rumor was true. "Did she really sing downtown?" he wanted to know. "Do you think she'd go to the Valentine prom with me?"

My mother's career at the Empire Room came to an end when Beckner asked her to go on tour with the band. "Can I go, Papa, can I go?" she begged. "I can make up school. I've got to go!"

Papa had to go downtown and confess to Beckner that his popular young singer was a fourteen-year-old kid. She didn't get to go on tour.

For my mother, the setback was temporary. She got a job singing at the Aragon Ballroom, a downtown club particularly popular with servicemen stationed at nearby Ellington Field. It was considered one of Houston's elite nightclubs, one of many that sprang up and flourished after the repeal of Prohibition in 1931.

At fifteen, this precocious teenager decided she was ready to test her talent in the big city. Shaking Sally awake one night, she made an announcement. "I'm going to New York," she said. "I'm quitting school, and I'm going to New York to sing."

"You can't go to New York," Sally, who was seventeen at the time, told her younger sister. "For one thing, you don't have any money."

"I do, too," Dawn said. "I've got thirty dollars. I borrowed it from Sister."

Sister, twenty-one and every bit the responsible eldest daughter, was working for Houston Power and Light. She kept her savings in a box on the top shelf of her wardrobe. She had no idea that Dawn had "borrowed" her money.

Sally knew she ought to tell Sister and their parents what Dawn had in mind, but she decided not to. She was afraid they might say no to what promised to be an adventure. She suggested to Dawn what she considered a reasonable compromise.

"Look, go to New Orleans instead of New York," she said, "and I'll go with you."

Dawn frowned at the suggestion, then said okay. She would try New Orleans, but just for a while. They agreed that Sister would want them to have her hard-earned money to finance such an important trip, so they decided not to tell her.

The next evening, Sally braided Dawn's hair to make her look young enough for half fare on the train. In the morning, the girls sneaked their suitcases out of the house and dropped them off at the neighborhood drugstore on their way to school. School seemed interminable that day. When the bell finally rang, they dashed over to the drugstore, grabbed their bags, and took the bus to the train station downtown.

Sally bought tickets to New Orleans. Dawn's braided hair worked. Once they were on the train, the blue-suited conductor punched her half-fare ticket without a second glance.

The train pulled into New Orleans the next morning. The girls took a cab to the YWCA—that was Sally's idea—and got a room. That afternoon Sally found a job at a little gift shop on Barone Street. She was promised eighteen dollars a week. After a couple of weeks at the Y, Sally found a room for them in a boarding house in the Garden District just off St. Charles. She enrolled Dawn in the eighth grade at school.

Sally called her parents after she and Dawn had been in New Orleans a few days. Mama and Papa didn't seem particularly concerned that their teenage daughters had run away from home to a place Sally liked to call Sin City on the Mississippi.

"Have a nice time," Papa said. "Oh, and Sally, look up Bob Wiggins if you have the time. He's an old friend of the family. A fine fellow. Tell him we said hello."

Every morning, Sally rode the streetcar to work, while Dawn went to school; at least, Sally hoped she was going to school. In the evenings, the sisters wandered through the exotic old French Quarter. They listened to the sounds of jazz and blues and swing wafting into the narrow, musty-smelling streets from the clubs and bars and restaurants. They were too young to go inside.

On a Sunday afternoon, Sally and Dawn wandered into the Walgreen's near their apartment. A gang of teenage boys hung out at the drugstore, and one of them, a friendly, freckle-faced kid named Eddy Klonhaur, struck up a conversation with the two pretty girls who had come into the store. He was sixteen, Eddy told them, and he had just come home from the Navy. He had enlisted at fifteen, but shortly before he was to be shipped overseas, his mother informed the Navy of her son's real age. Eddy got shipped home. To his neighborhood buddies, he was a hero, even though he hadn't done any fighting.

Eddy Klonhaur, proud son of New Orleans, offered to be the girls' guide to the city. That afternoon, they boarded the St. Charles streetcar and rode out to the zoo. Sally and Dawn and Eddy got to be friends that day, strolling past the elephants and tossing peanuts to the monkeys, talking, laughing and teasing as they sat together on the promenade above the Mississippi.

Over the next few weeks, Eddy Klonhaur showed them his New Orleans. They were close friends by the time the girls left town. Eddy was especially close to Dawn, perhaps because she was more outgoing than Sally, but also because they were almost exactly the same age. They weren't girlfriend and boyfriend exactly, just friends. Maybe because he had sisters of his own, he was relaxed around girls; he knew how to be a friend. He and Dawn vowed to keep in touch.

One afternoon while Sally was working, Dawn wandered into the large and luxurious Hotel Roosevelt. She found the Louis Prima band rehearsing in the ballroom. Prima and his band were featured each night in the hotel's famed Blue Room, "the oldest supper club in America," the poster in the hotel lobby proclaimed.

As in Houston with Denny Beckner, my mother talked her way into an audition. Prima, a jive-talking, finger-snapping New Orleans jazzman, hired her that afternoon. She could hardly wait for her big sister to get home from work. She forgot about school.

Sally was in awe of her talented younger sister. Some nights she would stand in the hallway and peer into the Blue Room at the fashionably dressed couples drinking and dining at round tables with crisp white tablecloths, under golden chandeliers. She observed what the beautiful women wore, how the men held their lighters while they lit the ladies' cigarettes. She watched them talk and laugh and glide gracefully across the dance floor. She felt awkward and immature and wondered if she would ever be so graceful and knowing and sophisticated.

She tried to make herself inconspicuous long enough to watch Prima strike up the band with a loud and lively jazz number featuring his raspy voice and one of his skittering riffs on the trumpet. After a few pieces, he would introduce his new singer, the lovely Dawn Elgin.

Sally listened to the polite applause as the room darkened and a spotlight found Dawn. She stood at the microphone in her low-cut white cocktail dress, a dress that Sally had helped her buy. The light played off her shiny, shoulder-length blond hair, her smiling, pretty face. She slid into "Star Dust," giving the Hoagy Carmichael hit a quiet, wistful treatment.

After the applause died down, the band broke into a bouncy "Fascinating Rhythm." Prima, standing off to the side with a manic leer on his face, did a kind of Groucho Marx shuffle toward Dawn. Fist jammed into his jacket pocket, grinning crazily, he made what appeared to be an obscene gesture inside his jacket pocket. The audience laughed, and Dawn stifled a giggle. She nearly tripped over the lyrics.

I have a brittle, yellowed photograph of my mother at the microphone, with Louis Prima at her side. She certainly doesn't look fifteen. As Sally remembers, she didn't sound fifteen, either.

The girls were having fun in New Orleans. With Sally's gift-shop job and Dawn's singing, they made enough money to get out and enjoy themselves. Occasionally, the large Klonhaur family had them out for dinner, looked after them from a distance.

My mother was always talking herself into interesting new places or meeting interesting people at the hotel. Sally followed along.

"You'll never guess who was in the audience tonight," she told Sally. "Charlie Chaplin, Jr.! He wants us to have dinner with him tomorrow night!"

They did have dinner, the three of them, at Antoine's. They stayed in touch for several years.

Prima took his band to L.A. after a few months. He left Dawn behind because of her age. Disappointed and restless, she decided to follow through on her original plan. Sally gave Dawn a week's salary, quit her job at the gift shop, and boarded a train back home to Houston. Dawn, not yet sixteen, took the train to Manhattan.

In New York, Dawn got in touch with some of her prosperous Gehring relatives. She stayed with them for a few weeks, but she wasn't able to catch on with a band, perhaps because the Gehrings kept a closer watch on her than Mama and Papa did. They bought her a fur coat, took care of her for a while, and then sent her home.

At sixteen, my mother's course was set. I can imagine her waiting on the platform at Grand Central Station. The train pulled in, she wrapped her new coat around her and stepped on board. The train may have been taking her south, but she wasn't really going home again. Looking at her reflection in the glass, she must have believed that childhood and school and girlish dreams were over. Like her great-grandfather nearly a century earlier, she was ready to begin her new life, her real life. She could hardly bear to waste a minute.

Back in Houston in the spring of 1945, she hooked up again

with house bands at the Aragon Ballroom. Like a morning glory reaching for the sun's first rays, like a child too excited to sleep on Christmas morning, she kept her eyes open, yearning for the big break that would take her out of Houston for good. She would be the next Margaret Whiting or Helen O'Connell or Jo Stafford. She had no doubt.

The Elgin girls—Hollywood, 1945: Marian, Betty Lee,
Sally, and Dawn.

CHAPTER FOUR

Every Christmas and every Thanksgiving, Auntie and I made the rounds of our Houston relatives. I loved these outings. Not only did I get to be with cousins and other children, but I always knew I might hear something about my mother. I was a spy, always listening. Squeezed between adults on a couch or lurking in the next room, I would listen in on conversations on the off chance that my mother might be mentioned. Even better, someone might pull out old photo albums, and I would plant myself next to the relative holding the thick volume. I would linger over pictures of my mother as long as it was allowed.

I remember a Thanksgiving at Sister's. Mike, Sally's former husband, was having dinner with us. (Even though Sally had remarried, Mike was still part of the family.) We had finished eating, and my aunts were clearing the table, but Mike and Uncle Don and some of the other men were still at the table drinking coffee and talking. I wasn't listening particularly, until I heard Mike say, "She was such a beautiful woman! And so voluptuous!" He was looking off into the distance, a little smile on his handsome face.

Smoke drifted slowly up from the cigarette in his hand. I wasn't sure what voluptuous meant, but I realized he was talking and thinking about my mother.

The story he was telling was inconsequential, but I was captivated. I listened for every detail. I would take the grains of information he was offering and polish them into shiny pearls of knowledge about the person I cared for most in the world.

I was constantly trying to piece together the puzzle. I was obsessed with this woman who, to me, was more than just my mother; she had become a goddess. I felt great shame about my obsession. At some point, I had begun to understand that she was not to be talked about. To other members of the family, she was a symbol of darkness, of something forbidden. She represented pain and regret and aching loss. Auntie didn't seem all that reluctant to talk about my mother, but her sisters, my aunts, did, and they were the ones who knew the truth.

As I got older, I gradually came to realize that Sister and Sally and Betty Lee weren't consciously trying to keep my mother's life a dark family secret, although they did feel a need to protect me. They may have been in mourning for their younger sister, for Dawnie, for their shining star who fell to earth. It was hard for them, painfully hard, to sit down with me and tell me what I desperately wanted to know.

Only in recent years have they begun to open up to me, even though they still find it painful to talk about what happened. Sally in particular. Sally was closest to my mother when they were growing up, but it has been years since she has seen her younger sister. Remembering the Dawn she adored, she can't bear to see the Dawn my mother has become.

The obsession that began when I was a little girl has never really ended, after all these years. With my aunts' help and with the help of my mother's old friends—Eddy Klonhaur, for example—I have at last begun to piece together Dawn's story. Some of it has been confirmed, some is imagined, and some I guess I'll never know for sure.

Eddy Klonhaur had one great worry that summer, the summer of 1944. He was afraid the war would end before he got a chance to do his patriotic part. One morning, not long after Sally and my mother left New Orleans, the sixteen-year-old washed-out Navy veteran marched into the Marine Corps recruiting office on Canal Street and told a jut-jawed Marine he had just had his eighteenth birthday. The recruiter didn't ask for proof, even though the wiry little red-haired kid standing before his desk hardly resembled the recruiting-poster leatherneck who would strike terror into the Japs.

Three months later, after Parris Island and Camp Lejeune, Private Eddy Klonhaur, USMC, found himself in Honolulu, then Guam and Tsingtao, China. Eddy was a machine gunner with the 6th Marine Division.

Through it all, he and my mother kept in touch. "Your letters keep me going," he wrote. "You'll never know how grateful I am to you."

She was headed back to California, she wrote Eddy in the summer of 1945. Betty Lee was driving out to Bakersfield to be with her husband, Bennett, who was in the Army Air Corps and stationed at a base nearby. Twenty years old and the mother of two infants, Betty Lee needed help with the children on the drive out, so my mother volunteered.

She had no intention of staying in hot, dusty Bakersfield, in the middle of nowhere. A few days after Betty Lee arrived and got settled, Dawn persuaded her older sister to drive her on to Los Angeles. Sister and Sally were also back in L.A. Sister was working at Twentieth Century-Fox. Ever the responsible one, she found her younger sisters a place to live in a Hollywood rooming house for single girls. The rent was seven dollars a week.

Almost immediately, Dawn found a job singing at a seedy little bar in downtown L.A., just off Broadway. The Tiki Ti, it was called.

"Tacky Ti's more accurate," Sally wrote Betty Lee. "I'd like to hear her sing," she wrote, "but I'm scared to go down there."

Nothing frightened Dawn. Every evening about five, she put on one of several nice dresses she had worn when she sang at the Aragon and took the trolley downtown. The little bar was cool and dark, the only light coming from recessed blue bulbs in the corners of the room. The motif was ragtag South Pacific, with dusty fishing nets on the wall and dingy little Chinese lanterns at the tables.

Dawn would linger at the bar for a while chatting with Gin-Gin, a heavyset Hawaiian who assured her that he was her body-guard. As customers began to drift in, she took her place at the back of the room on the tiny platform that passed for a stage. After warming up with her trio, she swung into her repertoire of the latest jazz tunes. On the wall above her head was a dusty old blue marlin, stuffed and mounted many years ago.

"I guess the musicians look after her," Sally wrote, "but it's a real dive. She rides the streetcar downtown and rides it back at night. She knows her way around. As far as I know, no one's ever asked about her age, and if they do, she'll just lie about it."

Single-minded as ever, my mother was doing what she had to do. And it wasn't just the Tiki Ti. The war had made L.A. a round-the-clock town. Defense industry plants started running twenty-four hours a day, and "swing shift" dance halls sprang up for late-night workers. Bands played from two in the morning until dawn. Dawn was working constantly.

Tara Elgin Holley with Joe Holley

92

Like so many song stylists of the time, both male and female, she was honing her basic skills, learning her craft. When she wasn't singing, she was listening—to Jo Stafford with the Tommy Dorsey Orchestra, Doris Day with Bob Crosby and then with Les Brown, June Christy and Chris Connor with Stan Kenton, Helen O'Connell with Jimmy Dorsey. She was picking up little tips from the musicians around her and developing a smoky-voiced style that was her very own.

Dawn was sixteen. Sister kept nagging her to finish school. "You never know how your singing's going to turn out," she would say. "You need that high school diploma."

"You're probably right," Dawn told her older sister, so one morning she walked over to Hollywood High and enrolled. She even showed up for class for a few days, but it didn't take her long to realize that she wasn't interested in learning what high school had to teach. Besides, it was hard to get up and make it to school every morning after working until two the night before. She dropped out after a few weeks.

A few mornings later, barely awake after working the night before, she opened the front door to a sober-looking man in a brown suit and a hat. He was from the Los Angeles Independent School District, he said, showing her a badge. He was a truant officer. When Dawn told him there were no parents at the address for him to talk to, he told her to get dressed. She would have to accompany him downtown. He took her to the juvenile detention hall and handed her over to a police matron. The matron accused her of being a prostitute and ordered her to strip. "I have to see if you're really a virgin," the woman said.

"What did you do?" Betty Lee asked her later.

"I didn't do anything," Dawn told her. "I said, 'How dare you!' "

Sally, who had graduated the year before and had gotten a job at Twentieth Century-Fox, had to take off work and go downtown to bail Dawn out of detention hall. She almost ended up in custody herself.

"How old are you?" a snippy little social worker wanted to know.

"I'm old enough to be on my own," Sally said angrily. Before the social worker would agree to release Dawn, Sally had to sign a document stating that she would send her little sister back to Houston.

"Can you imagine what that prune would have said if she knew about the Tiki Ti?" Dawn said to Sally on their way home from the detention hall that afternoon. She and Sally laughed so hard the bus driver glanced at them through his rearview mirror.

Dawn did go back to Houston for a few weeks to visit Mama and Papa, but she never went back to school. Except for a few jazz extension classes at UCLA, she was never in a classroom again.

Back in L.A., her singing gigs were getting better. She got a job at a little place on Vine, where she hooked up with the band leader Harry Wham. She was a hit at Lake Arrowhead and at Big Bear. She spent several weeks at Lake Tahoe singing with the Harry Wham band. She hooked up again with her old New Orleans mentor, Louis Prima. One night she sang with the Dorsey Brothers Orchestra at the Hollywood Bowl, and then she caught on at a place called Ciro's, a little club across the street from Mocambo on Sunset Boulevard. The stripper, Lili St. Cyr, famous for her bathtub act, was on the same bill.

Dawn was singing regularly at Ciro's with the Harry Wham Orchestra. ("It looks like wham, Eddy, as in whammo," she explained, "but it's pronounced wahm.") Gary Cooper hung out at Ciro's. So did Bugsy Siegel and his mobster friends.

On Monday nights, she was a regular at the Palladium, the flashy Hollywood ballroom that provided a venue for some of the best big bands in the country. Stan Kenton and his orchestra were the regulars at the Palladium, although the Les Brown Orchestra, with Doris Day on the vocals, were also headliners. Dawn sang with the Tommy Jones Orchestra.

"Did you see that guy I was with last night?" Sally asked her one night after a date at the Palladium. "He couldn't believe that was my sister up there on the stage. He kept saying, 'She can't be seventeen!' He could hardly dance for looking at you."

Betty Lee remembers a night in 1945 when the two of them were hanging around outside the Palladium with several other girls when Nat King Cole walked out. The girls squealed and asked for his autograph. He spotted Dawn. "Could I take you home?" he asked.

Almost without thinking, she blurted, "Oh, no!" She was shocked that the famous singer had asked her out. Dawn responded the way she did because she was surprised, but Betty Lee remembers Nat King Cole's response. "I'll never forget the look on his face," she says. "He was very hurt.

"She was naive, bubbly, and cute," Betty Lee recalls. "She was always getting traffic tickets, but the policemen who stopped her usually ended up asking her for a date. Once she ran into a telephone pole, and the pole fell down."

Once, when Dawn was sixteen, someone wrote Universal Studios about Betty Lee's beauty. A man named Williams called. He was a talent scout, he said, and he invited her out for a screen test. Dawn went along.

Williams asked dark-haired Betty Lee a few questions and looked at her through a range finder. "Do you ride?" he asked.

"Ride what?" Betty Lee responded.

Williams noticed Dawn. She told him she was a singer.

"We'll be in touch," he told her.

"In Hollywood," my mother told me years later, "everyone was looking at everyone."

"She was as cute as could be," Betty Lee remembers. "She was blond, she had beautiful teeth, a great figure. She was always worried about her eyes being too small and her nose being too big. I think an agent told her that. She was worried about her ankles, so she would sit and do rotation exercises."

Dawn wrote a letter to Papa back home in Houston, thanking him for a box of Valentine candy he had sent.

Well, here I am in Hollywood for a little while. I was thinking about you and Mama and how much I'd love to see you again, but I am so glad you both are together, and I hope everything is swell. I know I feel pretty wonderful with my job, and I'm singing at the Palladium now. It's just an intermission band, but oh it's wonderful. Then Harry and all of us are going to Balboa and play I think but nothing is definite yet. Incidentally, Palladium is the biggest, best ballroom in the U.S.! We broadcast too.

My mother was seventeen, and the war was over. Eddy Klonhaur was back in the States, stationed at Camp Pendleton, an hour's drive south of L.A. Although the war was over, he had decided to stay in the Marines and was now part of a newly formed reconnaissance unit based at Pendleton.

"My buddies couldn't believe that little Eddy Klonhaur was getting letters from this beautiful blonde in Hollywood," he told Sally later. "To tell you the truth, I couldn't, either."

"I'll drive down to see you," Dawn wrote him when she found out he was coming home.

He was in his barracks one morning in the Headquarters Battalion of the 1st Marine Division. He was folding his laundry when he got a message that his wife was at the base guest house. Curious to see this mystery woman, he also was apprehensive. He knew Marines who had been ambushed by women they thought they had loved and left. "Come go with me," he asked a couple of buddies.

Even before they got to the guest house, Eddy's companions started grinning and slapping him on the shoulder. There at the curb in front of the house was a tall, blond beautiful girl, her wavy, shoulder-length hair glinting in the sun. She was standing beside a new Ford convertible, shiny and red.

"She drove me back to the barracks so I could pack some things, and all my buddies were drooling, so was my CO," Eddy told Sally when the three of them had dinner in Hollywood the next night. "See, they never really believed the beautiful Hollywood gal existed. And here she was in the flesh."

Two or three weekends a month, Eddy would take the train up to L.A. to see my mother. They went everywhere in her little red convertible—to the beach and pier at Santa Monica, to restaurants and clubs, to Palm Springs and Lake Arrowhead. One Friday evening, when Eddy didn't have a weekend pass, my mother smuggled him off base in the trunk of her car. As in New Orleans, they were friends, nothing more really. They were two kids who enjoyed life and being together.

One afternoon, she took him to the races at Santa Anita. Eddy had never been to a racetrack, but Dawn, laughing and friendly and outwardly mature for her age, seemed to know her way around. They ran into several musicians, guys from the orchestra she was singing with, who took them into the private club high above the turf.

"They were what you call high rollers," Eddy told Sally as the three of them sat around Sally's tiny apartment just off La Cienega late that afternoon. "They wanted to parlay twenty bucks apiece, but I knew the maximum money I had in my pocket was thirty-five or forty bucks. I was thinking that would leave me twenty bucks."

"The guys pitched in twenty dollars apiece for us, and I picked the horses," Dawn said, giggling.

"And this is what we won," Eddy said, pulling a roll of bills out of his jacket pocket. He laughed and shook his head. "I don't know how she does it, but she always comes up a winner."

Dawn particularly liked having Eddy in the audience when she was singing. "The people in the band loved her," he told me years later. "They took care of her. She had a soft, bluesy-type voice, real distinctive. When she sang 'Summertime,' it was just an amazing experience."

Along the Sunset Strip in the late 1940s was one little supper club after another, each with its own personality, its own cast of regulars. Players, owned by the director Preston Sturges, was one of Dawn's favorites. Actors and studio people frequented the place. "Ruth Roman, Betty Grable, and Maureen O'Hara—they're there just about every night I've been there," Dawn told Sally.

In addition to Ciro's, my mother liked Trocadero, just down the hill from the house on Miller Drive. She liked the Garden of Allah, where Dorothy Parker, Robert Benchley, and other *New Yorker* types stayed when they came to L.A. Her favorite was Mocambo. One night at the chic little supper club, she and Eddy sat at a table near Edith Piaf and Maurice Chevalier. She wanted to go over and say hello to the legendary songstress, but for once her courage failed her.

Tara Elgin Holley with Joe Holley

"Who was the new guy on the drums?" Eddy asked one night.

"Oh, that's Mel," Dawn said. "Mel Torme. He's actually a pretty good singer, but the guys all laugh at him 'cause he always wants to play the drums. Personally, I think he ought to stick to singing."

One weekend, Eddy took two paychecks and bought a blue suit, a white shirt, a tie, and a new pair of shoes. The next weekend, he found himself sitting alone at a table at Ciro's while Dawn was singing. He noticed Vincente Minnelli, Lana Turner, and Stevie Crane all sitting at tables nearby. He wondered if he ought to pinch himself.

Harry Wham at the piano marked the downbeat with a nod of his head as his five-piece orchestra broke into the first couple of bars of "My Funny Valentine." There was a smattering of applause from the regulars in the audience, including Eddy. He dared to wonder if his friend was singing just for him. She wore a clingy green velvet dress, and as she looked down at the mike, there was a little smile on her face. She glanced up and gave a wink in his direction. He could feel his face blush.

This, he knew, was her signature song. She had a special way with it. With her sultry, expressive voice, she caressed the words, shaped the phrases in a way that no one had ever taught her. She reached out, and the audience was with her.

Eddy enjoyed being with Dawn, but after a while, he felt uncomfortable with her always picking up the tab. His sergeant's salary just didn't allow him to live the fast life she thrived on. They were strolling the pier at Santa Monica one afternoon when he tried to say something to Dawn about how he felt. He could feel his face turning red beneath the freckles.

Dawn laughed and gave him a hug. "Oh, Eddy, that's ridiculous," she said. "I've got the money; it's a crime not to spend it."

She walked over to a food booth. "Here, buy me a pretzel," she said. "Maybe that'll make you feel better."

Eddy laughed, but he still felt awkward about it. He began to spend occasional weekends in L.A. without telling Dawn he was in town. They stayed friends.

The last time he saw my mother, it was April 1948. He had decided to stay in the Marines. He had become a diver, and his unit was being shipped to the Middle East to secretly survey the beaches of Saudi Arabia. He spent his last weekend stateside with Dawn and my grandparents. He slept at the house on Miller Drive Saturday night and had to get to the docks at San Pedro by eight on Sunday morning. Everyone overslept, and he missed his bus.

My mother, Eddy remembered, threw a robe over her nightgown and drove him to the docks. Mama also came along on the mad dash to get him to the ship. When they got to San Pedro, he and my mother embraced, then he hoisted his duffel bag and boarded the ship, leaving Dawn and Mama waving to him from the dock.

I met Eddy many years later. He was married, with grandchildren, living in retirement on a lake north of Dallas. He turned out to be such a nice guy, I halfway wished that he were my long-lost father. I even looked for some resemblance. But my birth date didn't work out, and he insisted that as much as he adored my mother, they were never more than friends. "Your mother just wasn't that kind of girl," he said. "She was a real classy lady."

They lost touch, Eddy explained. That day on the docks at San Pedro was the last time he saw her. He was in China for a while, then Guam, looking for Japanese prisoners, then Saudi Arabia. He heard from his sister Rhoda a couple of years later that Dawn was in New Orleans, and he tried to look her up. Rhoda told him she heard that Dawn was seeing someone, so he didn't try too hard.

More than forty years later, he still wondered what had become of the beautiful girl who brightened his life with her smile, her energy, her vivacity, who made his life in California so exciting. His recon unit got together for a reunion every couple of years, he said, and his old buddies still asked him about Dawn.

"I just couldn't believe that someone like her would choose to spend time with me," said the old Marine, who still wore his hair chopped military short. He shook his head and smiled. "She was amazing," he said softly. "She'd walk into a room and just light up the place. All eyes would be on her."

He remembered one last thing. After he shipped out to the Far East, he heard that Dawn had begun to date his best friend, a fellow Marine named Johnny Wakefield. He and Johnny had grown up together in New Orleans.

"Johnny lives in Florida," Eddy said. "We still see each other now and then. His wife was mentally ill. Schizophrenic. They've been divorced for years, but he still looks after her."

"Dawn was always falling for some guy," Sally would eventually tell me.

"There were always men in her life, from junior high on," Sister said. "I guess it had to do with her illness." (Sister is not known for her subtlety.)

There was Nestor the band leader. There was tall, handsome Ed, an ex-Marine going to school, his father was a professor at the University of Oklahoma. There was Johnny Wakefield, Eddy's friend. And there was Lars, the tall, blond Dane who smoked a pipe, wrote travel articles, and was trying to break into pictures. Betty Lee remembers that in addition to Dawn, he was dating a girl who was seeing Robert Stack. Dawn remembers that he often borrowed her car and drove it out to Pacific Palisades, although he always brought it back. Lars was the man who broke my mother's heart.

And then there was Roy. Slight and soft-spoken, Roy William Hurst was not at all the flashy sort of fellow who usually caught her eye. As Sally remembers, Dawn met him on the rebound from Lars, probably in the fall of 1950.

"He's in Naval Intelligence," Dawn told Sally as they dressed for dinner one night that fall. Roy was taking them both out. "He's really a nice guy," Dawn said. "I like him a lot."

On their way to dinner, Roy was polite and gentlemanly. He seemed nice enough, Sally decided, though he didn't have much to say. Maybe he's shy, she told herself. He was in his early twenties, she guessed. He spoke with the hint of an accent, an accent she couldn't place, though it sounded vaguely Hispanic.

He pulled over to the curb in front of a drugstore. "Be right back," he said, and dashed into the store. When he came back to the car moments later, he presented them with two large bottles of Chanel No. 5.

"That's strange," Sally thought to herself, realizing that the perfume he had bought was probably the most expensive in the store.

The restaurant was expensive, too. He ordered lobster for the three of them and champagne. He insisted on picking up the tab. Sally decided that he was anxious to impress Dawn, and she wondered if he really had the money. He was trying too hard, she thought. It made her uncomfortable, but Dawn squeezed his arm and smiled into his eyes. She didn't seem to mind.

Sally felt better about him when he mentioned one night that he was worried about Dawn. He had come by the house at a time when he knew Dawn would be working. "I think she's drinking too much," he said, his dark eyes earnest. "I've tried to talk to her, but she doesn't listen to me. Maybe you can get her to stop?"

Sally had noticed it too, and it worried her. She assured him she would talk to her sister. My mother, it seemed, was living so intensely, and her drinking was only part of it. She seemed to be in such a hurry to sing, to make a name for herself, to be a star. But she had always been like that, Sally reminded herself. Whenever she threw herself into something, she could not be deterred.

But these days, it seemed different. She was sharp with people, particularly with members of her family. She came in at all hours, even on nights when she wasn't singing or wasn't out with Roy. Her impatience and her intensity bordered on the desperate. Sally feared she would career off a cliff, or that, like a shooting star, she would crash into the earth and burn. Still, my mother's career was continuing to soar. She had made some demo records, and RCA-Victor was interested. There was talk of a movie role.

Mama and Papa were back in Hollywood, living in an apartment. In the summer of 1947, Dawn persuaded them to buy a house she had discovered while driving in the hills above Hollywood one day. It was a lovely, brick split-level on Miller Drive, perched high above the hotels, clubs, and restaurants on Sunset. For the down payment, Mama and Papa sold forty acres they owned in a Houston suburb, and Dawn agreed to make the monthly payments. A couple of months later, the three of them moved in together. My mother was twenty-one.

One afternoon that fall, Dawn dropped by the Twentieth Century-Fox studio where Sally worked. They walked over to the canteen for a Coke.

"Can you take me to the airport tonight?" she asked. "I've got a late-night flight to New York."

"I guess so," Sally said. "But why New York? And why tonight?"

"I've got a job," Dawn said. "I'll be singing at a place called Club Onyx. It's just for a few months."

That night, Sally stood on an outdoor balcony and watched Dawn climb the stairs of the plane. It would be her first flight ever. At the door, she turned and waved. Sally smiled and waved with one hand while she held her wind-blown hair out of her face with the other. The drone of powerful engines drowned out other sounds.

Her sister looked so smart and confident, so sure of herself, Sally was thinking, but also so alone. Sally remembered their New Orleans adventure and thought fleetingly that she should be flying off to New York with her. She wished she had talked to her, the way she had promised Roy. She wondered why Roy wasn't with her. She hoped her little sister was okay.

For weeks, Sally heard nothing from Dawn, or from Roy. Neither did Mama and Papa. Nobody worried. Mama and Papa, of course, never worried. They all had their own lives to live, their own cares and concerns. They knew that Dawn had been obsessed lately with her singing and her career. They knew she had a way of blocking out everything and everybody else. She could take care of herself.

Sally called Betty Lee a couple of months after Dawn left. "Have you heard from Dawn?" she asked her older sister, who was back in Houston.

"Not since she went to New York," Betty Lee said. "She told me she'd be in New York awhile, and then she was going to Paris. Said she had a singing job in Paris. Or else she was going to get one; I can't remember. You think she's there yet?"

That was the first Sally had heard about Paris. She felt uneasy.

She tried calling Roy in L.A. although she wasn't sure he was still in Dawn's life. His phone was disconnected.

Papa managed to get in touch with Roy's commanding officer at the naval base in Long Beach. The officer had disturbing news. Roy had been arrested, Papa reported to Sally. It involved embezzlement, but the officer wasn't at liberty to go into detail. He refused to tell Papa whether Roy was still on the base or whether he was in custody somewhere else. There was even some question about whether Roy Hurst was his real name.

Was he stealing money to impress Dawn? Sally wondered. She remembered the expensive bottle of perfume. It gathered dust on her dresser. She felt terribly uneasy.

A few weeks later, the phone calls began. They were from Dawn.

"They're watching me," she told Sally, her husky voice almost a whisper, as if someone were listening. "People here are watching me."

"*Who* is watching you?" Sally said, near tears. "Where are you? Why don't you come home?"

"I can't tell you," Dawn said. "It's better for you and for me if you don't know."

Dawn called Sally every couple of weeks. Each time, she sounded strange, distracted, maybe even paranoid. Between calls, Sally desperately tried to figure out what to do. She tried to make sense of the calls. Did they have something to do with Roy, she wondered. Was Dawn in trouble with the FBI? Should she call the police?

For a while the calls stopped. It was the day after Christmas, 1951, and Betty Lee and her three children had come out to Hollywood for the holidays. They were at the Miller Drive house when the phone rang. Betty Lee answered.

"My name is Sergei," a heavily accented voice announced. "Sergei Du Brotin." The man spoke slowly and precisely. "I'm a friend of Dawn's," he said. "I am calling to let you know that she has been ill for the past several weeks. You shouldn't worry. She is better now. She's been staying in my home for a while."

"Is she there?" Betty Lee asked, trying to keep her voice under control. "May I speak to her?"

"Of course," the caller said. "She has been, I suppose you would say, a little nervous lately. But now I believe she is fine. Here she is."

"Merry Christmas," Dawn said. "Yes, I'm fine," she said. "I was just down for a while. I guess I was working too hard."

She told Betty Lee that Sergei was an older man she had met at Club Onyx. He was a Russian count, she said. He lived in a big house at 36 Riverside Drive. She had been staying in his house for a while.

"I feel fine," Dawn told Betty Lee, "except I've been having bad dreams. It's the same dream every night. I see this angel in my room. He's the angel of death, and he has come to take my soul. He sits at the end of the bed and talks to me." She gave a nervous little laugh. "I try to close my eyes and shut my ears, but in the dream I can still see him. I can't make him go away."

"That's scary," Betty Lee said. "I don't know what to tell you. Why don't you come home? We've been terribly worried about you."

"I'm planning to," Dawn said. "It won't be long."

"Whose baby is that I hear crying?" Betty Lee asked. "I can barely hear you."

"Oh, just some people visiting Sergei," Dawn said. "I think they're getting ready to leave."

The telegram for Mama and Papa came the next week. It was from a doctor in New York, a psychiatric resident at Bellevue

Hospital. YOUR DAUGHTER IS ACUTE PARANOID SCHIZOPHRENIC, the message said. NEEDS HOSPITALIZATION.

Papa immediately called the doctor, who tried to explain what schizophrenia was. It sounded terribly frightening. The doctor also told them about the baby.

"She's at least three months old by now," she said. "A little girl. Her name is Tara."

"Sara?" Papa asked.

"No, Tara," the doctor said. "Like in *Gone with the Wind*."

The family was sick with worry. "I think I should go get her," Sally said. "We have to bring her home."

"No, I have to go," Mama said. "She's my baby." She immediately walked to the phone and made train reservations on the *El Capitán*, the Santa Fe Railroad's cross-country passenger train. She left, traveling alone, the next day. She brought us both home.

Sometimes I try to imagine that train ride back across the continent. In my mind's eye, I see the two women sitting across from each other—one of them elderly, the other young and pretty, an infant in her arms. I imagine the long days, the *tick-a-tack* sound of the tracks, the baby crying. The two women talk, tend to the baby. A nation flickers past outside. Mama, terribly anxious about what lies in store for her youngest child, watches.

I imagine the nights, when the coach is quiet. Mama dozes sitting up. The baby—it's hard to imagine that it's me—is at peace in her mother's arms, sleeping. My mother looks down at her little girl, then stares out the window into a reflection of herself. Whom does she see looking back? Who is she becoming?

Betty Lee was waiting at Union Station when the train came in. "I can still see Dawn getting off the train," she told me long afterward. "She had on this beautiful gray dress and a flowing black cape and a black velvet hat. She had this perfectly beautiful little baby in her arms. She looked fine."

My Mother's Keeper
107

CHAPTER FIVE

She may have looked fine, but she was not. I can imagine Mama and Papa trying to wish away the disturbing signs, but her sisters could not. Once my mother and I got home, Betty Lee could see immediately that the young woman who sang and danced and kept people laughing with her funny stories about the people she worked with, the people she met in the clubs—that young woman had not come home to Hollywood. Dawn now spent days moping around the house.

She would put on a record, Sinatra maybe or Ella Fitzgerald or Jo Stafford, and she would sit on the living room floor and listen, over and over, day after day. For nearly a month, she was obsessed with one song, the theme from *Kismet*, the rich baritone sound of Howard Keel inviting her to escape into paradise. She didn't sing along, as she had in the past. She just listened, staring down at the floor.

I think of an intricate jigsaw puzzle in an empty room. The table has been jostled, the tiny pieces scattered and scrambled. No one seems to know how to put it back together.

The new baby in the house made the picture even more complicated. I must have been like a Christmas doll, loved and cared for and passed around from one pair of arms to another. My aunts tell me that Mama tended to me those first few months, increasingly so as the months became years. Papa helped and occasionally my great-grandmother Theresa. My mother drifted in and out.

"Maybe it's postpartum depression," Sister suggested in a letter to Betty Lee. "After all, she's been through a lot."

And maybe it was, but postpartum depression could not explain the frightening, infuriating symptoms: the hallucinations that took control of my mother's mind; the nightmares that shook her awake at night; the metallic, echoing sounds in the chambers of her mind; the dizzying, ghostly objects that flew and buzzed and bounced like pin balls before her eyes.

Postpartum depression did not induce the two lions that kept watch for many years at the foot of her bed. They were grave and solemn, but they did not frighten her. The angel of death did. He sat at the foot of her bed and waited, patiently waited. Unlike the lions, he would eventually rise and take away her soul.

What could explain the paranoia, the feeling that whenever she went out, the FBI or the police or spies—or somebody, she didn't know who—was always watching her. How did she know they were watching? The voices were telling her. Insistent, insinuating, they chattered, they screamed, they bored into her consciousness, drowning out everything else. No one could persuade her they weren't absolutely real.

Occasionally, she would try to describe to her sisters what she was experiencing, but words were so infuriatingly inadequate, and often she would break down in tears. She must have wanted to tear her hair out trying to explain the turmoil in her head, the frustration of trying to concentrate and the mind mocking every effort. What would people say if she told them that somebody in the deepest chambers of her mind was talking to her in a barely audible monotone? Like a radio left on in another room, the voice was unrelenting, tireless. She knew what they would say. They would say she was crazy.

Betty Lee, her long, dark hair done up in a braid, came bouncing into the living room one afternoon. "Tennis anyone?" she sang out. She was wearing her tennis whites, her racket in hand. Despite the ditsy facade, she was worried sick about her sister.

My mother, as usual, was listening to one of her records. Betty Lee knelt beside her. "Come go with me, hon," she coaxed. "I've got a court reserved over at the Beverly Hills."

Dawn, honey-blond hair hiding her face, shook her head. With two fingers, Betty Lee gently pushed the hair aside. She looked into her sad, brown eyes. "Please," she begged. "You know you'd enjoy it."

Betty Lee would not give up, and finally Dawn agreed. She changed into her shorts and tennis sneakers, found her racket, and rode with Betty Lee over to the beautiful hotel. It was a glorious L.A. day, and my mother seemed to be her old self. It took her a while to get her stroke down, but she smiled and bantered with her sister, even when most of her serves thudded into the net.

Then, as if a cloud had drifted over the court, she changed. A ball got past her, and as she trotted toward the fence to get it, she suddenly stopped. With her back to Betty Lee, she seemed to be staring at the tall green fence. She dropped her racket, buried her face in her hands, and sat down heavily.

When Betty Lee got to her, she was sitting with legs crossed, Indian-style, her chin cupped in her hands. She was sobbing.

"What is it, honey?" Betty Lee asked, kneeling beside Dawn on the hard-packed clay and putting her arm around her shoulders.

My mother began to shake her head. She grabbed Betty Lee by the arms. Her reddened eyes opened wide. "What is happening to me?" she asked, her fingers gripping Betty Lee's arms as if she were drowning. "What is happening to me?"

The two sisters knelt on the court together, crying and holding on to each other. A man and woman on the next court glanced at them between serves.

"I don't think I can stand it anymore," Dawn said in a whisper. "It hurts too much."

She looked into Betty Lee's eyes as they sat beside the tennis court. She seemed to be pleading for help. Betty Lee, the big sister, had never felt more desperate. She wanted more than anything to tell her that things would be all right. That she would make things right. But she couldn't. All she could do was hold her and try to keep from crying.

A few weeks later, in the middle of the night, Dawn got in her car and drove away with David, Betty Lee's infant son. Where she was going, why she took David, who could say? Maybe she thought David was me. Betty Lee rushed next door and awakened the neighbors, two older men who wrote musicals for Alice Faye. They found Dawn at a tennis court, sitting on the ground, her hands crossed in her lap. Little David was fine.

Later that week, Betty Lee found an unfinished letter from Dawn to the doctor in New York who had diagnosed her illness. In one part of the letter, she had written: "Please, doctor, you must tell me. What will become of my little girl? Can you assure me that she will be okay? Will I be able to care for her? Will they have to take her away from me?"

*　　*　　*

Tara Elgin Holley with Joe Holley
112

Sally was living in Houston again, but that summer, the summer of 1952, she came out to Hollywood to stay with us for a while. She and my mother had been the closest of the four sisters. Sally tried to get her to talk about what had happened in New York, what she was experiencing now.

"Why did you run away?" Sally asked one evening. "And why New York?"

They were sitting on the red-brick front steps of the Miller Drive house. Sally remembered how quiet it was in the gathering dusk. They could hear the soft soughing of doves in the eucalyptus trees behind the house. The lights on Sunset were just cutting through the haze.

My mother looked down the hill at the lights, as if she hadn't heard Sally's question. "I was angry," she said after a moment, her voice so soft she seemed to be speaking to herself. "I was angry at Roy. When I told him I was pregnant with his child, he just looked at me. Then he said, 'How do you know it's mine?' That's what he said, 'How do you know it's mine?' I was so angry. It hurt, so I just left."

When Sally compared notes with Betty Lee about the story my mother had told her, she was left even more confused. Dawn had told Betty Lee that she decided to go to New York and Roy had decided to go with her. She then planned to go on to Paris. Harry Wham had put her in touch with some club owners who might have work for her, and she hoped Roy would accompany her. When she left L.A., she said, she wasn't pregnant. The two of them had been in New York for several weeks; she was singing at Club Onyx. And then the FBI arrested Roy. He was charged with embezzling money from the military to pay off gambling debts. She had known nothing about it. He was on the run when he was arrested.

"Who was following you?" Betty Lee had asked my mother. "Was it the FBI?"

"The FBI? Yes. It was the FBI," Dawn said. "I had dreams about the FBI. They made me dream."

It was vague and confusing to her family as well. Except for Dawn and perhaps the man they knew as Roy Hurst (which may have been an alias), no one knew what really had happened. No one else knew why Dawn went to New York, whether she went alone or with Roy. No one knew where she lived or how she supported herself during the year she was alone in the city, although she has told people over the years that she did indeed sing at the Club Onyx. No one knew how she ended up at Bellevue Hospital. Or later, how the two of us came to be living with the mysterious Sergei.

Many years later, my mother lifted the veil for me just a bit. She decided to tell me about Sergei. The two of us were sitting on a park bench beside a lake in Austin; I had signed her out of the state hospital for the afternoon. "His name was Sergei Du-Brotin," she said. She looked at me and smiled. "He called you Tarushka."

"What did he look like?" I asked.

She thought for a while. "He looked Russian," she said.

She was living in Sergei's house when I was born, my mother said. At 36 Riverside Drive. She remembered some of the other people who lived in the house. "Mario Pescara, a good-looking Italian." Rita Venay. "She was from France. Very sophisticated."

I imagine Sergei at the Club Onyx. Night after night, Dawn notices him. He is a tall man, wearing a dark, well-tailored suit. His dark hair is turning to silver, and his white mustache is full but neatly trimmed. He sits alone at the same table every night. Neat, precise, elegant—for my mother, he is the epitome of a gentleman.

One night, he sends a note to her dressing room. He adores

her singing, the note says. Would she do him the honor of joining him for a drink?

He takes her to the Wedgewood Room of the Waldorf-Astoria. Sinatra is the headliner. He is a count, with an estate outside Moscow, Sergei tells her. He emigrated to America in 1920. He has built a prosperous business in New York as a furrier, but his passion, from the moment he encountered the Gershwins, was jazz.

"And do you know?" he tells her with a smile. "The Gershwins are my neighbors!" He has celebrated his seventieth birthday, he says. His wife died some years earlier; his children have moved away. He now has time to indulge his passion.

Perhaps it was only natural that Sergei, Dawn's devoted friend, found out she was in trouble. Did she end up on his doorstep? Did she break down and tell him that she was pregnant? That she was sick? Or did he find her, find us, at Bellevue? I cannot answer those questions. The veil came down again that afternoon at the lake. Her attention began to drift.

I still wonder. Whenever I'm in New York, I walk by the house on Riverside Drive. It's a big, imposing brownstone, with rounded stone turrets two stories high. I never go inside, but the place looks and feels familiar. Two stone lions guard the front steps, just as my mother said they did. And George Gershwin really had lived around the corner.

I discovered a bit more about Roy William Hurst, though not from my mother. Although Sally was extremely reluctant to tell me anything about him—she did acknowledge that he was Hispanic, probably Mexican-American. She remembered that maybe six months after the two of us came back home to Hollywood,

Papa and Mama got a letter from him. He was in federal prison in Illinois, but he expected to be paroled soon. He wanted to know about Dawn and about their child. He wanted Papa's advice. Should he come back to California when he got out of prison? Was Dawn willing to be his wife?

Papa read Roy's letter over and over. He and Mama sat at the kitchen table late at night; while my mother and I slept, they pondered a response. They talked to Mr. Smith, the Christian Science "practitioner" who had befriended them. They got in touch with Roy's parole officer, who told them Roy was doing well.

One Sunday afternoon, Papa sat down at the table and wrote out a response in his old-fashioned, flowing script.

> You should know, that Dawn is not well. God willing, she will get better, but we think it best for the both of you that you not try to get in touch with her. You are young and still have a chance to make something of yourself, despite your misfortune. You do not need the added burden of a wife who is having difficulty. I believe it is best for all concerned for you to go back home when you are released from prison and start a new life. We are an old Southern family. We will do our best to care for Dawn and little Tara. We are praying for God's help.

Papa didn't tell Dawn about Roy's letter, or about his response. No one in the family heard another word from Roy Hurst, this man who I assume is my father.

Years later, I wrote the Federal Bureau of Prisons about Roy William Hurst. Weeks later, I got a reply: "A search of our current and historic files indicate no record of incarceration in the Federal Bureau of Prisons."

Tara Elgin Holley with Joe Holley

"I need to know what happened to him," I told my mother not long ago.

"Well, that would be good," she said, "because then we could find out what happened to me."

When, as an adult, I pressed Sally for information about my father, she wrote:

> Even those who were called by those titles were not always so deserving. Is our Father or Mother only those who bore us? I don't want to get metaphysical here, but perhaps you should look for the more spiritual meaning of these titles. Maybe it would help you in your fruitless concern regarding the man who impregnated Dawn. You are who you are, never mind who are the parents. Your beauty, talent, and intelligence are yours alone. Your true being is your true self; it does not belong to any physical mommy or daddy.

Maybe Sally is right, but still there's so much I want to know—so much more than "He played the guitar" and "He had an accent." Did he know that my mother would soon be unable to care for me? Did he abandon me? Did my grandfather's letter give him the reason he needed to walk away and make a new start?

I don't want to sound tragic, but the questions don't go away as the years pass. They grow more insistent. Sometimes I wonder whether my interest in Latin American culture, my ease with languages, and my work in ethnomusicology—a field where cultural identity is of primary importance—have something to do with my missing father.

I have a snapshot of him. He's a small, dark-haired man in a sport shirt and slacks, standing in front of a fountain. I think it's New York City in winter, on the Hudson, maybe in Riverside

Park. I have another photo of my mother taken in the same place, apparently at the same time. Wearing a knee-length coat, she looks heavier than usual. She is either newly pregnant or has just given birth. They both look happy.

I look a lot like my father. I'm small and dark, just as he is in the photograph. His ears stick out, like mine. From the photo, he could be Hispanic. I would like to know.

I like the way he looks. The snapshot, I suppose, is the closest I'll ever get to him.

She was acute paranoid schizophrenic, the doctor at Bellevue had said. She was mentally ill, her bright and agile mind bedeviled by a brain disease as terrifying as it was mysterious.

The symptoms were growing more severe. Some days the family would see a flicker of the person she had been before fleeing to New York. My aunts remember how she would take me to the park or play with me in the yard. She would be the old Dawn, the happy, fun-loving Dawn, and that flicker of personality would ignite flames of hope. Then the cloud would reappear, and the young woman they knew and loved would withdraw into a twilight existence no one else could penetrate. For days at a time, I would be in my grandparents' care, not my mother's.

At first, it must have been like an infant's game of peekaboos, deliciously thrilling as my mother's smiling face was there in front of me, then not there, there in front of me, then not there—until she tired of the game and hugged me to her breast. As I got to be three and then four, old enough to have memories of my own, the pattern continued, and she was away for longer and longer periods of time. I eventually came to understand that it was no game we were playing. The effect on me of her sporadic comings and goings, both mental and physical, would be deep and long-lasting.

Mama and Papa refused to acknowledge that their daughter was sick. Sin and pain and disease were mortal illusions; so was matter itself. So was death. Dawn would snap out of it, they assured family members. We must trust in God, they told each other. God *is* love.

Mr. Smith would help. Mr. Smith, the Christian Science practitioner. Sally remembers a short, stocky man, soft-spoken and unfailingly polite, who always wore a white shirt, a plain brown tie, and a sober brown suit shiny with age. It was almost a uniform. Though only a fringe of gray hair was left on his head, flecks of dandruff invariably clung to the shoulders of his dark suit.

He came by the house at least once a week. He sat in a chair in the living room, his tan felt hat in his lap. In his quiet, insistent voice he talked, first to Mama and Papa and then to Dawn. He talked about her faith, "our faith," he would say. He encouraged Dawn to follow Mama and Papa's example and do her daily readings from *Science and Health*.

My mother sat in a chair across from Mr. Smith. She listened quietly as he told her about God's love for her. "As Mrs. Eddy reminds us," he would say, "we must entrust ourselves to His care and safekeeping. He will keep us ever safe. You must realize that God is all. He is our healer, not man."

My mother must have wanted to believe in this earnest, caring man of faith. He must have felt genuine concern and affection for all of us. But the disease was like a cruel thief. It was making off with her sanity, and Mr. Smith's prayers and admonitions couldn't do a thing to stop it.

It saddens me to think about what might have been. If only

Mama and Papa had listened to my aunts. If only someone had intervened—as someone did with Sister when she was a little girl and dying of pneumonia. I've learned that acute schizophrenia is occasionally arrested if dealt with early enough, and I've never believed that my mother's case was the most extreme. If only it had been different in those early days with my mom.

Her lingering depression began cycling into something more ominous. She and Sally were in a drugstore one afternoon, sitting at the counter having coffee. Sally was trying to get Dawn to talk about resuming her singing career. She thought if she could just get her interested in something again, she might not feel so depressed. Dawn, resting her cheek on the palm of her hand, listlessly stirred her coffee with a spoon. She wouldn't look up, wouldn't talk.

Sally looked away for a moment, and then she heard her sister say, in a low voice, "What are you staring at?" Sally started to answer, "Nothing," but then she noticed in the mirror that Dawn was looking at the young man behind the counter. "What are you staring at?" Dawn repeated, this time louder.

The young man realized she was talking to him. His face under his white paper cap turned bright red, and he stammered something about how he wasn't looking at her.

"You *were* staring at me!" Dawn said again, banging her fist down on the table. Her cup clattered off the saucer. Coffee puddled on the counter, dripped onto her dress. Sally grabbed at napkins, then tried to pull her sister away from the counter. Dawn was crying. They made it out the door, Dawn crying and mumbling to herself about "that nasty boy."

What was happening to my mother was symptomatic of the early stage of schizophrenia. Her mind was beginning to lose its ability to distinguish between what was happening around her and what was happening inside her head. Her own fears and obsessions were being expressed, as far as she was concerned, through the thoughts and actions of those around her. And it wasn't just voices. The phone, the radio, the phonograph—all the noise around her, all the confusion of everyday life, blended into the cacophony in her mind.

Sally was frightened and angry and confused. She tried to get her parents to understand that Dawn was in deep trouble. Mama didn't want to believe her. "She's just upset," she would say. "It's not easy having a little one to take care of. You should know that, Sally. We have to give her time. Time heals all."

Dawn had her good days, when she seemed almost like her old self, but the troubling incidents continued. She began staying out late at night, sleeping all day. Once she came home with a black eye and a torn dress. Sally feared she was drinking again.

I know now that my mother feared she might harm me, though nothing like that ever happened. I believe I was her salvation, her last link with the normal life she had known. Playing with me in the park, singing the songs I remember to this day, she was clinging to the last semblance of our life together. She wanted so much for us to be together, and I wonder if she ever considered catching me up in her frantic arms, clutching me to her breast and stealing away into the night. Or did she know even then that she could never outrun the shadows?

It was 1952, and Betty Lee brought her children out to Hollywood for Christmas. It had been nearly a year since she had seen Dawn. "She looks like a different person," she told Sally in a worried voice. "We've got to get her some help." Still, Mama and Papa resisted.

One morning, my mother was in the bathroom for a long

time. When she came out, Sally was horrified to see what she had done. She had taken scissors to her long hair. She had chopped it off, leaving deep, jagged gashes where beautiful wavy curls had been. She looked like a concentration-camp victim.

"I hope you're satisfied now," she said to Sally.

Betty Lee remembers a Saturday evening some weeks later. My mother had slept until almost noon and then stayed around the house all day. It was nearly dark.

"Where's Dawn?" Betty Lee asked. No one had seen her for a while. Outside, they heard shouting, a scream, and then a torrent of curses. Dawn was on the front lawn, yelling at the top of her lungs at the elderly couple who lived next door. They had just driven into their driveway and were standing beside their car. They were staring at the distraught young woman with the short, scraggly hair. Obscenities were spewing out of my mother's mouth.

Betty Lee rushed out the front door and tried to gather Dawn in her arms. Papa followed, carrying me. My mother was able to push them both away, all the while shouting "No! Leave me alone, you bastard!" She begin striding toward the man and woman next door; she was shaking her fist and shouting. Betty Lee regained her balance and rushed after her. She managed to slow Dawn down, and the neighbors scurried into their house. Up and down the street, people were peering out of windows, stepping into the narrow, winding street to see who was disturbing their quiet, stucco-walled privacy.

Betty Lee, with Mama's and Papa's help, began to herd Dawn toward the house, but when they got her to the front porch, she broke away and ran down the steps. She stood in the middle of the hilly street and shouted curses at the people watching her. "What are you looking at?" she screamed. "Get away from me! Leave me alone!" In the middle of the street, she began a frenzy of pacing, back and forth like an animal in a cage, all the while cursing and mumbling and scratching at her forearms.

A black-and-white LAPD patrol car nosed its way around the corner and up the steep hill. It stopped in front of the house. Two officers approached warily. Betty Lee and Papa tried to explain to them that Dawn was sick, but the officers were unmoved. They had an arrest warrant, they said. The neighbors had complained.

They took my mother by the arms and handcuffed her. Head down, exhausted, she went quietly. They led her down the steps and put her into the patrol car.

Mama, wringing her hands and moaning, suddenly ran down to the car. Crying, she got the back door open and began trying to pull Dawn across the seat. The officers had to pry her hands from Dawn and from the door handle. One of them escorted her back up the steps while the other stayed with my mother.

Papa handed me to Betty Lee. He put his arms around Mama to keep her from going back to the car. "It'll be all right, Marian," he said softly. "God will watch over her." He held her tightly. Together, they watched the car move down the hill. My mother turned to look back at us. The car went around the curve.

Days pass. I can imagine Papa and Mama in their Sunday clothes sitting in a doctor's office at the Metropolitan Hospital. Leaving me in the care of one of my aunts, they have ridden the bus for over an hour to the L.A. suburb of Norwalk. It is the site of the only mental hospital in L.A. County, the place where my mother has been committed. She sits quietly between Mama and Papa, her hands in her lap, the nails of one hand trying to peel strips of skin from the palm of the other. She is wearing a blue hospital smock. She has been a patient for a week.

My Mother's Keeper

"The disturbing-the-peace charge has been dropped," the doctor is telling my grandparents in a calm, officious voice, "but, of course, your daughter is in no condition to be released. I'm sure you will agree. What we would like to do is keep her with us for ninety days of observation and treatment. We believe we can help her."

He asks questions about Dawn's health, about her family, about me. He wants to know her life history. He wants to know about mental illness in the family.

My grandfather answers in a quiet, refined voice. "No," he says. "We are from an old Houston family. There has never been any mental illness in my family. Nor in Mama's."

My grandmother is politely defiant. She cannot imagine what this smooth, self-assured fellow in a white laboratory coat can do for her daughter; all she wants is to take Dawn home. She is afraid her child will disappear into the maw of this frightening institution; they'll never see her again.

But it does no good to resist. The doctor has a pen and a pink official-looking document. My grandparents are to sign. Just sign. My grandmother knows what is happening. She knows they are signing over their daughter's fate. But what else can they do?

The doctor stands and comes around from behind his desk. This is the signal that the interview is over. My mother and my grandparents get to their feet. The three of them hold each other tightly. They are crying. A nurse comes into the office and leads away my mother, who balks at the door of the office. "You've got to get me out of here," she pleads. "I don't belong here!" The nurse pulls her through the door. The desperate plea is one my mother will repeat, thousands of times, for the next forty years. Those words echo in my dreams.

*   *   *

Tara Elgin Holley with Joe Holley
124

In the early 1950s, antipsychotic drugs were just coming into use, not as a cure for schizophrenia, but as the first effective weapon against the teasing, tormenting delusions and hallucinations, the disordered thinking. Researchers were first surprised and then amazed at the results. Nothing else had ever worked.

Thorazine and other so-called miracle drugs offered another benefit: They kept patients calm, sedated. Mental hospitals became relatively more civilized; restraints and straitjackets and padded cells were no longer so necessary.

When my mother was led away by the nurse that day at Norwalk, she already was on medication. She was sedated; knowing her as I do, I am sure that she despised it. Like most patients, she has always hated the mental fuzziness more than she fears the delusions.

Although the new drugs were no cure for schizophrenia, most doctors forty years ago assumed the disease *could* be cured, or at least kept under control. Most believed that the patient had some control over her illness, that family environment or the patient's own willfulness or some neurotic quirk was at the core of the problem. Extended conversation with the patient would peel back the secret at the heart of schizophrenia.

Over the years, my mother has spent countless hours with psychiatrists, particularly in the early years of her illness. As they earnestly tried to explore with her those early childhood experiences that, in their opinion, caused her schizophrenia, they likely exacerbated the symptoms. I remember as a nineteen-year-old reading Freud; he said that schizophrenic patients "are inaccessible to psychoanalysis and cannot be cured by our endeavors." Still, some psychotherapists are stubborn. They continue to insist that the disease is amenable to their treatment.

Other doctors investigated the family. In the late 1940s and early 1950s, the so-called schizophrenogenic mother was considered a likely culprit. The theory was that child-rearing attitudes caused schizophrenia, and pathogenic mothering was probably the key factor, with no reference to genes. Granted, Mama was hardly June Cleaver when it came to mothering, but it's hard to imagine the gentle, childlike artist who was my grandmother actually causing her daughter's illness.

Mama must have carried a heavy burden of guilt; most parents of schizophrenics do. Whether any of my mother's doctors suggested to her that she could have caused her daughter's illness, I do not know. It would have broken her heart. Fortunately, it's difficult to find any reputable psychoanalyst today who still subscribes to the schizophrenogenic mother theory.

One other incident in my mother's life may have had some connection to her illness. As a nine-year-old, she was sexually molested. For months, a friend of the family who ran a little grocery store in Houston gave her quarters to buy her silence about what he was doing to her each time she came in the store. She finally told Sally, who told Mama and Papa.

Whether there is any connection between that traumatic childhood episode and the onset of schizophrenia years later is impossible to determine. Sexual abuse, I have read, affects every victim differently, depending on gender, the age of the child, and the child's relationship to the molester. Whatever the effect it had on my mother—and it was no doubt profound—it was not the sole cause of her illness. On the other hand, this type of "emotionally intrusive experience"—to use the phrase of an internationally known expert on schizophrenia—could have been a trigger of some sort, even years after the actual experience. It can't be proved, but it can't be discounted, either.

Whatever the cause, or causes, doctors still looked for a cure in the early 1950s. They no longer relied on spinning chairs or bloodletting, but some of the so-called treatments they put my mother through were hardly more advanced. One was called hydrotherapy.

I can imagine her on the ward, perhaps lying on her bed in the middle of the day. Suddenly she realizes that two men in white are hovering over her. They help her up and lead her down the hall to what looks like a communal shower room. The room is bare, with cold gray cement walls and floor. Sounds echo. Since she is sedated, she allows herself to be undressed and laid out on a cot made of hard rubber. The attendants strap down her arms and legs.

They drape her with towels, and while she lies, wide-eyed, on her back on the hard rubber, they approach from behind and suddenly douse her with pails of ice-cold water. She screams. She is crying, sobbing, struggling to get her breath. They drench her over and over. She strains against the leather belts that hold her to the cot. They seek to shock her into sanity.

Sometimes I imagine this naked, humiliated young woman, my mother, after she has endured one of these so-called therapy sessions. I watch her stumbling down the hall between two attendants, her hair soaked and stringy, a white robe plastered to her wet skin. She is trembling violently from the shock and cold. The attendants are almost dragging her back to the ward, and away, far away from any semblance of sanity.

"You've got to get me out of here! I don't belong here!"

Through the years, I've seen this image of her suffering over and over, in one form or another. In my dreams, my nightmares, I see her being led, stumbling, head bowed, along a harshly lit endless corridor. She is lying on a narrow bed, along an endless row of beds, and she hardly dares sleep, lest she awaken into a nightmare even worse than the one she is experiencing. This will be her life, she must realize. It will never end.

My Mother's Keeper

Of course, we're always trying to help her. It's always for her own good. Or so we tell ourselves.

Nothing worked. Doctors resorted to stronger measures. On numerous occasions, probably dozens of times, my mother was led into an examination room, stretched out on a table, and strapped down. A nurse attached an electrode to each temple, and an alternating current of 90 volts leaped between the electrodes for a fraction of a second. My mother was shocked into senselessness.

Electroconvulsive treatment, ECT, or electroshock therapy, it is called; it is still used on people who are severely depressed. It had an effect on my mother. It transformed her, for days at a time, into a zombie. Pieces of her life disappeared. Days and nights became a gray blur. The treatments left her nauseated and, like any sane person, she came to dread and fear them. Robbed of memory, stripped of emotional response, she sank more deeply into the half life that is the lot of so many schizophrenics.

"You've got to get me out of here! I don't belong here!"

I suppose I should be grateful; it could have been worse. Insulin-induced coma. Starvation. Dialysis. Even lobotomy. All were standard therapies my mother might have endured not so many years ago.

My grandmother, and to some extent my grandfather, never believed that any good could come from "putting Dawnie away." Mama wrote Betty Lee: "Please do not feel disturbed when I tell you I take Dawn out. The doctor and the nurses all o.k. it. I myself don't see anything the matter with Dawn. In some ways she has much more poise than I have—talks as intelligently, is calm and like her old sweet self."

Mama and Papa would take the tedious crosstown bus ride to

the hospital at least once a week. Along with bus fare, they would scrape together enough change for a treat for Dawn, usually a Hershey's chocolate bar with almonds. They would stroll with Dawn on the grounds or share a cup of coffee with her at the canteen. They must have told her about me when I was living with them as an infant. They probably told her about the little songs I sang, the funny little things I said and did.

Sometimes they arranged for Dawn to come home on weekends, to a small Hollywood apartment they had moved into after having to sell the Miller Drive house; with their sick daughter, they could no longer make the payments. They tended to indulge Dawn's every whim and looked for signs of improvement, which they inevitably saw. They reintroduced their daughter to her own daughter.

After I went to live with Auntie in Houston, Mama was still writing about Dawn and me: "I think she and Tara should be together. She speaks of Tara all the time, and I know Tara wants to see her mother, but I wonder sometimes how it is going to turn out."

On Sunday afternoon, they would take Dawn back to the institution—or maybe they wouldn't. Mama, in particular, was bad about abetting Dawn's escapes.

The cycle would begin again. My mother would be with us at home for a few weeks, maybe months, and then something would happen. Maybe she would pick a fight in a bar or cause a disturbance in some public place, and she would find herself back at Metropolitan Hospital. That's where she would stay until Mama connived, yet again, to get her out.

The cycle continued for several years, until finally even Mama and Papa conceded that their difficult, disturbed daughter and her five-year-old child were too much for elderly people to handle. Sally and Betty Lee and Sister were all back in Houston; so were all the aunts, uncles, and cousins, the close friends of a lifetime. Except for Mr. Smith, the practitioner, no one was around to help. Maybe the two of us would do better in Houston, they decided. It was 1956. My mother had been sick for nearly five years.

CHAPTER SIX

The phone rang one autumn afternoon in 1958. Auntie and I were downstairs in the living room. She was sitting in her rocking chair peering closely at the newspaper through her gold-rimmed bifocals. I was seven years old. Home from school, I was stretched out on the floor, entranced by some imaginary adventure with my dolls. Soon I would have to begin my homework. Auntie picked up the phone on the little table by her chair. It was Mama; I could tell by the tone of Auntie's voice.

At least once a week, Mama called Auntie, usually to report on the latest financial crisis she and Papa were enduring or to talk about Dawn. Mama was in her sixties by now, but as far as Auntie was concerned, she was still the wayward, flighty niece she always had been. In many ways, I suppose she was.

I could be totally involved in playing with my dolls or reading a book, but once I realized it was Mama calling, I tuned in. I knew I would be hearing about my mother. Much of what I knew about her, I learned from Auntie's end of their long conversations.

Sitting on the floor at her feet on this particular afternoon, I sensed Auntie stiffening, heard the little intake of breath. "Marian," she said after a moment of listening, her voice angry and reproving, "how in the world could you let that happen? What did you *think* would happen when you and Alfred let that man visit her?"

I still wasn't sure what disturbing news she had heard, but I did know that Auntie fought a continuing battle with my grandmother over my mother. Time after time on the phone, Auntie would insist to Mama that Dawn was sick, that the doctors wanted to keep her committed. And time after time, Mama would be assuring Auntie that Dawn was almost back to normal.

I can hear Auntie's snort of contempt as Mama expressed some such notion over the phone. For Auntie, the refusal to accept the fact of Dawn's illness was yet another example of my grandmother's disconnection from reality.

I wanted every shred of information I could find about my mother, but it hurt for her to always be a problem that had to be solved, a burden for someone to bear. To hear Auntie say unkind things about my mother was an insult to me. I would hear relatives describe her as somehow damaged, maybe even bad, and I would want to grow up to be a woman just like her. To spite them. Talking about her, as far as I was concerned, was the same as talking about me.

As Auntie sat with the phone to her ear, one of her three daily newspapers now spread on the floor beside her, the story gradually came out about the latest problem my mother had caused. I got the details when Auntie hung up.

My mother was pregnant. She was going to have another child. Who the father was, Mama and Papa didn't know, although they suspected it might be a man named Assif.

Tara Elgin Holley with Joe Holley
132

I remembered Assif. He was from Lebanon, and he had a little candy shop on a side street a block off Hollywood Boulevard. Papa and I had dropped in often, and I remembered him as a friendly, pleasant man. In fact, Mama and Papa considered Assif a friend of the family. He even came by the house occasionally.

His name had come up before. Mama had apparently mentioned to Auntie that Dawn had gone out with Assif during her furloughs home—or her escapes. "He's such a nice young man," she would say. "And he cares so much about Dawn."

"That's ridiculous!" Auntie would say. "Dawn is very sick, and the man is simply trying to take advantage of that poor, unfortunate girl."

"That's not true," my grandmother would argue. "He's even encouraged us to get some help for Dawn. He doesn't think Mr. Smith is enough. I don't agree, but at least it shows he cares about her."

"The candyman some time back wanted to marry Dawn, but we wouldn't listen to anything like it," Papa wrote Auntie. "He went to a Dr. himself (not ours) about Dawn, asked all about her."

Auntie would turn Mama's argument against her. "See, Marian," she would say, "even this fellow Assif can tell she's not fine, as you say. Now, you listen to me: You get that girl into a hospital where she can receive constant care and attention. You get her there, and you keep her there. Do you understand?"

Auntie was horrified that Dawn was having another child. She was on the phone daily trying to find out all she could—when Dawn had missed her period, whether Assif was actually the father, whether it had happened while Dawn was on furlough. Auntie suspected the father was someone at the hospital—a fellow patient, maybe even one of the doctors. Something similar had happened when Dawn was a patient in the hospital in Galveston, she reminded my grandmother. A patient, it seems, had sexually assaulted her. Or had it been a young doctor? It was a story I had never heard, and, as usual, the details were blurred.

Auntie was determined to prevent yet another child being tossed pillar to post the way I had been. I know she was trying to prevent another child from totally losing contact with its father. She believed that if she could persuade Mama and Papa to investigate who the father was, to ask around, maybe the second child would grow up with at least some knowledge of its father, which was certainly more than I had.

Auntie may have been aghast at what had happened, but I was delighted. I longed for a little sister or brother. I loved it when people from the outside world came into our house, whether it was a cousin or the occasional boarder. A baby in the house would be wonderful. I could just imagine a little brother who would toddle along behind me while I skipped through the garden, a little sister who would play dress-up with me in the attic or romp and play with the dogs.

Only one thing bothered me: If my mother was having another child, didn't that mean that my father had come back into her life? And if my father had come back, why hadn't he come for me? I asked Betty Lee, but she had no answer. She just bent down and hugged me, stroking my hair as she held me tight.

Once the child was born, and Auntie realized that Mama and Papa intended to take care of him, as they had tried to do with me, she began musing about adopting the little boy. "Maybe it would be for the best if the two of you could grow up together," she mentioned occasionally. Although she herself was nearly eighty, she saw herself as a more capable guardian than my grandparents. She, after all, was the caretaker, and always had been. She could not imagine Mama and Papa, at their age, having to cope with bottles, diapers, sleepless nights.

The boy's name was Harold. My mother named him after her first serious heartthrob, a boy she had known in junior high. Apparently she continued to insist until the time of her delivery that she wasn't pregnant. "How could I be," she said to Mama, "when I haven't done anything?" Little Harold was born in an ambulance.

After four days in the hospital, Dawn went back to her ward at Metropolitan Hospital in Norwalk. The baby went home to live with Mama and Papa. "They gave us formula for the baby, and we have been following that precisely," Papa wrote Auntie. "We are up two or three times a night feeding Harold. He sure is a fine looking child in every respect. I sure wish Tara could see her brother. It so touched me when I heard her voice on the phone, I could hardly talk to her or you."

To Mama and Papa, the baby was a miracle, yet another sign from God that the world is good and that life, existence, is joyous. Every week they carefully dressed little Harold in his Sunday best and took him on the bus with them to the hospital so Dawn could see her baby. "A great many patients down there are quite rational, and they hold him and play with him," Mama told Auntie. She would go on about Dawn giving him his bottle and changing him. "She just adores him," she would say. "She can't wait to see him."

Auntie would scoff. "She no more knows that's her child than a man in the moon," she would say. Then she would remind Mama about the pregnancy, the mystery of the father, all the accumulated evidence that to Auntie proved that my mother— and my grandparents—were incompetent, ineffectual, and irresponsible. With my eavesdropping, I was learning a lot!

Auntie was right, of course, but it was equally absurd to imagine that she herself could care for another child. It was more and more difficult, physically, for her to take care of me. For the first couple of years I was with her, she got around relatively well, and she kept up her busy routine, but by the time I was ten, I was the responsible one.

We walked everywhere. In the Village—a shopping area as well as a residential neighborhood—everybody knew us. They would see the tall, white-haired woman in the wide-brimmed hat walking slowly on stiff old legs, leaning on her cane and on the shoulder of the little dark-haired girl in the white lace socks and too-long dress. For lunch, we might head to One's a Meal, a friendly little café around the corner from the house. While we ate our creamed-egg-and-bacon club sandwiches, Lola and Frieda, the waitresses, would lean over the counter and talk about husbands and children and goings-on in the neighborhood.

At least once a week, we left the house and walked over to Victor's Village Cafeteria for dinner. The black women who did the cooking at Victor's would come out and sit with us. "Howya doin', Miss Elsa?" they would ask, smiling. "My, this little girl's growin'!" Maybe they would have a glass of iced tea while they fanned their sweat-beaded faces and rested from laboring over hot stoves. Usually, Victor himself would invite us to sample what his family was having that night. It would be homemade lasagna or manicotti or ravioli, since Victor's mother, who had immigrated from Italy, was the one who cooked for the family.

Across the street from the house was Rose Behar's World Toy and Gift Shop. Rose Behar had survived a concentration camp; I was concerned about the faded blue number tattooed into her arm. Auntie would be watering the front yard when Mrs. Behar, large and slow-moving, brought the trash out to the curb. The two women, one German and one Jewish, paused to talk every morning, often about what had happened during the war.

On Sundays after church, when the store was closed, Mrs.

Tara Elgin Holley with Joe Holley

Behar would invite me in. She was a special friend. I knew she was concerned about my life with Auntie; she asked lots of questions. She wasn't reluctant to ask about my mother. I had the run of the store while Mrs. Behar talked about the bad old days in Germany. She painted and repaired Dresden china and Limoges figurines as she told me about how she and her husband had endured and survived life in the camps.

As the years passed, Auntie spent more and more time in her rocking chair, the library table beside her cluttered with her pill containers, her correspondence, her newspapers, and her books. I became her legs. That was fine with me. I lived for the opportunities to break away from her supervision.

Some evenings, she would send me to One's a Meal or Victor's for takeout. I loved going on errands by myself. Skipping along the sidewalk in the gathering dusk, the air warm and rich and heavy, I imagined I was flying. I was careful not to step on the cracks. I would peer into the window at World Toy and Gift Shop and pick out what I would buy if I could have anything I wanted. Mrs. Behar would wave. I would cut through the service station driveway and breathe in the gasoline fumes and then slow down at Moeller's Bakery, where the odors made my stomach hollow. Sometimes I imagined running and never stopping, never going back to Auntie's. Maybe I would run to Hollywood. I would join my mother. I would be like Dawn, as I imagined she was.

I was free on those errands, if only for a little while. Free from the all-seeing eye that was always looking, always assessing, always judging the way I moved and the way I thought, never letting anything slip by unnoticed.

Despite the growing responsibility and Auntie's rigid ways, my life was good. I enjoyed the responsibilities I had. I even enjoyed the constant work we had to do on our house. More and more each year, I was realizing that it was truly *our* house. For a few more years, it wouldn't matter that Auntie was my whole life and that my peers at school, when they noticed me at all, thought that I was odd. I had my dogs and my yard, my dolls and my books. Everybody in the Village knew us, and I knew them. I had a place in the larger world, and I was gradually coming to realize that the life I led was so much more interesting, more textured, than the lives of my cousins. I stood apart, and that wasn't always bad.

And out in California, I had a baby brother. The idea that there was another version of me in this world, an extension of me, was pretty wonderful.

Papa and Mama sent pictures. In the photos, Mama and Papa are posing in what appears to be a park, though it is probably the hospital grounds. Cars from the fifties are blurs on a busy street behind them, on the other side of a high chain-link fence. It's probably a Sunday, because Papa has on a dark suit, a white shirt and bow tie, and the hat he wore when he got dressed up. The baby is wearing a white suit with a white knit cap that ties around his little fat chin. Papa's big hands are cradling him against his chest.

Mama wrote about how beautiful the baby was, "his little shoulders just like a man's, with a tiny fuzz of golden down on his back, just a little on his shoulders but prophetic of coming manhood." His eyes were big and brown, "just like Brother's," she wrote us. "His little chin and mouth and nose are beautiful—so much so that it is commented on by strangers."

I so very much wanted to see my baby brother; my grandparents occasionally suggested that they bring him back to Houston. They wanted to bring my mother, too. "I think Dawn needs Tara and that Tara needs her mother," Papa wrote Auntie. "This touches a tender spot in me, for Tara to be with her mother. Like

Rob, my brother, used to say, 'The children in daytime might want their father, but when night comes, it's the mother they want and should have.' "

I fully expected to see Papa and Mama on our doorstep, babe in arms—with or without my mother. I got a warm, cozy feeling just thinking about it.

Another letter came shortly before Christmas. "This is some bad news," Papa wrote. "Harold passed on during the night last night."

I remember Auntie sitting in her rocking chair, the letter in her lap, shaking her head. I remember going to her and putting my head in her lap. We both were crying. How could this be? My baby brother just got here. I never even got to see him, and now he no longer existed.

He had been coughing for several days, Papa explained. Sometime after ten, he died. He had been coughing so much and breathing so heavily that Papa had rushed across the street to call Mr. Smith, the Christian Science practitioner. (Apparently, my grandparents were in such financial straits by this time, they no longer had a phone.) When he hurried back ten minutes later, the coughing had ceased and the baby was asleep. He and Mama laid him in his crib.

"In the night about two A.M.," Papa continued, "I awakened, as I always do, to see if he was covered. I felt him, and he was as cold as ice."

Papa woke Mama, and she hurried into the baby's room. He rushed back across the street to call Mr. Smith. When he came back to the house, he found the baby still lying cold in his crib, but Mama had disappeared. He went into every room looking for her, and then went outside and called her name, but he could not find her.

She was gone for two hours, wandering the dark streets of

Hollywood, crazed with grief. For the third time, she and Papa had lost a child in their care. It was almost more than she could bear.

As the sun came up that morning, Christmas Eve, she finally made her way to a friend's house, but she could not bear to go back home. She never did. She and Papa stayed with friends for a while and then moved to another apartment.

After Harold's death, she wrote to Auntie: "I miss the care of Harold so, and I have nothing to fill my days. . . . I wished I had not dashed out into the street like a crazy person but had worked with the practitioner. I saw Julia Page bring Papa back from the dead, and I know of an instance similar."

The baby was buried in a pauper's grave. "Putting him away," Papa wrote to Auntie, cost $42.70.

"When Harold was with me, I was very happy, even with Dawn in the hospital," Mama wrote. "I felt like a young woman again. It comforts me to write about him."

Something else she wrote still haunts me. "Had we had a doctor for Harold, and he had passed on, I would have felt we had murdered him. We would never have given Harold away."

"I haven't told Dawn yet," Papa wrote. It was April, four months after the baby's death. Dawn never asked about the child. I'm not sure he or Mama ever told her that he had died.

A long time afterward, I began to understand the impact on my grandmother of losing Harold. She was always delightful, and yet underneath the outwardly cheerful demeanor, I could detect a quiet sadness. Perhaps her feelings about her other lost children drove her to try so hard to hold on to her youngest daughter.

Auntie and I were glum that Christmas. Even as we made the rounds of family visits, with me collecting presents at each stop, I remember the weight of sadness. I remember feeling, without being able to put it into words, how precarious life felt, especially for the children in this family. I was glad to be with Auntie.

It remained for the old family friend, the one who insisted that Auntie should tell me my mother was dead, to put Harold's death in its baldest perspective. In her frankness, this woman could be even more cruel than Auntie.

"I know the sick girl is not having the care she needs," she wrote Auntie.

If you had not sent Dawn a picture of little Tara, she would have forgotten her as she has forgotten the baby. Mr. and Mrs. Elgin used to drag that tiny baby out there almost every week in all kinds of weather to have Dawn know her baby. But Dawn doesn't even remember "her" baby. And it would be better for Tara if Dawn could forget her little girl, and she would if Marian and you did not keep that mother instinct and ownership alive. That baby had two strikes against it. If he grew up, he faced it—illegitimacy and an insane mother. So it was best he passed on. Two senile people should not rear a child, in these times anyway. A baby is not a toy. It is a responsibility and needs training and nursing constantly.

How I hated her! I hated the truth of what she had to say.

Life for me, of course, went on. I still went to church on Sunday, still sang in the choir. On a Saturday each spring, we would board a bus with other elderly ladies and take a day tour along the dogwood trails of East Texas. I still had my art classes in the summer. Auntie and I had our rituals, our rarely varying routine. We had our housework and our shopping to do. We had our garden to tend and our dogs. We had each other.

When I was nine, one of Auntie's nieces died, and the husband sold the large family home. Auntie and I took the bus over to the house to sort out who got this piece of furniture, what should go in storage, who wanted what. The two girls in the family had a collection of five hundred dolls, not to mention an incredible library of children's books. They had the complete Nancy Drew, Nurse Jane, the complete Dickens, the complete Poe, and Dante's *Inferno*, with the Doré illustrations.

"Find boxes for these things, dear," Auntie said. "They're yours now."

For once, I was almost speechless.

Like her father, who had brought his Shakespeare collection with him from Germany more than a century earlier, Auntie treasured books. On the shelves of her antique secretary were lovely old gold-leaf books with fascinating titles I immediately memorized: *The Fall of the House of Usher*, *The Iceman Cometh*, *For Whom the Bell Tolls*, *Death of a Salesman*, *Wuthering Heights*. Somehow I knew that all the real answers to the many questions I had about life were waiting for me in those books.

Every night before going to sleep, we read. At seven, after dinner, chores, and a bath, I would get my next Louisa May Alcott or Nancy Drew and stretch out on the floor beside Auntie's rocking chair. Sometimes I would get so caught up in the story, I would read until I finished the book. Reading was the one thing I was allowed to do past my eight-thirty bedtime. I could read late into the night.

"Goodness gracious, she goes through those books like a tornado," Auntie told people. "She's a gifted child," she bragged. "Never needs entertaining." I loved to hear her compliments. I wondered what other children did. Did they read, too? Did they imagine they were Nancy Drew? Since I rarely got to play with them, I didn't know.

Television was a rare treat, except for Lawrence Welk on Saturday night and occasionally Mitch Miller. Usually, the house was quiet in the evenings—no TV, no radio, no other people. The only sound was the soft swish of turning pages.

During the school year, I knew not to ask permission to visit a friend from school or to have someone over. Auntie had a stock reply. "You don't need to be around children every hour of the day," she would say. "You're with them enough at school."

Occasionally, one of my aunts dropped her children at Auntie's—for an afternoon, for a weekend, sometimes for several weeks at a time. I was thrilled to be with my cousins. They were frightened of our stern old great-great-aunt—most people were—but not so much that they didn't enjoy visiting. The house was more fun than a carnival scary house.

"Take us to the attic!" Greg and David and Donna and Conrad would shout as soon as they scrambled out of the backseat of the car. We would clamber up the steep stairs to the third floor, shushing each other as we went. It was terrifying; that's why we loved it. Terrifying because of the trunks and the mothball-scent of age, the peculiar slant of the attic ceiling, and because of several little doors in the wall that provided access to the wiring and the roof.

And terrifying because of the mannequins. Ed Nirken, who ran Ed Nirken's Men and Boys Shop next door to Rose Behar's World Toy and Gift Shop, stored his out-of-season offerings in the attic, along with at least two or three mannequins. My cousins and I knew they were up there, but just to pop up into the attic and see a gathering of nude men lurking in the shadows always gave us a delicious little fright. Those were the times in my childhood that I forgot about my mother's absence from my life. I could just be a child.

What my mother was experiencing, I had no idea, although I suspect now that she had reached the absolute nadir of her existence about this time. Whether anyone ever told her or not, I have no doubt she knew she had lost her child. She knew she had lost both her children. Whatever support Mama and Papa had been able to provide was beginning to diminish. As they got older, they were less and less able to care for themselves, much less Dawn.

She was thirty years old. She had been sick for nearly a decade, for nearly her whole adult life, for *all* of my life. She had endured shock treatments, repeated hospitalizations, and the loss of her self. Despite being on Thorazine, she was still tormented by voices. At some point, they were brazen enough to offer a new suggestion. "Why not kill yourself?" they asked. "What's the use of living?"

At first my mother must have had answers. She talked back. She *had* to get well, she told the voices. My baby needs me.

The voices jeered. My mother gave in. And why not? In those moments of lucidity she was still capable of mustering, she saw that every incredible dream of her life had been dashed. Her artistry, her career, her children—all had vanished.

She took a knife and raked it across her wrist. It wasn't a neat slice. It was a jagged, punishing wound, but not deep enough to kill her. On two separate occasions, she tried to put an end to her misery. Each time, help arrived before she bled to death.

Papa died when I was ten. "He woke up one morning, put on his suit, and had his coffee," Mama told us. "Just like he always did. Sally was there, and he told us, 'I'll be leaving this afternoon. I love you all.' We didn't know what he meant, but that afternoon, he lay down on the bed, still in his suit and tie, and he just went to sleep. He never woke up."

That was Papa, it seemed to me. In his thoughtful, dignified way, he didn't want to cause trouble for anyone. He was eighty-six.

Mama brought him back to Houston for a funeral at the Christian Science Church, the white pews with their dark red cushions neat and tasteful, the natural light streaming in through the windows to banish any thoughts of darkness. *God is Love*, large gilt letters on the back wall reminded us.

When it was time to view the body, my aunts wanted me to stay in the pew, but Auntie said no. "She hasn't seen her grandfather in a long time," she whispered, and she took me by the hand. We walked slowly up the aisle to Papa's coffin. I looked at him for a long time, and then I touched his hand, the big hand that had held me and bathed me and wiped away my tears. I noticed the liver spots and the large, perfectly shaped nails. I almost expected him to look at me, to smile and take my hand in his. He had been so kind and so good, and he had loved me so much. How could he go away and leave me before I had a chance to see him? Auntie put her arm across my shoulders and led me outside.

My mother didn't come to Houston for the funeral. She was in the hospital in California. At least, that's what Mama told everyone. Her daughters had persuaded my grandmother to stay with Betty Lee for a few days after the funeral, until they could help her decide whether it was better to stay in Houston permanently or go back to California to be with Dawn or to bring Dawn back to Houston.

Betty Lee was upstairs one afternoon a few days after the

funeral when she happened to glance out a back window. There was her mother, hurrying toward the tall shrubbery at the back fence. In her hand, lifted high like a waiter, Mama carried a large tray. Betty Lee looked more closely. The tray was piled high with golden-brown fried chicken.

Betty Lee was mystified, but then, as Mama opened a back gate and slipped through, still carefully balancing her bountiful tray, Betty Lee suddenly understood that her mother was up to something. On the other side of the fence was Old Spanish Trail, a busy commercial street, with several motels. Somehow, Mama had gotten Dawn from California to Houston and had secretly installed her in a tourist court just down the street from the house. That explained her answer when Betty Lee had asked her about the trip when she had picked her up at the bus station. "Oh, we— I mean, I—did just fine," Mama had said. Betty Lee smiled, shook her head and waited for her mother to slip back through the fence, without the tray of fried chicken. The decision about what to do with Dawn and Mama was already made.

I didn't know that my mother had returned. No one told me until they had met with Auntie to see how the reunion was to be handled. I had hoped I would see her at the funeral, but when I didn't, I went on as usual. I wasn't supposed to ask about my mother too often; to ask would mean that I didn't appreciate Auntie. She also knew that if she told me that my mother was in Houston I would pester her hourly until my mother finally arrived.

When I finally heard that I would see my mother, I decided that she must be well. As I understood it, she had been in the hospital, the doctors had taken care of her, and then they had let her go home. Hadn't Mama told Auntie: "You'll be amazed when you see Dawn. You won't see a thing wrong with her!"

I had always known how our reunion would be, and I would feel a delicious thrill whenever I thought about it. I had fantasized for five years about this moment. She would be pretty, like Betty Lee, except her hair would be a deep golden, like honey. The doorbell would ring, I would clatter down the stairs, fling open the door, and there she would be, pretty and fresh and smiling down at me. She would sweep me into her arms and hug me, and we would never be parted again. She would take me back to Hollywood, and we would live happily ever after.

The day finally came, a Saturday morning. Auntie and I were sitting in the upstairs kitchen. The red-and-white room was cheery and spotless, the breakfast dishes put away, the breakfast table cleared, a tall vase of sweet peas in the center. I had been dressed for hours, and Auntie had found it necessary to remind me repeatedly to eat my breakfast, to quit fidgeting, to quit asking when they would arrive. I wanted to go outside and sit at the end of the driveway, but Auntie kept me in. "I don't want you getting that dress dirty," she said. I sat at the breakfast table and stared out the window, looking, waiting for that moment when my life would change forever.

It was nearly lunchtime when I spotted two women walking slowly down the driveway toward our back door. One was my grandmother, small and birdlike, a bit grayer than I remembered but still an attractive older woman.

The other woman was larger and heavier than my grandmother, and she looked almost as old. She wore what looked to me like baggy old-women's clothes, a bulky brown jacket, and a shapeless dress. Her shoulder-length hair, dull and brown, was parted on the side and plastered with bobby pins across her forehead. She clung to Mama's arm as if frightened and unsure; eyes lowered, she looked up now and then as if expecting someone to hit her.

"That's your mother, darling," Auntie said. "Don't you recognize your mother?"

CHAPTER SEVEN

When I was ten, Carrie Lou Arnold Smith, the Roberts Elementary principal, sent a message to my teacher in the middle of the day. "Mrs. Smith wants to see you, Tara," my teacher explained. "You should take your books with you."

Hurrying down the deserted hallway, my books in a satchel over my shoulder, I tried to imagine what I had done to deserve a trip to the principal's office, but nothing came to mind. I had learned, with Auntie's help, to curb my talking, so I didn't run afoul of the law as often as I had in earlier grades.

Mrs. Smith was waiting for me at the door of her office. "Honey, we need to get you home as quickly as possible," she said with a concerned look on her broad, rosy-cheeked face. She took both my hands in hers. "Miss Gehring is quite ill."

Mrs. Smith's secretary drove me home. As she pulled up in front of the house, I was surprised to see several neighbors standing in the driveway, gathered around something or someone lying on the pavement. I began to whimper as I realized it was my aunt, her head cradled on Mrs. Behar's arm. I ran and knelt beside her.

"Auntie, what's the matter?" I cried. "What happened?"

"She just had a little fainting spell," Mrs. Behar said, putting her arms on my shoulders. "We're waiting for the ambulance."

Auntie looked at me without saying anything. Her eyes behind her glasses stared wildly. She didn't know who I was.

"Auntie," I pleaded, "it's me, Tara. Please, Auntie, say something." I was frightened. I couldn't imagine anything ever happening to Auntie. Even though I had soaked her feet in Epsom salts, reminded her nightly to take her digitalis, and listened to her heartbeat, I always thought she would stay the same. She was an old woman, of course, but it seemed to me she would always be old, ageless as it were, and always there for me.

"That's all right, honey," Mrs. Behar said, gently smoothing a wisp of white hair off Auntie's forehead. "Your aunt just tried to do too much, and she fainted. Ambulance'll be here in a minute."

Sally drove up just as the ambulance arrived. We watched as Auntie was placed onto the stretcher and loaded into the ambulance. I noticed that Auntie's fragrant white daffodils were blooming along the border of the driveway. "She didn't know who I was," I kept saying to Sally. I couldn't stop crying.

I stayed with Sally and my cousins while Auntie was in the hospital. "Hardening of the arteries," the doctor said. He prescribed medication, and after ten days Auntie was home again, propped up in her bed like a duchess. I cooked for her, ran errands, helped her out of bed and into her milk bath, scrubbed her back. She was weak but getting better, she said. Soon she would be her old self.

She was able to get up and about after a few days, but she was never the same. She could no longer do the things she had done for the first five years I was with her. More and more, she depended on me to do the cooking, shopping, house cleaning.

Tara Elgin Holley with Joe Holley

And more and more, she began to exhibit extreme, irrational behavior.

Once I was sitting at the kitchen table doing my homework while Auntie puttered about the kitchen. Betty Lee dropped by and happened to notice that I wasn't doing my homework after all. Inside the notebook, I had hidden a comic book. It was a teenage romance comic book, one that my cousin Joanna had left at the house. I had never seen anything like it.

"Well, honey!" Betty Lee said, giggling.

"Please, Betty Lee," I whispered, quickly shutting the notebook. "Don't tell Auntie."

Betty Lee thought it was her duty to tell. As far as she was concerned, Auntie represented all the things that Betty Lee admired—education, distinguished family, the Old South. "I just happened to glance down at what she was reading, and I saw this magazine," I heard her telling Auntie in the next room. She gave a little laugh, as if to say, "Kids will be kids."

It wasn't funny to Auntie. Betty Lee left a few minutes later, and I took the dogs for their evening walk. When I came back, Auntie was in her bedroom, sitting in her rocker. "There's something we have to talk about," she said, glaring at me over her bifocals. "I'm going to ask you a question, and I want you to tell me the truth."

I knew what she was going to ask, and I got a sinking feeling in my stomach.

"What did you have in your notebook when Betty Lee was here?" she asked.

"I didn't have anything in my notebook," I lied. "I was doing my homework."

"Don't lie to me, young lady," she said, struggling up out of the rocker. I knew she had seen the pinch of guilt in my face.

I wasn't accustomed to lying. "Betty Lee saw what you were looking at."

I looked up at the old woman looming over me and decided to confess. "It was a comic book," I said. "One Joanna left over here. I'm sorry. I won't ever do it again."

"You're still lying to me," she said, lifting me by the arm out of my chair. She pulled me onto the porch. "What you were doing was dirty. It was sinful, and I will not have it in this house."

I began to cry as Auntie dragged me down the stairs. "I'm not lying," I said. "I was looking at Joanna's comic book."

On the downstairs back porch, she took a belt from a hook on a wall, a belt with small, pyramid-shaped metal studs. She forced me to kneel on the stairs, and she began to swing the belt against my back and bare legs.

"I know what you were looking at," she gasped as she swung the belt. "You were looking at those magazines, those dirty, filthy magazines."

Kneeling on one step, my head resting on my folded arms on a higher step, I couldn't imagine what she was talking about. I knew she thought comic books were cheap and crude, but surely Joanna's comic book wasn't that bad.

The blows continued, and suddenly I remembered. A few days earlier, Auntie had taken the trash out to the street and had found a torn and crumpled magazine lying at the curb. She had picked it up, began to leaf through it, and discovered that it was filled with grainy black-and-white photos of naked men and women. I had heard her telling Mrs. Behar about it.

Instead of throwing the magazine in the trash, she had brought it back into the house with her. She had tossed it onto the floor at the back of the hall closet where we kept the bottles of Scotch and the fancy tins of cookies or boxes of chocolates that people sent us every Christmas. I would explore the closet every now and then just to examine the goodies, and I found the magazine. I examined the pictures of naked men and women playing volleyball and cavorting at the beach. It was a little strange but didn't really interest me.

That was the magazine Auntie was sure I had been reading when Betty Lee caught me. What she herself wanted with it, I had no idea.

"I'll teach you to lie to me," she muttered, breathing in labored gasps, "even if it means I have to beat the living hell out of you!"

That's exactly what she was doing. Never had a beating lasted so long. With every lash of the belt across my back and bare legs, she was beating back the hell, the evil, the waywardness that had destroyed my mother. I carried the demon seed, and this old woman, in a rage of righteous indignation, was going to beat it back.

"Are you going to tell me the truth?" she shouted, continuing to swing the belt at me, her face red, her eyes wild with fury.

"I am telling you the truth," I sobbed. I tried to claw my way up the stairs, but the enraged old woman continued to hit me as I lay sprawled on the steps. The chopping strokes bit into my skin. There was always a place for the belt to land no matter how I ducked or writhed.

Over and over, she insisted that I tell her the truth, and over and over I screamed that I was telling the truth. The belt seared my skin, but I was trying to be strong. I thought I was standing up for honesty. I thought I was behaving the way Auntie had taught me to behave. I screamed, but still the blows fell.

Lying on the steps, I turned around to beg Auntie to stop. She swung the belt just as I turned, and I felt the metal part slash my eye. My eye burned, and everything blurred.

"All right," I moaned, "I'll tell you the truth." Auntie paused, the belt upraised. "I got the magazine out of your closet."

My Mother's Keeper
153

Auntie dropped the belt. She sat down heavily on the steps and drew me to her. She was breathing so hard she couldn't speak. She began to rock me. I was afraid she would have a stroke right there on the back steps.

"See how easy that was?" she finally managed to whisper. "If you'd just told the truth from the beginning, all of this could have been avoided."

I glanced down at the fiery red stripes across my legs. I was seething inside. I had been whipped many times, but this time it was different. This time it seemed as if childhood itself had come to an end. She had beaten a lie out of me, not the truth. I would no longer be so trusting. I would take care of myself.

The strength this sick and weakened old woman summoned must have been the last-gasp strength of panic and fear. As she weakened and as I grew older, she realized that she was losing control, she desperately feared that despite her most arduous and determined efforts to shape me and direct my future, what was in the blood would prevail, that shared blood meant shared susceptibilities. I was going the way of my mother, and she could do nothing about it. At school the next day, my teacher asked about my black eye. I told her I had opened a kitchen cabinet and bumped into the edge. She didn't question my story.

The old feelings of unease were creeping back into my life. This stalwart old lady I had learned to trust, this strong woman who had provided me with predictability and routine, was becoming as unpredictable as my grandparents had been a few years earlier. Senility was settling in, and her eccentricity began to evolve into the bizarre. There were the dogs, for example.

The dogs were Auntie's children: Buster, Suzie, Spot, Cubbie, Girlie, Sabu. They had been her children before I arrived, and like her, they were growing old and infirm.

Suzie, our big, beautiful dalmatian, was the first to die. I came home from school one spring afternoon, and Auntie was leaning, hands on her knees, over her body in the backyard. "She was old," Auntie said, while I knelt beside Suzie as she lay on her side, her legs stretched out stiffly before her. "It was time for her to go."

I smoothed the beautiful, spotted white fur. "Where can we bury her?" I asked, looking up at Auntie.

"We'll bury her in the yard here by the garage," she said, "but we don't have to do it right now. The ground's too wet."

We didn't bury Suzie that day or the next. Or the next. Auntie dragged her body into the garage and laid her on a mat she had made from old fabric. There it stayed for weeks. The smell was overpowering. Every day I would ask what we were going to do with Suzie, and every day Auntie had an excuse for not doing anything. After several weeks, Floyd the handyman buried the rotting carcass in the backyard.

Girlie, our little black-and-white fox terrier, was the next to go. She died in the house one day while I was at school. When I got home, I found Auntie in my bedroom. She had taken Girlie and laid her at the end of my bed, on a small blanket atop my maroon silk bedspread. "Shouldn't we bury her?" I asked a little later, dreading to repeat what had happened with Suzie.

"Of course, we will," Auntie said, staring down at the little dog. "But in a little while. Not right now."

The dog stayed in my room, on my bed. Again the smell was overwhelming. I stayed out of the room as much as I could, although I had to pass through it if I wanted to go down the front stairs and out the front door. I usually went out the back door.

At night, I slept with Auntie. "Just for a few nights," she said, "until the ground is dry and we can bury Girlie." That seemed reasonable enough to me, although after a while the image of that dog lying on my bed evolved into a dream and then a memory of having to sleep with the dog when Auntie continued refusing to dispose of it. After a week, the stench filled the whole house, and still the body stayed on my bed.

One afternoon after school, I had to get a book out of my room. I held my breath at the door, reminded myself not to look at Girlie's body, and walked in. I kept my eyes averted from the bed, but I had forgotten about the large oval mirror above the chest of drawers, on a wall directly facing the bed. In the mirror, I caught a glimpse of Girlie. The little white dog was moving. I couldn't believe it, but she must still be alive.

I turned toward the bed and saw what the movement really was. Greasy, white maggots, like wriggling grains of rice, were spilling out of her body, down the maroon bedspread and onto the carpeted floor. I rushed out of the room, afraid I was going to be sick. I ran to the kitchen, got a broom and dustpan, and ran back to my room. Frantically, I began trying to sweep up the maggots, but they swarmed out of the pan and onto the floor. I ran to the bathroom carrying the dustpan, and the maggots began scurrying up my arm. I flushed them down the toilet.

I should have told somebody, but whom could I tell? My aunts would never believe me. They were intimidated by Auntie as much as I was. I knew they cared about me, but I wanted them to rescue me. I wanted them to give me a home, but as far as they were concerned, I had a home.

Rose Behar and Ed Nirken and other people in the Village would see me doing the grocery shopping by myself and would stop to chat. "How's Miss Gehring?" they'd ask. "How are you?" Even as a child, I could tell they weren't just being friendly. They would look into my eyes, searching, it seemed, for any signs of distress.

My friends at church would see me get off the bus alone on Sunday mornings and would ask the same questions. But what could I say? That my mother's mentally ill and I'm living with an old lady who does things no one would believe? I would walk home from school alone, staring down at the sidewalk and wondering what I should do, what to say.

I wanted to tell someone about Floyd also, but I was afraid to. I certainly couldn't tell Auntie. She would say that what happened was my fault.

Floyd had worked for Auntie for years, doing odd jobs around the house and yard and sometimes driving me to school. Occasionally, he'd do the grocery shopping for us or drive Auntie downtown. On the days he didn't work for Auntie, he was a dishwasher at One's a Meal. His wife was a nurse. A kind, matronly woman who rarely smiled, she seemed older than Floyd.

Floyd was a handsome, friendly man in his early thirties. I liked him a lot. Once, when he was working around the house, I heard him singing, his deep, rich voice filling the house with joy. I ran to get a hymnal we had, and we sat on the couch and sang hymns together.

Sometimes he brought his two children to the house, and we played together. I liked the way he was attentive and affectionate with his children, a little boy and a little girl about my age. When he was playing with the three of us in the yard, I wished he were my daddy, too.

Auntie treated him in a typically southern, patronizing way. Sometimes she would refer to him as her big, black stevedore because he was so muscular and strong, and she would order him around as if he were a child. He was always deferential and smiling, but behind his smile and elaborate courtesy, Floyd must have simmered with rage.

One afternoon, Auntie had taken the bus downtown to the bank, and I was left at home with Floyd. Auntie was remodeling the first floor of the house, so all the furniture had been moved

My Mother's Keeper

out of several rooms. Floyd was doing some painting, and I was puttering about downstairs chattering and singing. I wandered into the room where Floyd was working.

"Want me to swing you around?" he asked.

I thought that was a great idea. It was a game we played outdoors when his children came over. He would grip us under the arms with his big hands, turn in a circle, and we would fly ever faster, our feet off the ground.

He put down the paintbrush, dried off his hands, and put his hands around me as we stood facing each other in the center of the empty dining room. He began to turn, faster and faster, leaning back as he turned, and soon I was flying, the walls and floor spinning so fast I had to close my eyes. After a moment, he slowed down, lowering me down his leg to the floor. I looked up at him. He was breathing quickly, almost panting, and there was a strange look in his eyes. Suddenly I felt frightened. Something was wrong, but I didn't know what it was.

I told him I didn't feel good and that I didn't want to play. He reached down and helped me up, then put his big, strong hands around my waist and lifted me atop the radiator. I sat there, my feet dangling. Floyd looked at me, saying nothing. I watched him unzip his khaki pants, and with his erect penis in his hand, I watched him move slowly toward me. I didn't know what was happening. I fell back against the wall.

I must have fainted, because when I came to, I was lying on my back on the kitchen floor. Floyd was kneeling beside me, a worried look on his face. He peered into my eyes. "Now, don't you tell Miss Gehring what happened," he said in a low voice. "You understand?"

I nodded, got up, and brushed past him to the back door. I sat on the steps, my knees pulled up to my chin, my arms around my knees. I tried to fold myself into a ball. I felt cold. I was trembling inside and out, and I could not stop. Auntie, I knew, wouldn't be back until six, and I couldn't go back into the house where Floyd was still working. As far as I could tell, he hadn't done anything to me, but I hated him for what he wanted to do, although I wasn't sure what it was. I hated him for making me be quiet.

I lay in bed at night trying to sort it all out. Was this what Auntie meant when she said I was just like Dawn? Was this what she meant when she warned me about being suggestive? But what did it mean to be suggestive? I remembered what Mr. Sweeney, the jeweler in the Village, had said about me. "She's going to be a gorgeous girl when she grows up," he told Auntie.

The compliment made Auntie angry—at me. "Those come-hither looks are going to get you in trouble," she warned. "You're no different from your mother and from Betty Lee." I was seven years old and had no idea what she was talking about.

With Floyd, I was ashamed but couldn't figure out what I had done. I said not a word to Auntie about what had happened, but at night I plotted to get rid of Floyd. "I just don't think Floyd works as hard as he ought to," I would mention to Auntie. Or I would try to convince her he was stealing from us. I had nightmares about him.

On those days he took me to school, I would open the back door of his older-model Chevrolet, and as soon as I touched the yellowed plastic that protected the backseat, I would begin to feel nauseous. I'd look down at my hands on the plastic, and I would feel bile coming up in my throat. Often Auntie would be with us in the front seat, talking to Floyd as he drove. Before Floyd's attack, I chattered all the way to school. Afterward, I always sat quietly in the back, trying not to vomit all over Floyd's yellowed-plastic seat covers. I was cool toward him; I tried to seem threatening.

Floyd quit working for Auntie about a year later. Maybe he was afraid I would tell, although I never did. Auntie never knew what happened. For me it was like a bad dream, dark and shadowed, that I never forgot. I kept it to myself for ten years.

Sometimes I would tell my cousins what was happening with Auntie. I'd tell them about the dogs or the frequent whippings, and they would tell my aunts. As I got older, Sally and Sister and Betty Lee must have assumed my complaints were typical adolescent gripes. They didn't take me seriously, and no one ever sat down with Auntie and asked her what was going on. She was the family matriarch; she had known my aunts since they themselves were children. No one ever questioned Auntie.

Whatever was happening to Auntie's mind, senility or hardening of the arteries or whatever it was, she was increasingly distressed with me. Approaching adolescence and every day more independent, I was no longer the docile creature she had worked to mold. I resolved never to take another beating like the one she had given me. Flush with my own power, I began to talk back.

"I was a teacher for forty-three years, and never did I have trouble with children talking back to me," she grumbled, her mouth grim. But I was different. I was rebellious and headstrong—just like my mother. She would tell me yet again about my mother sitting in her upstairs window as a child and singing to the boys. I was turning out just like her.

She still whipped me, though never as severely as the time on the stairs. Sometimes after a whipping, I would threaten to go away and leave her alone. "Mama and my mother want me to come live with them," I would tell her. "That's what I'm going to do, and you can't stop me."

"Go right ahead, young lady," she would say. "See how you like living in a pig sty with no one to care for you." As she turned away, I would hear her mumble, "Give young people enough rope, and they'll hang themselves."

The tears would come, no matter how hard I tried not to cry, and I would run out of the room. I knew she was right. I had known it from the morning I watched my mother walking slowly down our driveway with Mama. My mother was a crazy woman, and she could no more take care of me than she could take care of herself. My grandmother was almost as helpless.

My aunts had rented a garage apartment for them three blocks from our house. Auntie allowed my mother to visit once a week, usually on Saturday morning, and Mama would come along. While we did our Saturday household chores, Mama would sit in the kitchen and drink coffee and talk to Auntie and me.

Auntie treated my mother like a child. As soon as she came into the house, Auntie made her take a thorough bath and shampoo her hair. Dawn didn't protest, and she almost always needed a bath.

After the bath, she would sit in a rocking chair, murmuring softly to herself and laughing. Since Mama never insisted that she take her medication—as far as Mama was concerned, she wasn't sick—she was more attentive to the voices in her head than she was to me. I would stand beside her chair, showing her my school-work or something I had drawn, but my mother couldn't concentrate. Rocking back and forth, she would stare at the papers and nod, and then she would whisper and laugh to herself, making up word games from the things I said and talking about Hollywood.

I would try to have a conversation with her, but after a while I would give up and go to my grandmother. I enjoyed being with Mama as much as ever, but she would gently shoo me back to my mother. "Go on, honey. She's been dying to see you," she would say. "You two need to be together." If Auntie heard her, she would shake her head at such foolishness. "Oh, Marian," she would say.

Once a week, Auntie allowed me to visit Mama and Dawn in their garage apartment. Auntie herself went once and vowed never to go back.

I would ride past One's a Meal and Moeller's Bakery, park my bike in the backyard of the house where they lived, and walk up the dark, musty inside stairs to their tiny apartment. Sometimes my mother would be sitting on the stairs waiting for me. "Hi, honey," she would say as I hugged her around the waist.

They lived over a garage in two rooms, a combination living room/kitchen and a bedroom. The apartment was small and close and foul-smelling. A ratty old couch and a small table were the only pieces of furniture in the living room, except for an easel and tubes of oil paints. In the other room were two single beds covered with books and papers. The house was always filthy, with roaches scurrying over moldy scraps of food and food-encrusted dishes scattered about the room. I hated the way they lived.

Mama seemed oblivious to the filth. Although she still kept herself clean and fresh-smelling, no one had ever expected her to keep house—that's what hired help was for—and she wasn't going to start now. As far as I was concerned, she was still a delight. She read stories to me, asked me about my schoolwork, and made me feel like I was the prettiest, smartest little girl in the world.

She got up before sunrise every morning and walked through the quiet neighborhood, breathing in the fresh morning air and marveling over the miracle of the sunrise. She took the bus to the downtown library and checked out a dozen books at a time, which she kept in a tall, precarious stack by her unmade bed. She still wrote poetry and painted and played the violin. To her, music and art were still the essence of life. Scurrying about cleaning house and preparing meals, paying the bills, and balancing the checking account—all the practical, everyday things that occupied the lives of most people—were, to Mama, as bothersome as gnats. They distracted her from the only things that mattered.

Aunt Betty, one of Papa's two sisters, died, and Mama inherited some money. She and my mother immediately bought a piano. Now, when I visited, my mother and I had something to share. I stood beside her at the piano and watched her hands—her nails bitten off in ragged edges—range knowingly over the keys. I felt her sway with the music, and I listened to the voice, to the full, honey-coated sound that filled the room and filled me up inside. When she played, when she sang, she was her old self. It didn't matter that she no longer looked like a princess or that most of the time she retreated to a world forever closed to me. Just for a little while, she was the mother I remembered, the one I had dreamed about all my life. Her voice soothed me and allowed me to forget all my discomfort with the surroundings.

A song would be dancing through my head as I clambered up the dark flight of steps, maybe one I had heard from a musical at the Delman Theater the week before, maybe something from *Gigi* or *Oklahoma!* "Out of my dreams and into the hush of falling shadows/ . . . out of my dreams I'll go/Into a dream with you," I would be singing as I pushed open the wooden door at the top of the stairs. My mother would hear me and pick up the tune on the piano, and then she would lead me through the lyrics. She would work with me on the other songs, singing for me in a voice as lovely and expressive as the voice I heard on the records I had at home.

Then she would teach me. Again and again, we would go over the pieces phrase by phrase, me singing, she playing the melody and looking into my eyes as she lip-synched the words along with me. She coaxed the music out of me, helped me mold and shape it the way you would shape smoke floating through the air. I was a quick learner. In fact, I seemed to know the tunes already.

I lived for those moments when my mother would clap her hands delightedly, pull me to her and tell me that I sang like an angel. Then we would go on to another song, maybe one I'd never heard, from her repertoire that I was so eager to imitate. "Listen to this," she would say. She would cock her head, wink, and launch into "You Made Me Love You." It was uncanny the way she could invest a song with meaning. She was singing, but at the same time speaking just to you, as if the words and the emotion were fresh and immediate. I would have given anything to sing the way she did.

We would sing and play for a couple of hours together on those Saturday mornings, and then I would give her a hug, say good-bye to my grandmother and hurry down the dark stairs to my bike. I would ride through the neighborhood along the streets lined with oaks, pecans, magnolias, past sturdy brick homes, older homes set back from the street on shady, green-carpeted lawns, and I would imagine what it was like to be a little girl in a normal family, with a mommy and daddy, brothers and sisters. My mother would be playing the piano in the living room and singing when I got home from school every day, and later in the afternoon, my father would drive up in his car, home from the office. "How was school?" he would say, bending down to give me a hug. He'd have his suit coat draped over his arm, and his tie would be loosened, his top button undone. I would take his briefcase with both hands, and we would walk into the house together, his hand on my shoulder.

Then I would see my mother in that dark, smelly apartment, my mother alone with her music, alone with the voices that did not sing. The fantasy became more and more difficult to conjure up.

Tara Elgin Holley with Joe Holley
164

But if she could sing, if she could still make music, didn't that prove that she could still get better? I held on tightly to the hope that she was still sick only because she hadn't received the proper care. I had heard Auntie and Katherine Ball and my aunts lament over and over again that Mama would not keep her on her medication, that she wouldn't cooperate with Dawn's doctors. That's why she was sick. She just hadn't been given a chance to get better.

I would be the one to give her that chance. I would rescue my mother and lead her out of the darkness that kept her confused and off balance. After all, I was taking care of Auntie more and more. I was taking care of myself. Why couldn't I take care of my mother as well? Then, when she got well, she could take care of me the way other mothers did. She would bake cookies the way my friend Hallie Welborn's mother did. She would brush my hair and help me with my clothes. She would visit my school and talk to my teachers. We would make music together every day and talk. All those things that other mothers did, my mother would do too, if she just had the chance.

One afternoon, Auntie decided to go to the grocery store by herself. I told her I'd stay home and finish my homework, and when she got back I'd be ready to help her with dinner. I waited on the sidewalk until I saw her hobble slowly around the corner, and then I dashed back into the house. I went to the phone in the hallway and called an 800 number I had seen on TV. It was a number to call if you needed help, and I had memorized it.

My hand was trembling as I dialed, and I wasn't sure I would be brave enough to talk if someone actually answered. A woman came on the line. "My mother is . . . my mother is . . ." I couldn't get the words out. I tried again. "My mother is mentally ill," I said. "Can somebody help me?"

The woman began to ask me questions, but I barely heard. I

My Mother's Keeper

kept hearing the words I had used to describe my mother. Mentally ill. It was like a confession. It was as if I had confessed the most horrible of sins. The words themselves were horrible. I was betraying my mother, telling an awful truth to the world.

The woman wanted to know my name, but I was afraid to tell her. I was afraid Auntie would find out. I hung up the phone.

CHAPTER EIGHT

One afternoon after school, a few days after my thirteenth birthday, Auntie called me into her bedroom. "There's something we need to talk about, dearie," she said. "Help me get up."

She was sitting in her rocker, as usual, so I walked over and held the chair still while she gripped my forearm and pulled herself up. She steadied herself and slowly led me over to her antique rosewood chest of drawers. She bent down and opened the bottom drawer, the drawer where she kept her lingerie. The silk night gowns and corsets and slips were folded in neat layers, each layer separated by a long, filmy piece of tissue paper. Tucked among the clothes were silk packets of sachet in pastel colors. They gave off a rose fragrance. From underneath the bottom layer, she retrieved a bulky cotton pad.

"This is a Kotex," she announced matter-of-factly, "for when the bleeding begins." She explained what would soon happen to me, how to use the Kotex, how to keep it in position. I pretty much knew what to expect from discussions with my teenage cousin Joanna, who had stayed with us a few months, but I never realized I would have to wear one of those bulky things. I could just see myself walking into class with a big bulge under my skirt. Auntie must have had it in her drawer for at least thirty years.

"It's no fun having to wear it," she said, smoothing out the wide elastic belt that went with it, "but it's certainly an improvement over what we had when I was your age." She explained how she and her sisters had to use rags, and how they put the soiled rags in buckets to soak, and how their black servants had to wash them out. I took the pad to my room and waited for the day I would have to use it.

Even my mother noticed I was changing. One Saturday morning when she was at the house, she poked my tiny budding breasts. "Will you look at my little girl?" she exclaimed. "She's growing up."

Her gesture made me uncomfortable, and I got the feeling that my growing up disturbed her as well. I think she still had some idea of herself as a young woman, the young woman she had been when she got sick, and it just didn't seem right to her that she was old enough to be the mother of an adolescent.

She looked at her daughter's body and saw her younger self. We were separate, and yet the same.

Of course, I felt the same symbiotic identification that she felt. But if I was a reflection of my mother's younger self, she was, for me, a clue to my future self. From her, I needed assurance and acceptance. These were gifts, of course, she was unable to offer.

My mother's response to my maturing body reminded me of the teasing I endured at school because I still had to wear little cotton undershirts instead of a bra. Auntie insisted. I would not wear a bra until I was at least sixteen, regardless of whether I needed one. Once in a junior high phys ed class, a gang of girls stripped me, so they could ridicule my undershirt. A girl named Brenda started it, Brenda and a couple of her gum-chewing, bouffant-haired friends—girls who wore caked-on black eyeliner and hung out with a motorcycle gang—but it wasn't long before the popular girls in the country club set joined in.

What happened to me could have happened to anybody, but then, as I struggled and cried and tried to fend them off, I was thinking, Uh-oh, they know. They know. Somehow they know that my mother's crazy and my aunt controls my life. They can tell by this stupid haircut and these old-fashioned clothes and this undershirt Auntie makes me wear that I am as weird as they come. What's happening to me now only confirms it.

A bell rang, and the girls dashed out of the dressing room to the gym, leaving me cowering in the corner, naked on the cold tile floor. With the sound of their laughter still echoing off the rows of mole-gray lockers, I sat on a bench feeling sorry for myself, relieved only by what the girls didn't know. They didn't know that Auntie still knelt painfully beside the tub every night and bathed me, or that she didn't intend for me to date or go to parties or wear a bra for years. They didn't know the sense of shame I carried with me, like the bulky, old-fashioned Kotex tucked away in my purse.

Actually, the girls knew little about me, and I doubt that any of them knew about my mother. Some of their mothers may have known, but none of the girls. They just knew that I was different. Queer, they called me. I had cooties.

I did have one friend at school, one who wasn't weird or queer or different at all. Her name was Hallie Welborn. She was friendly and popular, and amazingly enough, she wanted to be my friend, too. Skinny, with bouncy auburn hair, Hallie was cute rather than pretty. I made better grades than she did, but she had something I envied. She was at ease with herself, at ease in the world. She liked people, and they liked her.

What did she see in me? She borrowed my schoolwork, for

one thing, and I suspect she probably enjoyed feeling superior. But it was never a malicious thing. She had many friends, all kinds of friends. She was like her mother, who enjoyed inviting her daughters' friends into the Welborn household and getting to know them. Hallie was my junior high school savior. In the afternoons after school, I'd tell Auntie I was going for a bike ride, and I'd head for the Welborns' comfortable, two-story house a few blocks away. Hallie and her older sister, Joan, had movie magazines and the latest Beatles album, and they knew the latest styles. They would fix my hair, show me how to put on makeup, let me borrow their clothes. Of course, I had to stuff the clothes into my purse, so Auntie wouldn't see them. On the way to the school bus stop the next morning, I would dash into the Texaco rest room and hurriedly pull on the blouse or the skirt that Hallie had loaned me. It happened two or three times a week all through junior high.

Joan was old enough to drive, and her parents had given her a red Mustang. Sometimes she would take Hallie and me for a ride, although I had to warn her not to drive by my house. Auntie might be outside in the garden; if she saw me riding around in a red car with a teenager, she'd beat me within an inch of my life. We'd cruise around the Rice area talking about school and records and boys. "Johnny Weingarten thinks you're cute," Hallie would say, "but he's too shy to tell you." I was thrilled to know that a boy had actually noticed me.

Hallie was eager to pair me off with the Welborns' next-door neighbor, Robert Levy. I'd go see him occasionally, when I was visiting the Welborns. He would be at home alone, and we would sit at the piano together, our hands occasionally touching as we worked on simple chords.

The most fun we had was on Saturdays when Hallie and I would go into Scheppes Department Store in the Village and try on clothes. "Oh, Tara, this looks just like you!" she would exclaim, taking a dress my aunt would never let me wear and urging me into the dressing room. Moments later, I'd step out in a short little sundress, my shoulders bare, and I would feel like a normal kid.

Hallie always had money and often bought things at Scheppes. Not me. Auntie had to buy my clothes. We'd go on all-day shopping expeditions to Neiman Marcus, Battlesteins, all the best stores, but Auntie would invariably insist that I buy the dorkiest dresses, the clunkiest shoes. They were always expensive clothes, good quality, but I never saw another child wearing them. Maybe Princess Anne over in England might have worn them, but Princess Anne didn't go to Lanier Junior High School in Houston, Texas. If a salesclerk, trying to be helpful, picked out a dress and cheerily exclaimed, "This is what all the girls are wearing these days!" my heart would sink. I knew that for Auntie, the fact that it was "what all the girls were wearing" was the very reason I would never take it out of my closet on a school day and wear it with a delicious sense of anticipation as I strolled into homeroom.

Occasionally, Betty Lee would send over a box of clothes that Bonnie, her oldest daughter, had outgrown. Bonnie, who would eventually be a model, was eight years older than me—and six inches taller. Her skirts brushed my ankles—just right as far as Auntie was concerned.

Those days, trying on clothes with Hallie was as close as I ever came to wearing the latest styles while I was with Auntie. Oh, I could hastily pull on something of Hallie's in my Texaco dressing room, but somehow it wasn't the same. The girls at school probably knew I was wearing Hallie's clothes.

One Saturday, Hallie and I came out of Scheppes and started walking down Rice Boulevard toward One's a Meal. It was lunchtime, and we had decided to have burgers and fries. The sidewalk was crowded on this sunny Saturday afternoon. Leaning into each other, our heads almost touching, we were gossiping and giggling as we weaved in and out of strolling shoppers.

We were almost to the café when I noticed my mother coming toward us. I stopped laughing, and Hallie glanced at me to see what was wrong. I didn't say anything. Though we were the best of friends, I had never told Hallie about my mother. She just wouldn't understand—or maybe she would have, but I would have hated her pity as much as her scorn. Other people's pity marked me as someone different, as an outsider, a child deserving compassion at a time when I desperately wanted to be part of the crowd.

Mommy was alone, and as she shuffled slowly down the middle of the sidewalk, she mumbled to herself. She was wearing a wrinkled dress that belonged to Mama, misbuttoned so that you could see her bra. She had slipped into a pair of dingy old house slippers, the heels bent down beneath her feet. She occasionally looked to the side as if carrying on a conversation with an invisible companion. She had scraps of paper pinned to her dress, and as she walked she scattered rolled-up balls of the newspaper she was carrying. I noticed how people eddied around her, how they glanced back at her as they passed.

It wasn't unusual for us to run into each other in the Village, but I had always been alone when we met. I knew what would happen if she spotted me. "Oh, honey! Oh, darling!" she would exclaim, taking me into her arms. She would launch into a breathy stream-of-consciousness monologue while people passed by on the sidewalk and wondered what this strange woman had to do with this teenage kid. In the early 1960s, if you saw homeless people at all in Houston, they were on downtown side streets near the courthouse, certainly not on the streets of the Village. My mother stood out.

I panicked. If Hallie found out, she would know the truth

about me. I could imagine her mouth opening in shock as we stood there on the sidewalk. She would slowly back away, and at school on Monday, I would see the little sideways glances in the hallway, the brief lifting of the eyebrows, as the girls Hallie had told whispered and giggled as I passed. Hallie wouldn't like me anymore, and I wouldn't have a friend.

"I've got to go home!" I muttered. "I just remembered Auntie needs me at home." Before Hallie could say a word, I turned my back on my mother and on my friend, and I fled. I hurried around the corner and started running, and I didn't stop running until I was back home.

Breathing hard, I walked down the driveway to the back steps and sat down, chin in hand, tears in my eyes. I was so ashamed. I wanted to tear my hair out, kick down the garage, do something to gouge out the pain and anger and guilt I felt. I was embarrassed about deserting Hallie, but most of all I was ashamed of running from the person I cared about most in the world, the person who so desperately needed my love.

I wanted to love her—I did love her—but I was tired of carrying around this burden. I just wanted life to be normal. I wanted a mother and a father I could watch and know and love. I also wanted a glimpse of future possibility, a sense of who I would be in a few years when I was grown and on my own. To imagine my mother as my future was almost more than I could bear.

Much of the time at school or with Hallie, occasionally with my cousins, I could pretend to be normal, even though I worried almost constantly that I wasn't. In the hallway at school, I would listen to the laughing, chattering girls around me; I would notice their short skirts, their sweaters tight across their breasts. I would watch them huddled together, as if for strength, and they would seem to speak a language I really didn't understand.

I could keep my strangeness compartmentalized, but I had to work hard at it. Neither Hallie nor any of my friends ever came to my house. They never spent the night with me, never even came into the yard or climbed the stairs to my room to play. If I let them into my life, they might discover the Miss Havisham I lived with. They might find out about the dogs. They might find out about the real me, the lonely kid with the crazy mother.

Another junior high friend helped me begin the long, slow process of understanding that my strangeness didn't have to be a burden. Unlike all-American Hallie, Anita Kalpaxis was "queer," too. Tall and gawky, she had matured early and was the butt of locker-room jokes because she had to wear a bra even before junior high. Unlike me, she was strong enough to laugh it off.

Anita was a straight-A student and, like Hallie, was comfortable with herself. Perhaps without even realizing it, she helped to draw me out of the shadows where I tended to linger. Anita and I giggled and laughed and studied together. I would cry on her shoulder, and she would comfort me. I could even tell her about my mother and about Auntie, though I never took her to meet either of them.

As the eldest daughter of a Greek Orthodox priest, Anita was at the center of perhaps twenty Greek kids at school who did not belong to the blond-haired cheerleader/football player set. Part of a prosperous, close-knit community, Anita and her Greek friends seemed more intellectual than most kids at school. They read poetry and took part in debate and other esoteric activities, and they did not spend their summers beside the pool at the River Oaks Country Club. I admired them and through Anita I got to know them well. It didn't matter to them that I was different; in River Oaks, they were different, too.

So was Bernie.* That's what attracted me to him. The year was 1966, and Bernie and I were both fifteen. We were freshmen at Lamar High School, the most prestigious, tradition-encrusted high school in Houston. The River Oaks kids went to Lamar High—that is, those who didn't go to Kincaid, St. John's, and other exclusive private schools. Howard Hughes was an alumnus of Lamar High, and so were many of Houston's bankers, lawyers, and businessmen. These were the people who ran Houston, who occupied the gracious homes and mansions set back among the thick trees and shrubbery off the winding roads of River Oaks and Shady Side. The River Oaks Country Club is at one end of tree-lined River Oaks Boulevard; within sight at the other end is Lamar High School. In those days, both institutions were pillars of Houston society. My relatives—the children, grandchildren, and great-grandchildren of Auntie's brothers and sisters—were part of this world. Unlike Mama and Papa and my aunts, they remained old-line Houston. They were industrialists and investors and shipping company executives. We saw them at Christmas, but they weren't really part of our daily lives.

Bernie sneered at all that. Tall, thin, and slouched over, with silky blond hair that hung down to his shoulders, Bernie read Ken Kesey, William Burroughs, and Alan Watts. He wrote poetry and knew the lyrics of every song ever recorded by Jefferson Airplane, the Stones, and Mothers of Invention. He could make A's in any class he wanted to; in fact, he tested at near-genius level. Usually, he didn't want to make A's; that would be a concession to the system. One semester, he might make an A in physics and shop and flunk all the rest. He drove his parents crazy with his sullen defiance.

Bernie and his friend Jimmy Landis* were ringleaders for a group of a dozen or so boys whose mission in life was to get the whole world stoned. Like Bernie, they were extremely bright, though as far as they were concerned, high school was a *Mad* magazine joke, and earnest kids like me were the Alfred E. Neumans of the world. High school stifled every creative and rebellious instinct a bright and sensitive human being might feel. In class, while I was conscientiously taking notes and raising my hand to answer questions, Bernie and his buddies, strategically seated throughout the room, would be passing messages to each other in code, slyly driving the teacher crazy with their smart-aleck disdain.

Often they skipped school, which is how I got to know Bernie. I worked in the attendance office during fourth period, where one of my duties was to call students who were absent and find out why they weren't in school. Bernie was absent so often that he and I got to be friends over the phone. I gradually began to realize that he was more intelligent than he let on.

With Bernie, I assumed my accustomed role. I would be his savior. "You're going to blow it," I told him many a morning. "You need to be in school."

On one of those days that he deigned to be in school, Bernie was absentmindedly looking in my direction during biology class. Busily taking notes, my eyes focused on my notebook, I happened to prop my foot up on the rung of the desk in front of me. My long skirt—it was probably one of Bonnie's hand-me-down skirts—fell away from my leg. Bernie noticed, and to him it was like an epiphany. He suddenly realized that the class weirdo, the Goody Two-shoes who called him almost every morning when he stayed at home, was actually a girl.

In the summer of 1967, I began riding my bike over to Jimmy Landis's house to see Bernie and his friends. Auntie didn't know, of course. She would have been horrified. I remember the first time I stood in the side yard at Jimmy's house, waiting for him to throw down the rope ladder from his attic window—if he and his buddies deemed me worthy. I felt an anxious flutter in my stomach, wondering not only if they would let me enter but whether I had the strength and agility to climb up. After all, I was the class klutz, the last one to be picked whenever we paired off for team sports in phys ed.

Jimmy tossed down the ladder, and I gripped the wriggling rope and began my slow climb to the third floor. I managed to get close to the top rung when Bernie leaned out the window and pulled me through, into a dim lair reeking with pot smoke and incense, pulsating with the full-blast sound of the Mothers of Invention. In one corner, I noticed a guy named Sam* sitting on a mattress covered with an Indian madras spread. He held a roach clip to his mouth and drew deeply on what was left of a marijuana cigarette. He seemed to be blissed out on the music.

This was Jimmy's hangout, his crash pad, the attic apartment his parents had turned over to him in hope that whatever mischief he got into would at least happen at home. He had dropped out of school a few weeks earlier, shortly after the weekend he drove to Mexico to score some peyote and ended up getting arrested, not for the drugs but for having long hair.

I looked around the dimly lit room. Jimmy, an artist, had turned the walls of his room into vibrant psychedelic murals. Everywhere I looked, the spiraling, distorted images of his acid-stoked imagination leered back at me.

Jimmy and Bernie and their friend Ronny Calhoun*, whose father was a Pentecostal preacher, were arguing about Carlos Castaneda, about whether his transformations were real or merely products of his literary imagination. I had never heard of Carlos Castaneda, but I was fascinated. Bernie rummaged around in the pile of books on Jimmy's desk and found *The Teachings of Don Juan* for me. I wanted to read it, but I was afraid to take it home because of Auntie. I couldn't get over how intense they were. The same boys who slouched around school with scorn on their pimply adolescent faces—when they were in school, that is—were

My Mother's Keeper
177

afire with ideas. They were reading and thinking, bouncing ideas back and forth like lasers. I was thrilled by their passion. As I sat on a mattress listening, Tommy Gardener* passed a joint to me. I waved it away.

All through the summer, I kept going back to Jimmy's house. Jimmy and his friends gradually began to accept me, partly because I was Bernie's girlfriend, but also because I was different, as they were. I summoned the courage to tell them about my mom, and they thought it was cool. I had a story to tell, real-life experiences to share. They were artists, rebels, and they could see that I wasn't the little geek everybody thought I was. My mother's madness, my aunt's senility, my strange life—those were existential advantages, they insisted. My unusual experiences saved me from the bourgeois boredom and uptight hypocrisy that permeated Lamar High School and River Oaks.

Thus they released me from my childhood. In the marijuana haze of Jimmy's attic crash-pad, I could reinvent myself. I could command the power and attention I could never find at Auntie's.

"You know Allen Ginsberg?" Jimmy asked me one afternoon. I didn't, so he found a dogeared paperback of *Howl and Other Poems*, opened it, and began reading aloud about how Ginsberg had seen madness destroy the best minds of his generation. He read in a dramatic voice. Standing in the center of his cluttered bedroom, with his innocent face and his long brown hair and beard, he resembled a youthful Jesus. When he came to the end of "Howl," he told me that Ginsberg's mother had been mad. "She died in a mental hospital," he said. I began to feel proud to be different.

As the sultry Houston summer wore on, Jimmy became the neighborhood connection to the zeitgeist. Young housewives, educated and intelligent and curious about what they were missing, heard about what Jimmy had to offer. How they found out, I've never really known, but they began making the climb up the rickety rope ladder. Jimmy was eager to oblige them. He would start them out on pot and then, after a couple of weeks, introduce them to acid. Drugs, he reminded them, were a vehicle to a higher vision. They put you in touch with the intuitive, the spiritual, even the supernatural.

Sometimes these women invited Jimmy over while their husbands were at work, or they dropped their children at Southside Pool to swim and then strolled across the street to spend the morning at Jimmy's house. The minister's wife from down the street was a regular visitor, as was the next-door neighbor, wife of a Houston city councilman. She managed to seduce Jimmy, who at fifteen was still a virgin despite all his talk about the ecstasy and spiritual awakening of free love.

Suburban wives weren't the only Houstonians questioning the status quo. Parke, our youth minister at church, and his wife, Mary Alice, led us in discussions about drugs and sex and the war in Vietnam. Most of the Episcopal ministers were antiwar, and several were smoking marijuana. "If Jesus were alive today," Parke proclaimed, "he would be a hippie."

I kept trying to persuade Bernie to go to church with me, but he had read The *Passover Plot* by Hugh Schonfield, and he was convinced Christianity was a fraud. "It's not what you think," I'd tell him. "The people there are cool." One Sunday morning, he finally consented. As he walked beside me down the long, center aisle of Christ Church Cathedral, I knew the well-dressed men and women in the pews, the men in their dark suits, the women in their big hats and white gloves, were giving him the once-over. They saw his long, blond hair first, his ragged bell-bottoms and tie-dyed T-shirt—and then his bare feet.

I loved being around Bernie and his friends. I liked strolling into the dark and sweaty swirl of the Love Street Light Circus and Feel Good Machine in downtown Houston on a Saturday night. I liked losing myself in the psychedelic sounds of Jimmy's spaced-out friend Roky Erikson and his band the Thirteenth Floor Elevators. I liked peace and love, flower power, and the smell of patchouli, and I loved the Beatles, but the drugs frightened me.

I knew what the fear was. I had already seen the devastating effects of an altered state of consciousness, and I wanted nothing to do with it. Drugs messed with your mind, as Jimmy often pointed out approvingly; I had seen what could happen to a mind disturbed, a mind miswired by disease. Enough of Auntie's dire warnings about how my mother had somehow induced the condition she was in made me wary of losing control, whether it was to drugs or alcohol or simply letting go. I was afraid the drugs would take me to another place, just as Jimmy and Ken Kesey promised, but it wouldn't be a place where I would want to be. I was afraid that, like my mother, I would never get back.

I was a senior in high school before I would even try marijuana. Finally, after two years of urging, I sat cross-legged on Jimmy's Indian madras bedspread one afternoon, my drugged-out friends kneeling around me like devotees. They watched expectantly as I inhaled. Somewhere in the room, Janis Joplin wailed about freedom being just another word for nothing left to lose. It took two and half joints before I finally felt a tiny buzz. It hardly seemed worth the trouble.

As soon as I came down off my miniature high, I resumed my role as drug scold. "What you're doing is dangerous," I would tell them. "You're going to get in trouble."

"You don't understand," Bernie would say. "It's a religious experience. When I'm smoking, I'm alive! I get high, and I see and hear and feel! I know things! You're a religious person, Tara; surely you can understand that!"

High on morning glory seeds one afternoon, Bernie held my

hands in his and with his blue eyes shining like an Aquarian prophet's, he poured out his vision. As soon as we graduated from high school, we would buy a used VW van, he said, and like Ken Kesey and his merry pranksters, we would travel the country, only we would be looking for opportunities to swoop in and change things for the better. We would never surrender to money and status and lives of quiet desperation. A house in the suburbs, barbecuing in the backyard, me at home with the kids and Bernie working in an office downtown—it was a dreadful dream, unthinkable.

We were best friends, for life, and together we would drive our van into a town and feed little black kids in the ghetto. We would make sure that old people had love and companionship, that people like my mother had clean, safe places to stay. Together, from one town to another, we would change the messed-up world we had inherited. We would bask in the dawning of the Age of Aquarius. There were tears in my eyes as I listened.

Bernie and I never got our van. I went off to college and then to Europe to pursue a singing career; Bernie drifted in and out of college looking for a way to channel his rebelliousness and his brilliance. We never changed the world, though Bernie believes to this day that those years were the best of his life. He was lucky. He managed to avoid the calamitous fate I often warned him about. Despite never finishing college, he's now a successful electronics engineer in Austin. Several of our friends weren't so lucky. Years later, I counted up the toll. Ronny Calhoun, the Pentecostal preacher's son, was committed to Austin State Hospital. Our friend Lee*, whose mother was a devoted stay-at-home mother and his father a professor at Rice, was living in a shabby room in a college town two hundred miles from Houston when he stuck a pistol to his temple and killed himself. Cal*, maybe the brightest among us, became a cocaine addict. He died home-less on a Houston street. Wilson* drove his car into a concrete abutment; he was probably high on LSD when he crashed.

Of the ten boys who made up the core group during our own age of Aquarius, seven destroyed their lives. Maybe they were troubled before they began taking drugs; maybe that's what drew them together in high school. Maybe the drugs were a symptom, not a cause.

I was seventeen, a senior in high school, and life at home was becoming unbearable. Part of it was my own adolescent rebel-liousness, which Auntie, growing ever more senile, was ill equipped to handle. She was supposed to be taking digitalis for her heart, but at times the little brown bottle simply gathered dust on her table. When she wasn't taking the medication, she probably wasn't getting enough blood to the brain.

I realized that age and infirmity were working their inexorable transformation, but I didn't understand why cruelty had to be part of the aging process. She began cursing like a sailor. I was shocked. This dignified, convent-educated Episcopalian woman would stand rigid, hands on her hips, and rant, rage, and shower me with names I could not imagine she even knew. Once, when I didn't get out of bed as quickly as she thought I should, she doused me with a dishpan of water. She still expected me to endure her whippings, and I did, until one evening she raised a frying pan and threatened to slam me over the head with it. I grabbed her upraised arm, squeezed her fragile wrist until she winced, and told her I would never let her hit me again. I cried myself to sleep that night, picturing my thumb's red imprint on the soft, almost translucent skin of her wrist.

Tara Elgin Holley with Joe Holley
182

My mother and my grandmother also were cause for worry. Dawn had run-ins with the landlady. She would be psychotic, unruly. She would hear voices and wander through the neighborhood talking to herself. She would leave the house in the middle of the day and not come back for several days. She met a guy named Charlie during one of her jaunts away from the house, and, incredibly enough, she married him. He lived with another woman in a shabby house trailer on the outskirts of Houston, where Dawn would stay with him—or with them—for a few days at a time before making her way back to Mama. It was almost more than my aunts and I could bear, but fortunately Charlie drifted out of her life after a few months. The marriage was annulled.

Auntie, during those times when she was thinking clearly, would be on the phone with Betty Lee or Sally or Sister, trying to decide what to do with Dawn and Mama. Mama would come over to the house on Saturday mornings, sit at the kitchen table with a cup of coffee, and complain about how Dawn had mistreated her. She often had to borrow money from Auntie. She and my mother let the apartment deteriorate so badly, they lost their lease. My aunts bought a small house for them in Sister's neighborhood.

I was seventeen and coming to the end of my high school career. I was excited about growing up and being on my own. I had gotten an after-school job at a drugstore in the Village and was saving my money for college. Parke, the Christ Church youth minister, was helping me look for scholarship money. Sitting before his desk one afternoon in the church office, I told him I wasn't exactly sure what I wanted to do with my life, but I knew I wanted to be an intellectual. I can still see the hint of a smile on his face. He tried to explain that being an intellectual was a worthy aim, but it was more a habit of mind, a way of discerning the world, not an end in itself. Whatever, I remember thinking, I just had to learn everything!

At the same time these good things were happening, I couldn't ignore the fact that growing up, for me, meant I would have to assume responsibilities most of my friends would never have to think about. Lying awake at night sifting through my thoughts for ways to solve my mother's intolerable situation, and my own, I concluded that I had to be the one to take action.

At seventeen, it didn't seem to me that she had been sick all that long. Only a few years earlier, I had been certain that she would be well soon, that she would come and take me home. But time was passing, and she was still sick, and it seemed as if no one was going to do anything. My aunts had their own busy lives and were neglecting her. Mama was in denial. Or so it seemed to me.

I didn't realize that my aunts had tried for more than a decade to take care of their little sister. I just saw that things weren't getting better, and I blamed them for what I believed was their apathy. It seemed to me there was so much denial, so little hope. If that's the way the world worked, I told myself, I would make sure to change it. Bernie and I already had decided we weren't going to accept things as they were. Why should I accept my mother's dreadful world as it was?

Of course, it was Auntie, ironically enough, who was my inspiration. Even though she was part of my problem, it was her strength, her drive, and her decisiveness—those qualities with which I had lived day and night for ten years—that had instilled in me the belief that I could make things happen. She had always told me that someday my mother would be my responsibility. She had tried to prepare me for that eventuality. It seemed to me the moment had come, even though Auntie didn't realize it, would never realize it. I couldn't wait another day.

"Dawn's beautiful teeth are falling out," Betty Lee mentioned one day.

Watching my mother deteriorate almost before my eyes was like watching a child being abused or a house burning down with people inside—it was impossible to stand idly by. You have to take action, even if it's to preserve your own sanity. And I knew that I could make a difference. I believed that drugs and psychotherapy would cure her. I still held tightly to the dream, even though my mother was hideous in the condition she was in. I would not accept this horror as the way things had to be.

I really believed that if I pursued it, I could regain my relationship with Mommy, the bond that had been severed more than a decade earlier. I still believed that she might get well. She just hadn't been given a chance.

I also had to leave Auntie. I could not stand her tyranny any longer, and I couldn't see things getting any better. It seemed to me they would just get worse as Auntie continued to age. I talked to my aunts about staying with them until I graduated. I had less than a year to go, so it wouldn't be long. I reminded Sister that since Mama and Dawn were living nearby, I would be closer to the both of them if she and Uncle Don let me move in. I could look after them.

I knew Sister didn't really want me; she had her own kids to worry about, and she and Uncle Don had their own problems, but after constant pressure from me, they finally, reluctantly, agreed. I spent a weekend with them in the fall of 1968. I didn't tell Auntie I was leaving; I was afraid I wouldn't be able to carry through with my plan if I told her in person, so I called from Sister's and told her I wasn't coming home.

My Mother's Keeper
185

She was angry at first and then shocked, as she came to realize that this time I wasn't just threatening to leave. This time, I meant it. She promised me that things would be different. I told her no, though it was the hardest thing I had ever done. I could see her on the other end of the line, sitting in her chair, a desperate look on her face as she realized that all her plans for me were crumbling. I grieved, just as she did. At Sister's, I lay awake at night worrying about who would take care of her. I worried that I had betrayed her, and I lingered over all I had given up—our lives together, the plans she had for me, the house and my inheritance and my role as keeper of the family legacy.

When I went back to get some of my things a couple of weeks later, it was my turn to be shocked. Auntie seemed diminished, weakened, an old, old lady who could hardly leave her rocking chair. She cried and begged me to come home. I cried with her, and it took all the strength I had to say no. I had to get on with my life, and my mother's. I hurried down the stairs, walked out the front door, and tried not to look back.

CHAPTER NINE

Betty Lee told me the story long after it happened. It was the late 1950s, not long after my mother and I came back to Houston from California. Betty Lee was in graduate school at the time, working toward her doctorate at Rice University. Late evening, almost dark, she was in her bedroom upstairs, deep into a paper on Chaucer. Suddenly, she heard music, the rich, flowing sounds of a piano in the air, in her head, in the house. The sound startled her out of Chaucer's medieval world in mid-sentence. It was the radio, she thought, until she realized it was coming from the piano in the living room downstairs. Someone was playing "Clair de Lune," the lovely piece by Debussy. It was a piece that her mother had played all her life, one that was almost a family signature.

Betty Lee held her breath, listening. No one else was at home, and she hadn't heard a door open. She glanced at the phone on the bedside table, considered calling the police, but instead she walked slowly out of the bedroom and down the hall to the stairs, the music accompanying her every step. From the landing she could see Dawn, eyes focused on the keyboard as she enticed the sounds of Debussy from the instrument.

My mother had been committed a few weeks earlier to Jeff Davis Hospital in downtown Houston. Betty Lee herself had checked her in, and every afternoon Betty Lee's friend Tony Harris drove her downtown to visit Dawn. But on this night, Dawn, in a blue hospital-issue dress, had somehow made her way out the hospital door and walked more than five miles across Houston to Betty Lee's house.

Betty Lee stood on the stairs, trying to decide what to do. My mother must have sensed her presence. She glanced up, fear in her eyes.

"Oh, honey," Betty Lee exclaimed, moving toward her. Dawn bolted, tipping over the piano stool as she dashed for the front door. "Wait!" Betty Lee shouted, but Dawn was already out the door. Betty Lee paused to call the hospital, then ran out into the gathering darkness. She could see her sister running down the street, already a block away, but then she lost sight of her. Moments later, a neighbor called; she had seen Dawn on the next street.

Betty Lee got into her car, turned the corner and caught sight of Dawn again. Stopping the car, she ran up to a man watering his yard and asked to use his phone. She called the police and reported her location, then got back into her car and followed her sister, who continued to run. Minutes later, a police car passed her, passed Dawn, and drove up over the curb. An officer got out and opened the back door of his patrol car. Betty Lee watched as Dawn slowed to a walk and put herself in the car.

"I'll never forget the look on her face as that police car drove away," Betty Lee told me. "I cried all night."

That was the story Betty Lee told me years later. What she

didn't tell me until even later was her own ordeal at Jeff Davis Hospital, when she made daily visits to her sister.

It was the end of August, the tail end of summer, but not the end of the stifling late-afternoon heat. Betty Lee walked into the gritty downtown hospital and took the elevator to the top floor, to the mental ward. Through a large barred window, she could see downtown Houston. Stepping up to the counter, which served as a nurses' station, she noticed two nurse's aides sitting at a small table under an old whirling ceiling fan. A naked light bulb dangled from the fan. The women were playing cards. As she waited for the women to notice her, she heard the sound of knocking from somewhere nearby.

"You just shut that up," one of the women called out. "We're not paying you any attention, no matter how much you're wearing out that door."

The knocking continued, and Betty Lee watched as one of the women groaned, struggled out of her chair and picked up a big key ring on the table. As the woman walked toward a wooden door behind the counter, she noticed Betty Lee. "This here's the detaining ward," she said. "You must've got the wrong floor."

"Can I help you, honey?" the other woman asked. "We only got one patient up here."

"Where is she?" Betty Lee asked sharply. The knocking had stopped momentarily, then started up again, even more urgently. "I've come to see Dawn Elgin."

"Doctor says she can't have no visitors," the woman with the key ring said.

Betty Lee showed her the blue card she had been given when she had Dawn committed. "I'm family," she said, "her sister."

The woman dropped the big key ring on the table, fished in the pocket of her uniform for other keys, and walked over to the wooden door.

My Mother's Keeper

"She's in there?" Betty Lee shouted. "That was her, knocking like that?"

The women exchanged troubled glances, apparently afraid they were about to have another hysterical woman on their hands. The woman with the key unlocked the door and pushed it open. "Okay, sugar, come on out," she said. "You got a visitor."

Dawn stood in the doorway, a wild, hunted look in her eyes. Her face was red and wet with sweat. Breathing heavily, she held her right hand in her left one. "Betty Lee? You'll take me with you?" she asked, her voice a whisper.

"We can't just leave, honey," Betty Lee tried to explain. "I came up to see you, see how things were going."

"Get me out of here, Betty Lee," Dawn demanded.

One of the nurses leaned against the counter, watching and shaking her head. "Uh-oh, here she goes," she said. "She won't let up now."

The other nurse waved the room key at Dawn. "We're gonna put you right back in that room, you do any hollering."

"You leave her alone!" Betty Lee told her. She glared at the woman, then went over to embrace her sister. She took Dawn's hand, but Dawn winced and drew her hand back. "Oh, my God! Look at this!" Betty Lee exclaimed. Dawn's knuckles were scraped raw, beginning to bleed. "You've let her—how long has she—get the doctor up here!"

One of the nurses found a cloth and some kind of salve. She smiled as she took Dawn's hand.

"Miss Elgin, there's no doctors around," the other nurse said. "This is the detaining ward, not the regular hospital."

"I said get the doctor!" Betty Lee shouted. "Now! I want to talk to him now!"

"He's not gonna want to—" the woman mumbled, picking up

the phone. "That lady y'all let up here wants to talk to the doctor," she said.

Minutes later, the elevator doors opened, and a well-dressed middle-aged man got off. "I'm Dr. Wilson," he told Betty Lee. "What seems to be the trouble?" He glanced at Dawn sitting at the nurses' table but otherwise did not acknowledge her.

Betty Lee could barely speak. "Doctor, I think you ought to know what's going on up here," she said.

The doctor hardly waited for her to finish the sentence. "Miss Elgin," he said, "you may come to my office to discuss any such matters with me. My nurses are doing all they can. We all are."

"Haven't you seen her?" Betty Lee asked, taking Dawn by the wrist and holding up her scraped hand. "Do you have any idea what—"

"I'm sorry, Miss Elgin," the doctor said. "I'm on my rounds. You'll have to make an appointment." He turned on his heel, saw that the elevator door was closed, and walked briskly to a door marked EXIT.

"I think he means you can take her, if you want her," one of the women said.

"I can't," Betty Lee said, near tears. "She needs professional help. She may be suicidal. I had no idea she would be stuck in a place like this."

"We're just the detaining ward," the woman with the keys said. "This is just where everybody waits till they get sent to where they're supposed to go. We just hold 'em here till . . ."

It would be years before I knew how much my aunts had tried to do for my mother over the years—to find doctors who could help her, to find a hospital where she could live safely and comfortably, intervening when she got into trouble. I didn't know that they lay awake at night, just as I did. I didn't realize that my mother was a constant topic of conversation, a worry, as it is when anyone is chronically ill. She was on their minds, and her condition disturbed them deeply.

After a while, many families surrender. "We just can't cope any longer," they say. "There's nothing we can do. Our sister— our brother, our father, our child—is now dead for us."

Yet with mental illness, the person is not really dead. Unless the family member is institutionalized, she is sitting around the house all day having conversations with unseen voices. The family watches her do strange things with her clothes, forget to shower, develop odd little habits. Soon, every little thing she does drives you nuts, and you blame yourself for being impatient with a person who is just as sick as if she had cancer or AIDS or any other desperate illness.

After a while, the bizarre symptoms become too frightening, too stressful. Family members can no longer bear looking at the loved one they have lost, who is there but not there, who can no longer communicate. At least with mortal illnesses, you know it won't last forever. Schizophrenia lasts a lifetime.

As an adolescent, I assumed that my aunts had given up after a while, maybe because they found it so humiliating to have mental illness crop up in the family. Oh, probably they thought about Dawn, poor Dawn, now and then and felt a pang of regret and sadness, I thought, but they had their own lives to live. What more can we do, I could hear them saying, throwing up their hands.

I felt constantly on the verge of tears, and I didn't know why. I didn't really know for sure what my aunts' relationship to my mother was, though I understood that for each, the relationship was different. But that didn't matter; I couldn't understand why no one was trying to fix the problem. No one ever said to me: "Dawn has been sick since before you were born, and we tried for fifteen years to make her well, and nothing has worked. We don't know what else to do."

I believed that just admitting that my mother was sick would be an important first step. If we could come to grips with her illness, then we could keep her on her medication, and then she probably would get better. Why couldn't we all pitch in and do what needed to be done?

Occasionally, a friend or a relative would say something like this: "Honey, you know it's good that you're working on communicating better with your mother, and it says a lot about you that you care so much about her, but she will not get completely well. She may improve, but she'll never get well."

To hear that they had given up on my mother, and that they wanted me to do the same, infuriated me. When my voice teacher at the University of Houston suggested that bad karma was to blame, that my mother was probably living out some evil she had done to someone in another life, I was enraged, sad, and confused.

I was stubborn, too. No one was going to tell me my mother was not going to get better. I'd shut my ears and try to believe I could do what no one else had been able to do.

I was frantic about rescuing her, partly because I felt guilty. I had caused my mother's illness. Could there be any doubt? Wasn't it her pregnancy that had made her sick? After all, she was doing just fine before I came along.

Auntie had another take on the matter. "Your mother getting sick had absolutely nothing to do with you," she would say in an imperious tone of voice that suggested the question was settled once and for all. Then she would add, "She was on the wrong path from the time she was thirteen." She was lively, ambitious, devil-may-care. She was talented, focused to the point of obsession. She had all those qualities that Auntie had tried to beat out of me.

Auntie's observation was supposed to exonerate me, but it made me feel almost as bad as being blamed for her illness. I was Dawn's daughter; I loved this woman whose willfulness had led to her destruction; I wanted to be Dawn. Who could say that the same fate didn't await me?

Sister continued to blame her parents. "Dawn was drinking, boozing, partying, maybe she was emotionally unstable because of the broken affair, and Mama and Papa couldn't do a thing with her," I would hear her remind Auntie. "She got pregnant, and you know how the body chemistry changes when you're pregnant." She would glance at me, and I would wonder if she was thinking the same thing I was: if only Tara hadn't been born, Dawn would be okay.

My aunts never mentioned the childhood sexual molestation in Hollywood, although years later Sally admitted they always had suspected it had something to do with my mother's illness. I think it might have had something to do with her precociousness. As a teenager, she always seemed older and more mature than she really was.

"Every time I think of that man, I just want to kill him," Sally said, shuddering. "And to think, he was a friend of the family!"

Whatever had caused my mother's illness, nothing they had done or tried to do had worked. She was still sick, was probably getting worse. Sometimes I would look into her brown eyes, and I could hardly bear the pain and frustration of knowing she was right there, right there before me, and I couldn't reach her.

One Saturday morning, a few weeks after moving in with Sister and Don, I walked over to the little house where Mama and my mother lived. They were my first stop on my usual Saturday round of errands. It was a beautiful morning, not yet hot and muggy the way it gets in Houston in late spring. The yards were green, the flowers in bloom.

I could smell freshly cut grass, and it was suddenly Saturday morning at Auntie's. I was ten years old again, and we were mowing the lawn. Narcisso and Gilbert were getting the garden tilled, clearing out the beds for the sweet peas.

I snapped to: That was in the past. Now, Auntie scarcely left her bedroom. Later in the day, after I visited Mama and Dawn, I would try to find a couple of cousins, or maybe Bernie, and we would go over to check on Auntie. We would clean the house, help her with her bath, fix a meal for her. On two occasions since I had left, we had found the body of another of our dogs, unburied. It looked as if she wouldn't be able to stay in the house much longer.

A scarlet crape myrtle bloomed in the ragged little front yard of Mama's house. Inside, I found Mama and Dawn sitting at the kitchen table having coffee, Mama in a yellow springy dress, Dawn in baggy knit pants and a wrinkled blouse. She wore grimy house slippers, the heels broken down. On the dining room table were stacks of books Mama had brought home from the library. She had her easel set up in the middle of the living room. Splattered drops of many colors made an inadvertent abstract design on the bare wood floor, and a partly finished painting of a forest in the moonlight rested on the stand. The house was filthy as usual, but Mama and Dawn were oblivious to it. If it were commented upon, they would act surprised.

It wasn't the clutter and filth that caught my eye. I was long used to that. Something was missing, and it took me a second to realize what it was. "Where's the piano?" I asked Mama. "What happened to the piano?"

Mama looked down at the table and sighed. "A man came and

got it," she said with a sigh. "He and this boy he had with him just marched right in, put it on their truck, and drove away. I asked him, 'What is the meaning of this?' and he said we weren't making the payments."

I rushed downtown to Goggins' Music Company. "How much do they owe?" I asked the man behind the counter.

"Sixty dollars," he said. "They're three months behind on their payments. And I'll tell you one more thing, young lady. I shoulda charged them for an exterminator. That instrument was full of roaches when my men brought it in here. I'm still seeing 'em run around this shop."

I could feel my face burning. I was embarrassed and so angry I could barely look at the man. I didn't know how to deal with something like that. I wrote him a check for sixty dollars, using the money I had made from my job at the Interurban Pharmacy. I assured him that he would get his payments on time. He promised, reluctantly, to deliver the piano back to their house. Maybe he felt sorry for me, although he did insist that I pay an additional redelivery fee.

On Monday morning, I called a bug exterminator. I also called a rodent exterminator, because I had opened the kitchen cabinets one morning and noticed little holes in the back wall. I paid for a three-month extermination plan. The man came out a few days later and put pellets in little dishes near the holes in the cabinet. When my grandmother realized what the pellets were for, she was so horrified that she collected the dishes and threw them away. Protecting God's little creatures was more important to her than keeping the house rodent-free.

That was Mama. One hot, muggy afternoon, I dropped by the house and found her cooling off in the bathtub, in her dress. Dripping, she climbed out with a smile on her face, pleased that she had found a way to stay cool most of the afternoon. It made sense to her, and she seemed so pleased and unassuming, I had to laugh and give her a hug.

A few days before my high school graduation, my best friend Sarah gave birth to a baby girl. She didn't want to marry the father, and she wanted to keep the baby, so her parents decided it would be best for her to go to San Francisco and stay with relatives. They asked me to go along and help Sarah look after the baby, and—though it was largely unspoken—look after Sarah as well. I was still considered the responsible one among my peers. Sarah was not.

I was ready to go; after all, this was the summer of 1969, the summer of love, and San Francisco was luring young people from around the world. Only Auntie and my mother gave me pause. They both needed me. My aunts insisted they could look after both of them, so a few days after my high school graduation ceremony, Sarah and I and the baby flew to San Francisco.

We stayed with Sarah's relatives in Berkeley. Although I was only seventeen, I got a job waiting tables at a North Beach Irish pub and began socking away wages and tips for college. Since I had abandoned Auntie, she wouldn't be helping me with my college expenses, as we always had planned. I was on my own, although the church had helped me get a modest scholarship to the University of Houston.

When I wasn't working that summer, or helping Sarah with baby Lisa, I was communing with nature in Golden Gate Park. For a while, at least, I was a flower child, barefoot, braless, and happy to be free. Sometimes, wandering around town, or hanging out with hundreds of other young people on the Berkeley campus, I would flash back to turn-of-the-century Berkeley when a tall, red-haired woman from Houston was a student. I couldn't imagine Auntie wandering around; in my mind, she was always striding resolutely to class.

My Mother's Keeper

Sarah and I were not so focused. In our fringed madras dresses and headbands, our beads, sandals and tie-dyed shirts, we were part of a wandering, yearning tribe, a happy crowd of nomads searching for we weren't sure what. We browsed in the head shops, swayed, sang, and swooned at huge outdoor concerts, dipped into communal pots of spicy Indian food at Maharishi Mahesh Yogi feasts where everyone was welcome to eat all they wanted. Hare Krishnas with their bells and tambourines seemed to be background accompaniment for everything we did. We went to Fillmore West and danced under the mind-blowing strobe lights to the music of Grace Slick and the Jefferson Airplane. I browsed at City Lights Bookstore and kept an eye out for Ginsberg and Ferlinghetti.

I loved San Francisco, the hills and trolley cars, the cool, bracing weather. I enjoyed my first taste of real freedom. Yet I also had to admit that the teeming Haight-Ashbury scene bored me. I had seen what mind-blowing expereriences really do. Sarah teased me about still being the good little Episcopalian kid, and despite my flower-child inclinations, I had to admit she was right. I couldn't really get into it, and at summer's end, I flew back home and moved into the dorm at the University of Houston.

I enrolled for twenty-one credits that first semester. That was ridiculous, of course, but there were so many things I wanted to know, and no one told me I shouldn't take such a heavy load. I got a job working several nights a week as a waitress at Scene West, a loud, raucous bar on Westheimer favored by jocks and frat boys, most of them constantly worried about taking enough hours at school to avoid the draft. The guys who ran it were old University of Houston football players. They drank like fish, sold drugs on the side, and hit on all the waitresses.

Since I didn't have a car, I either had to bum rides with a couple of other U of H girls who worked at Scene West, or ride the bus downtown and transfer. The worst part of the job, other than fending off the owners, was getting back to campus at two in the morning. Since the dorm was closed at that hour, I either had to sleep over at someone's apartment or hitch a ride with a couple of university guys who worked as bartenders and hope that I could get someone to unlock the front door of the dorm.

Even though the owners, the bartenders, and the clientele were all into drugs—pot and cocaine mainly—they hated hippies. A few times Bernie borrowed a car and picked me up when I got off at two A.M. on a weekend night. We'd go to IHOP for breakfast, and he would tell me about the classes he was taking parttime at the local community college or he would read his poetry to me.

"Who's the long-haired guy coming around here?" one of the owners wanted to know, a sneer on his face. "You telling me you've got a hippie boyfriend?"

"He's just a friend," I'd answer, loathing every minute I had to spend in the man's presence. At least, I was saving enough money to get back to San Francisco the next summer.

Every weekend, I tried to see my mother. She was still living with Mama in the little house in Bellaire. I would try to take her shopping, to a movie, to eat at the Luby's Cafeteria downtown, even though I knew she was likely to laugh hysterically as we moved down the food line or start talking to herself—or to the voices that accompanied us everywhere we went.

Often, I caught myself getting impatient, as with a recalcitrant child. I would be trying to have a conversation with her, and she would be shuffling from one foot to the other, hands jammed into her pockets, humming, "Hooray for Hollywood" under her breath. I would explode.

"Stop babbling!" I'd shout, taking hold of her arms. "Be still!" I'd stare into her distant eyes, trying to will my way into her awareness. "Listen to me!" Like a child, she would look down at the floor, waiting for my reprimand.

I didn't want to be her mother. I was eighteen years old, and I considered myself oh so independent and mature, but I still wanted a mommy. I wanted to talk to her about my life, and she would be babbling about Hollywood, about Bogart and Bergman, Clark Gable and Lana Turner, the duke and duchess of Windsor, Charlie Chaplin, about people she had worked with at the studios. "Los Angeles, city of angels," she would say, sighing.

Invariably, she would mention the movie *Black Dawn*. I imagined her sitting in the theater and seeing that title come up on the screen. Was the movie about her? Did the title harbor some symbolic meaning for her? Was it a hidden message from those dark powers that controlled her mind, that taunted her with cryptic messages and spoke to her unbidden? She could not explain.

She had dreams about the MGM lion. "I wake up and it's in my room, and you wouldn't believe it! It's at the foot of my bed," she would say in a breathy whisper. She welcomed it. It was almost a religious experience. "Oh, you should see it!" she would say. Or she would ask, "Can you see it? Has that ever happened to you?" A look of wonderment would bathe her face. "Oh, baby, you just wouldn't believe it!"

"That's ridiculous," I'd say. "Let's go to your room." I'd take her hand and lead her to her cluttered little bedroom. "Look," I'd say, taking her by the shoulders. "There's no lion here."

But, of course, there was. I am ashamed, now. I believed she had more control over her actions than she actually had. I believed she was choosing to escape into a fantasy world that she actually preferred. I know now that she might have been more lucid if she had stayed on her medication, but no one was around on a regular basis to insist that she take it.

I was angry—at my aunts and my grandmother, and at my

mother. I knew that she had not chosen to contract the illness that had ravaged her mind or to leave me. But it had happened, nevertheless. She had made my life tangled and difficult. Her life was a living hell, and here I was, left to cope with the chaos that she left behind.

My mother was barely forty. The bright beauty of her early years was a sad and mocking memory. She had been sick for nearly half her life.

My favorite class my freshman year was introduction to psychology. Sitting in the large, crowded lecture hall, exposed for the first time to theories and ideas about the mind and how we think and feel, I quickly realized I had many more questions than answers—about my mother, about my family, about myself. I was thrilled to discover that people had thought deeply and systematically about mental illness, families, old people, all those things that vexed my life. In the spring, I took Abnormal Psychology, and though I didn't tell anyone about my mother, I found some comfort in the fact that others had similar experiences.

I asked my professor, Dr. McCarey, about counseling. He recommended that I see a former student of his, a Ph.D. candidate doing his residency in McCarey's office downtown. So one fall afternoon, I rode the bus to a medical center downtown and walked into the office of Donald Gautney, a young man not much older than myself who slowly and carefully, with tact and wisdom, led me toward the light.

Slight and soft-spoken, with thinning brown hair, Don was twenty-eight when I first met him. Once a week for nearly two years, I sat in a comfortable leather chair in his quiet, pleasant office, stared at the carpet or the prints on the walls, and for fifty minutes tried as best as I could to respond to Don's gentle, patient questioning. As we got to know each other better, he told me that he had lived with his mother all his life; for many years, she had been sick, so he understood the dynamics of caring for a parent. He was his mother's sole source of support. He understood the kind of hold that Auntie had over my life, and he encouraged my independence.

Don took almost anything I told him about what I was doing and showed me how I was taking positive steps. He knew that I felt weak, ineffectual, alone—about my life, about school, my mother. He encouraged me to completely open up and was never anything but trustworthy and encouraging. The better we got to know each other, the easier it was for me to talk to him.

One of the first things Don asked me was why I was coming to see him. I told him I needed help figuring out ways to help my mother. I told him I was having trouble communicating with her.

Don was able to explain why, and I was able to see my mother in a completely new light. "Your mother is ill, just as if she had cancer or heart disease or diabetes," he explained one afternoon after my session. We had gone downstairs to a little coffee shop to get a Coke. I was usually his last client of the day, so we often talked past my session.

"She happens to have an illness of the brain," he continued. "As you know, we call it schizophrenia. People don't realize it, but the disease your mother has is more common than a great many diseases we hear more about. Multiple sclerosis, muscular dystrophy, even more common than Alzheimer's disease."

Don smiled and took a sip of Coke. "Of course, with schizophrenia," he said, "you don't have any telethons or mentally ill poster kids. You don't need me to tell you it's a disease no one

Tara Elgin Holley with Joe Holley

202

wants to talk about, but what you have to keep in mind is that it is a disease.

"The way I see schizophrenia," he continued, "it's a negative image of Parkinson's disease." He took a pen from his shirt pocket and began drawing diagrams on a napkin. "With Parkinson's disease, what you have is an absence in the brain of dopamine. Dopamine is the neurotransmitter that allows the brain's ten billion neurons to communicate with one another. With schizophrenia, there seems to be too much dopamine activity; the brain over-transmits."

As Don continued his explanation, I couldn't follow all the details, but the underlying message was loud and clear: Something in my mother's brain wasn't functioning properly. She was sick, just as someone who has cancer or high blood pressure or tuberculosis is sick.

"How many people have schizophrenia?" I asked.

"As best we can tell," Don said, "maybe two and a half million people in the United States. That means one in every hundred people will become schizophrenic during their lifetime. Look around this room, and chances are you'll see somebody who will develop the disease. It's a lot more common than we like to think it is."

"But what causes it?"

Don looked at me across the table and shrugged his shoulders. "We don't know," he said. "We can talk a lot about schizophrenia's symptoms—the paranoia, the hallucinations, the imaginary voices, all those things that you know all too well. But when it comes to causes, there just isn't a whole lot to say."

It's a breakdown in the brain's chemistry, Don explained. That's about all we know for sure. It could be caused by a virus. It could be a gene. For all we know, it could be a head injury the person suffered years ago. It could even be something that happens in the womb. Whatever it is, it triggers the disease in late adolescence, just as it did with my mother.

Usually, it's gradual. Maybe it feels initially like an LSD trip—everything is vibrant, intense. Most of us have a natural capacity to filter out information we don't need. The person suffering from schizophrenia loses that ability. They are bombarded with stimuli; they hear voices, experience hallucinations. Fear, terror, panic, anxiety—those are all natural responses as the brain's disorders begin to manifest themselves.

"These people live in fear," Don said. "Fear of other people. Fear of losing their mind. Their mind, of course, is their core identity. As the illness progresses, there's a real struggle to maintain an identity. They are overwhelmed with feelings of uselessness and a loss of self-esteem."

I suddenly had this image of Mama clambering out of the bathtub in her dress. I remembered stories Sister had told me about the kind of parents Mama and Papa had been, and I remembered the uncomfortable feelings of chaos and disarray I had known as a child living with them. With Don as my guide, I began reading the literature about my mother's illness, the most profound and the most significant determinant of my life. I read about Emil Kraepelin, the German psychiatrist a hundred years earlier who had observed that most forms of insanity fell into two categories. One was manic depression; the other was what Kraepelin called dementia praecox.

Manic depression, Kraepelin observed, came and went. Between attacks, its victims were their full selves. Not so with dementia praecox, premature dementia. It was forever. I can remember the sadness I felt when I read what in my heart I already knew: that even in the rare cases of recovery, the rescued personality was less complete than the old one.

I read about Eugen Bleuler, the Swiss psychiatrist who in 1911 coined the term *schizophrenia*, split mind. He insisted that it was a more accurate description than premature dementia, and the term became universally accepted. Bleuler meant for his new term to suggest a split between the thinking and feeling functions of the mind, certainly not a split, or double, personality as the term has come to be misused. He had in mind the kind of inappropriate behavior I had seen with my mother—her tendency to laugh when tears would be more appropriate, for example. I also read that Bleuler attempted to treat Zelda Fitzgerald; she described him as "a great imbecile."

I dipped into books and articles by R. D. Laing and Thomas Szasz, psychiatrists who insisted that schizophrenia is a healthy reaction to an insane world, and may even be a growth experience. The person with schizophrenia is not really sick, they claimed. The schizophrenic is merely acting in a way that society labels "insane" as a way to survive in a truly crazy family, an unstable environment. My mother, Szasz seemed to be saying, made a conscious choice to be sick. The way she functioned in the world, or didn't function, was a healthy response to a world sicker than she was.

Szasz even went so far as to say that schizophrenics like my mother have a "fake disease." To be a true disease, he claimed, "it must somehow be capable of being approached, measured, or tested in a scientific fashion."

The theories of Szasz and Laing had been popularized in the late 1960s and early 1970s by such films as *King of Hearts* and Ken Kesey's novel *One Flew Over the Cuckoo's Nest*, works that posited the romantic notion that the insane were too gentle, too sensitive, for this world, and that their escape into what we call insanity was the only rational response to the craziness the rest of us tolerate and create.

I was perfectly willing to believe that my mother was too

acutely atuned to the world and had opted out, but one thing kept me from this theory: I had seen the torment and the anguish she had experienced, was continuing to experience. It was impossible for me to believe that her condition was a choice, conscious or otherwise, that she or anyone else would make. It was hard for me to believe that either of the good doctors had ever even seen a schizophrenic person, much less thought deeply about what they were experiencing. The theories of Szasz and Laing were no doubt more subtle and nuanced than I knew, but for me, it was easier to agree with a comment I once read from the singer/songwriter Dory Previn, who had been psychotic at one time. "Insanity is terrific on *The Late Show*," she said, ". . . but in the real world it's shit."

All the while that Don was answering my endless questions about my mother and her illness, he was focusing on the central issue as far as the both of us were concerned—me. He helped me talk about not only my mother but Mama and Papa, Auntie, my boyfriends, my dreams.

Sitting in his office one afternoon talking about my mother, about the latest psychological theories, I could feel the question I really wanted to ask forming in my mind. It was a question that had long been with me, but I was afraid to put it into words, afraid to hear Don's answer. With a hollow feeling in the pit of my stomach, I tried to summon the courage to ask it.

Slowly, haltingly, I began to phrase the question. Don helped me. "You want to know if you'll become mentally ill, don't you?" he asked. "What you're asking me is, is it hereditary?"

I nodded, tears pooling in the corners of my eyes.

Sitting in his chair a few feet from where I was sitting, Don was silent for what seemed like a minute. He clasped his hands around his legs crossed at the knee. I knew he was weighing his words carefully. "Schizophrenia does sometimes run in families, so there is a slim possibility, a very slim possibility, that you could become mentally ill," he said slowly, watching my face as he spoke, "but chances are we already would have seen signs. I have absolutely no reason to believe you'll get sick."

He handed me a tissue, and as I wiped my eyes, questions kept bubbling up—questions about heredity and genes and environment. Why, I wanted to know. Why did this happen to my mother, the brightest of all the Elgin girls, the most talented? Why her and not one of her sisters? What did she do to deserve such a terrible fate? Why her and not me?

And how did I know it wouldn't happen to me? I had asked the question all my life. Even my mother asked it. At times, she would put her hand on my shoulder, look into my eyes, and ask, "Are you sure no one talks to you?" I suppose she was expressing her concern, but I was offended. I had the feeling she was trying to draw me into her own delusions. "Of course I don't hear voices!" I would answer, shrugging her hand off my shoulder. "Why should I?"

Whether I was mentally ill, or would be, was a concern, I told myself, but it wasn't really a fear. And it certainly wasn't an obsession.

Don probably saw that the concern was more deep-rooted than I wanted to admit, and he patiently helped me get to the guts of it. "If it was happening," he asked, "what would you feel? What would you fear? How would you know it? Did you feel this fear of going crazy when you were little?"

He drew me out, trying to get me to describe what I imagined my mother went through. If I were mentally ill, I would explain, I would see things in my room that frightened me. Or I would feel totally out of control. Or I wouldn't be able to function. He was trying to get me to see that all of those experiences were foreign to me.

My Mother's Keeper

It is true, Don explained, that schizophrenia appears to have a genetic basis, although the linkage is not clear. Among twins from the same ovum, if one gets the disease, the other will not get it about two thirds of the time. In the afflicted twin, the normal spaces in the brain, called ventricles, will become enlarged. The afflicted twin also might show a variety of minor physical anomalies that express themselves before birth. You might see these anomalies in the fingers, the palm, the palate, or elsewhere.

In about one in ten cases, Don said, the children of a schizophrenic parent will get the disease themselves. But two thirds of the time, it strikes people with no family history of the disease. Once again, I thought back through my family tree. We had our share of eccentrics, I had to admit, but so did most families. As far as I knew, there was no history of mental illness on either side of the family, no weird uncle hidden away in a back room, no promising youngster stricken at an early age and put away.

To ease my concerns about my susceptibility to mental illness, Don gave me a battery of psychological tests. The tests showed that I was mentally and emotionally strong, independent, and self-reliant. Thanks to Auntie, my own constitution, or some combination of both, I really had nothing to worry about. I wasn't going to be mentally ill.

"I know you," Don continued to assure me. "Genetics aside, I know the person who's sitting here before me. I know your strengths. I know how you live your life, how you face your problems head on. You don't try to escape into drugs or dreams or whatever. Your mental health is just not a concern of mine."

Of course, I had problems, and Don was a trustworthy guide to help me explore them. He helped me understand that I had experienced the loss of my mother almost as profoundly as a child whose parent had died. That loss had become part of my emerging personality; it was a defining characteristic of who I had become. And from learning at such an early age that close relationships can be severed with the blink of an eye, that security is as ephemeral as the sweet peas in Auntie's yard, I had developed an adult's insight while still only a child.

I trusted Don implicitly, although there were some things it took me a while to share with him. The experience with Floyd was one of them. It took me months to tell him. Session after session, I would say, "I can't talk about that. There are things I have done, I'm too ashamed to tell anybody."

I was ashamed and embarrassed about my feelings toward Auntie. I had never told anyone about the dogs. I had never told anyone what I did when Auntie left me home alone: I would take my dolls, and I had dozens, and I would punish them even more severely than Auntie punished me. My dolls were my family. Like most little girls, I fed them and dressed them and had them interact with each other—and in secret I would torment them. I even dismembered a couple, jerked off their heads.

I was deeply ashamed, but Don thought it was great. "You were a helpless child," he explained, a smile on his face, "and you were acting out your anger. I'm proud of you!"

Don slowly and steadily led me through my story. He made me aware of my dreams. I was able to open up and see that I was unhappy and depressed.

Don was concerned that I didn't have someone looking out for me. I reminded him that I had Bernie. "Bernie is a nice person, a good person, and from what you tell me, he's brilliant," Don said in his quiet way. "But the truth is, he doesn't have anything to offer you. He's like so many other people in your life; he has a great many needs. I hate to see you saddled with another responsibility."

My responsibilities were a recurring theme. Don often encouraged me to focus more on taking care of myself and less on caring for my mother. It was tempting, but I just couldn't let go. I still believed that I was the one, perhaps the only one, who could help my mother get the treatment she needed. Mama and Dawn continued to be so needy.

After my first year at the University of Houston, I moved out of the dorm into an apartment of my own and got a job as a hostess and waitress at a wonderful little French restaurant called Ari's Grenouille. Soon, I was the restaurant business manager. Mama and Dawn began calling me, asking to borrow money. I felt bad for them that they had to rely on an eighteen-year-old. Every time I brought my mother to my apartment or took her out or visited with her in her little house, I felt she was trying to pull me into her craziness. I began to feel I had to do something drastic, either escape and never see her again, or get her the help she needed. I realized I couldn't escape, wouldn't escape, despite Don's advice.

I was a baby-sitter occasionally for Cornelle and Llewellyn Smith, Rice University graduate students who lived down the street from Sister and Don. They were aware of my mother's condition, and they often gave me wise counsel. They suggested she would be better off in the hospital for a while. I agreed, so one afternoon before work I took the bus downtown to Jeff Davis Hospital, where my mother had been a patient off and on over the years. I told the social worker familiar with my mother's case how she did not stay on her medication, how Mama continued to thwart any kind of treatment that might have helped, and how it seemed to me that my mother's condition was deteriorating. The social worker agreed that a ninety-day commitment might be beneficial. As my mother's closest relative, I was allowed to sign commitment papers.

The next afternoon, I showed up at the house. I didn't tell Mama and Dawn what was about to happen, and neither seemed to notice how nervous I was, how close to tears. I kept glancing out the front window; after about half an hour, a black-and-white police car drove up. Mama opened the front door and invited the two officers in. She was courteous, having no idea why they were there. One of them explained to Mama that Miss Elgin's daughter had given them permission to take Dawn Elgin into custody and commit her to the psychiatirc ward at Jeff Davis.

A look of horror passed across Mama's face. She hurried into the bedroom where my mother was and tried to close the door in the faces of the officers. I stopped her and led the policemen into the room. When Dawn saw them, she backed into a corner, shaking her head and wringing her hands. All of her paranoid fantasies had suddenly become reality, and she began babbling. "You can't take my baby away, Humphrey Bogart won't let you, it's the judge you want, in Hollywood. . . ."

The officers grasped her gently but firmly by the arms and began leading her to the door. Mama was crying, moaning, begging them to let her little girl go. "Stop them, honey," she pleaded. "You can't let this happen." Whether she knew I was the reason it was happening, I didn't know.

The officers got my mother out the door and into the car. I told them I would bring her things to the hospital later in the day. Suddenly, Mama rushed out the front door, wrenched open the back door of the car and began pulling Dawn by the arm. She was crying, and so was I, as I urged her to turn my mother loose. One of the officers got out of the car, put his arms around her waist and pulled Mama away from Dawn. Head down, twisting her hands in her lap, my mother mumbled intensely to herself. She never looked up as they drove away.

My grandmother was inconsolable that terrible afternoon, even as I told her over and over that what had happened was best for Dawn. I desperately hoped it was true. Two weeks later, Mama took the bus downtown to the hospital and helped Dawn escape.

Tara Elgin Holley with Joe Holley

CHAPTER TEN

I have mixed emotions about the entire thing. I feel that this is a big moment for my mother, and she should finally be given a chance to recover. I don't feel my aunts are going to give her that chance. It's too much of an old, sad story to them, and they have their own lives.
—Journal entry, March 1971

The sun had disappeared, and a cold, gray mist from the Zuider Zee had settled in. It was late March, close to five in the evening in Rotterdam. Already the streetlights were glinting yellow off the damp, cobblestoned street. I had been in Europe for nearly two years.

Biking down the street, my trusty all-weather coat buttoned tightly, I was thinking about how warm and welcoming the house would be and wondering what Arlene and I would do about dinner. While her husband was away, we didn't cook as elaborately or as often as we used to, although I had picked up cheese and bread and fresh meats from the small, cheery shops on the way home.

My European odyssey had begun during my freshman year at the University of Houston, while I was working at Ari's Grenouille, the little French restaurant on Westheimer. The Grenouille became my home, my family. Ari, who immigrated to America from Greece as a teenager, had made it big in Houston. He owned three restaurants and was committed to helping other ambitious, hardworking young Greeks who were determined to escape the hardscrabble villages of their homeland. Many of the restaurant employees had either jumped ship in Houston or had made their way to America to join a family member who already had a foothold in the country.

Ari's wife LeGay, from San Antonio, was ten years older than me and had become a good friend. The restaurant employees, from Greece, Morocco, Iran, Iraq, Mexico, and France, were like my brothers and sisters, and I loved hearing tales of life back home, particularly back home in Greece. I was already somewhat familiar with the Greek community in Houston because of my friendship with Anita Kalpaxis, the daughter of the Greek Orthodox priest. I felt such an affinity for the culture that I began to fantasize that perhaps my father was Greek.

Every Monday morning, Ari handed me the keys to his big white Cadillac. Even though I could barely see over the steering wheel, I managed to drive down to the docks to buy seafood or to the farmers' market to buy produce. I kept the books during the day, with LeGay's help. While we worked, we listened to the complete works of Chopin and Beethoven, chatted about writers we loved, or read poetry aloud. At lunch time, we ordered expensive items and good wine from the restaurant downstairs.

If Ari was short on staff, I would rush home to shower, put

on a chic dress, and return to spend the evening working as hostess at Ari's other restaurant, the Bacchanal. After work, a gang of us would drive down to the Port of Houston to the restaurants and clubs the Greek sailors favored. After hours of eating and drinking and swirling about the room doing Greek folk dances, I would stumble back into my apartment only a few hours before the sun reappeared.

Ari couldn't understand why I wanted to stay in school. "You have a future here," he kept telling me. "The next restaurant I open, you're going to run it." It was to be called the Marco Polo.

He wanted me to marry Jimmy, his young partner in the business, have lots of children, and become part of the family. Although Jimmy and I were soon involved with each other, I wasn't interested in marriage and children, and I certainly wasn't interested in giving up my dreams of a life in music.

One day after class, my voice teacher Arlene Thiel mentioned that she would be leaving at semester's end. "I'm going to Holland," she said. "Sammy's got a position with the Rotterdam Philharmonic." Sammy, her husband, was an accomplished French horn player, and she would be teaching privately.

Thinking about the classical music I had listened to all my life, the stories I heard every night from my European friends at the Grenouille, I told Arlene how much I envied her. "I would love to go to Europe!" I told her.

A couple of weeks later, Arlene had an idea. "Why don't you come with us?" she suggested. "You can study voice in Holland just as easily as you can here, and I know you could find work."

Could I really do such a thing, I wondered. Could I leave my mother, who seemed to need me more than ever? Did I want to leave Jimmy and my life at the Grenouille? I had misgivings, particularly about leaving my mother, but I decided to jump at the opportunity. A few months later, I was living in a tiny, one-room walk-up in a building near the docks in Rotterdam, working as a barmaid every night at a place called the Rhodos Bar, and studying music at the Royal Conservatory of Music in The Hague.

At first, it was hard. I was barely twenty years old, I didn't know Dutch, it was cold and wet all the time, and I was desperately lonely. Except for Sammy and Arlene, who were often away, I knew no one. Once, in the middle of winter, I came down with the flu, and for three days I lay in my bed burning up with fever and too weak to totter down the stairs. No one knew I was sick, and I didn't know where to find a doctor.

Gradually, of course, things began to change. I began to study Dutch—even though the Dutch themselves insisted on speaking English. I began making friends. Thanks to the sailors from around the world who frequented the Rhodos and the two gruff old Greeks who ran it, work began to take on a bit of color.

In Amsterdam one Saturday morning, I wandered into the Rijksmuseum, met a Dutch painter, and was easily persuaded to pose for him, in the nude, of course. On a student Eurail pass, I took off and traveled for three months. I hitchhiked across France and Italy, caught a ride across what was then Yugoslavia with a crazy Frenchman in a Volkswagen, endured a night trying to get some sleep next to him in the cramped front seat of his car, and eventually made my way to the close-knit mountain village where Jimmy had grown up. The whole village came out to greet me. Jimmy's ancient grandmother prepared a hot bath for me in a tub she set up in the kitchen of the tiny family home. It was a bath I badly needed. That weekend I attended a family wedding, and amid the drinking and dancing and food and the friendly people, I fell in love yet again with the Greek culture.

A couple of months later, I left my three-story walk-up and moved into the beautiful town house Sammy and Arlene were leasing from a Dutch professor who was on sabbatical in the United States for a couple of years. My new life was looking up.

I let myself into the house and walked toward the kitchen with the groceries I had picked up. Arlene was sitting at the kitchen table reading a letter from Sammy. He had been in Vienna nearly a month.

"Telegram came for you," she said. She put aside the letter and slid a brown, official-looking envelope across the table. She had a worried look on her face. "I signed for it," she said. "I'm afraid it's bad news."

I dropped my book satchel in the chair and picked up the telegram. Inside I found a white piece of paper. Green print around the border read: TELEGRAAFANTOOR ROTTERDAM.

Holding my breath, I scanned the message, in English: YOUR GRANDMOTHER HAS BEEN SICK IN HOSPITAL. FUNERAL TUESDAY MARCH 27 4:30 P.M. AT SETTEGAST KOPF FUNERAL HOME. LOVE AUNTIE.

Mama was dead? I reread the cryptic message to make sure. How could this be? I didn't even know Mama had been sick, and here I was going about my business as if nothing had happened. We had been such kindred spirits, I halfway believed that when Mama died, some breath would go out of myself. Somehow, in some spiritual way, I would know.

I was crying as I put down the telegram. Arlene came around the table and put her arm around my shoulders. "I'll make you a cup of tea," she said in a quiet voice. There were tears in her eyes, too.

As Arlene filled the kettle with water, I suddenly realized the date, March 28. Mama's funeral had been the day before. No one had thought to let me know that Mama had died until after the funeral. Maybe I could have flown home and said good-bye.

"Why couldn't one of my aunts have called?" I kept asking Arlene as we sat at the table. The teapot began its whistling.

"Try not to blame them," Arlene said softly, her hand over mine. "It was their mother who died. They must have been devastated. You know they had a lot on their minds."

I realized she was right, though once again it seemed I was merely an afterthought. I was hurt and bitter; I began crying for myself as much as for my grandmother.

I was crying for my mother as well. With Mama gone, what would she do now? Where would she live?

I canceled my lessons for the next few days. "I don't know what to do," I wrote in my journal. "Am unsure of why I should go or if."

I called Bernie, my old boyfriend. He got in touch with Don, the psychiatrist. Bernie called back the next day to tell me Don saw no reason for me to come home.

In the emotive style of a twenty-year-old, I wrote in my journal:

> Another reason I think I want to go home is because I feel that everyone has rejected me. I've never felt like part of that family. I don't know whose fault it is. I see myself going home and saying, "This is my mother, and I'm going to help her." "Leave us alone" is in there somewhere.
>
> Also, I don't think Mommy has been as totally alone as she is now. I want her to want me so much. If she is feeling very alone, I want to help her.

And then I wrote: "Hell if I know what I want."

"We didn't want to worry you," my aunts told me later. From

them I learned that Mama had suffered a collapsed lung and a blood clot, neither problem life threatening if she had been willing to see a doctor—but Mama was a Christian Scientist to the end.

In her eighty years of existence, she had never spent a night in a hospital bed, despite having given birth to six children. Only near the end, when her daughters forced her to go, did she place herself in a doctor's care. By then she was too weak to lift herself out of bed—or even to protest. The doctor hospitalized her immediately, but she was too weak to live. She told her daughters toward the end that it was the doctors and the hospital that were killing her.

I couldn't sleep that night. I thought again about going home. Even before Mama's death, even when my life was going well, I would occasionally feel depressed about how far I was from my family. I occasionally felt anxious and guilty about running away from my responsibilities. Shades of Auntie, I suppose. Weeks of dreary Dutch skies and constant cold and drizzle didn't help.

Usually, though, the morning routine—rushing to class, working, hours of practicing my music—chased away the homesickness. That and a glimpse of sunshine, when the rain finally ended. I would suddenly be aware of a brilliant light peeking from behind gossamer clouds, the bluest sky I had ever seen. The sixteenth-century Dutch painters had captured it, and it was mesmerizing. Unlike the clouds, however, the anxiety about my mother never dissipated.

The previous Christmas, during my first year in Holland, that anxiety had compelled me to fly back to Houston for the holidays. I was aglow with plans to spend time with my mother. I would take her Christmas shopping. We would see *The Nutcracker Suite*. I couldn't wait to tell her about my new life in Europe.

I bought a Christmas tree and took it to the little house where she and Mama were still living. I tried to talk to her about my singing, but she couldn't understand. I remember insisting that Sister have her over for Christmas dinner. Sister agreed, reluctantly, but Mama came alone. Dawn, she said, just didn't want to come. We fixed her a plate of food and covered it with tin foil, which Mama took home with her. Nothing worked the way I had planned, and I ended up spending little time with my mother.

During my Houston stay at that time, I visited my aunts and cousins and old friends. I saw Bernic and settled back into my old routine, but it wasn't enough. "This is what I've been missing?" I asked myself after a couple of weeks. As soon as the holidays were over, I hurried back to Holland, where life was *gezellig*, a distinctively Dutch word that means cozy, friendly, and comfortable.

Now, my grandmother's death gave me reason to think more seriously about going home to stay. I'll give myself a deadline, sort through my options, I decided.

On a Saturday in early April, the first really lovely spring day of the year, I was up early and having a cup of coffee, careful not to wake Arlene. I heard the clink of milk bottles at the front door. There's something Houston doesn't offer, I said to myself. Fresh milk, fresh butter, wonderful cheeses—all delivered to your doorstep. Maybe it was a sign.

Walking along Adrianne van der Doesland, I watched the sun peek over the three-story town houses. I smiled and nodded a *"Gute morgen, mefrau"* to neighbors, square-shaped Dutch women with red cheeks and brightly colored aprons, already hard at work in their postage-stamp front yards. They were scouring the sidewalks with soap and water and stiff brooms. I knew that later in the day they would be polishing the front window and laundering the white lace curtains. Still later, in the golden glow of the afternoon, the curtains would be pulled back and passersby could see the families sitting in their cozy parlors. Except for the dim blue glow of the TV, it was a domestic scene straight out of Vermeer.

A couple of blocks from our house, there was a beautifully manicured park with a small lake and tall, slender linden trees that bowed gracefully in the spring breeze. Their luminous green leaves were just beginning to appear. I walked through the park twice a week on the way to my piano lesson with Rhein, a tall, handsome Dutchman with blue eyes and a blond, neatly trimmed beard. Rhein was an accomplished concert pianist, the student of a student of Liszt. I had a mad crush on Rhein, but alas, he was in love with another pianist.

Strolling along the edge of the lake, watching the ducks float and bob, I could see a cross section of my adopted home. Across the lake was an open field where wide swaths of tulips grew in red, yellow, and purple glory. On the far side of the field stood three sturdy Dutch windmills, their long blades turning slowly. Beyond the windmills were tall modern apartment buildings, the abode of necessity for many residents of this most densely populated nation in Europe. Everything was so clean and orderly and beautiful.

I strolled along a gravel path near the water's edge. Joggers and families with straw-haired, pink-cheeked children veered around me. Now that I was no longer staying alone in a cramped room close to the docks, I was beginning to imagine making a life for myself in Holland. It also helped that I was no longer working in a dingy, smoky bar, having to sidle past boisterous sailors every night, all the while balancing a tray of drinks above my head. I smiled to think of Danielle and Willje and the other barmaids at the Rhodos. All of them prostitutes, although I didn't know it for the longest time. When the huge fishing boats were in port often for weeks at a time, the captain and a few of his officers would rent a small pleasure craft and engage the services of my Rhodos friends. I wouldn't see them for days at a time. I didn't know where they had gone; I just knew I worked extra hours when they weren't around.

Danielle and her friends lived lives far different from mine, but they had been good to me. In a way, they had protected me, although they never told me I was working in the middle of a prostitution ring. It was Iannis, an old Greek sailor who warned me that I had to leave the Rhodos. Iannis, who had retired to Rotterdam and spoke perfect English, came to see me every day. He didn't say why I had to leave; he just said it wasn't a good place for me. He felt I could find a safer way to pay for my musical training.

I had a growing circle of friends outside the Rhodos Bar. Like Rhein, Arlene, and Sammy, they were busy, bright, and deeply involved with music. It was their passion and their profession; I so desperately wanted it to be my profession, too. It always had been my passion.

In addition to my Dutch lessons, I was studying French privately in the city, taking guitar two nights a week with a conservatory teacher, and studying voice with Arlene. Arlene was convinced I was nearly ready to move on to the acclaimed Jo Bollekamp, former teacher of the famed soprano Elly Ameling.

Yet Holland was still not quite home. The telegram about my grandmother's death was a painful reminder that I missed my family, however fractured it was. As reluctant as I was to admit it, I missed the familiarity of Houston and old friends.

I surprised myself occasionally when some European pseudointellectual attacked America's crazy politics, its misguided Vietnam policy, or its brutish race relations; though I agreed, I didn't like hearing it from someone else. I didn't like their condescension. Afterward, I would shake my head and wonder what had happened to the long-haired, barefoot hippie who had spent two summers of love in San Francisco protesting the war and Richard Nixon.

I was twenty, and though I hated to admit it, I wasn't as worldly-wise and sophisticated as I pretended to be. I needed to finish college. I was homesick.

My anxiety about my mother was like a dull ache. The pain wasn't incessant, but I was never really free of it, either. No matter how far away I got from her, no matter how caught up in my music, my travels, or my various boyfriends, my mother was always lingering in the shadows of my mind. I would hear a song on the radio, and there she would be.

Now that Mama was gone, I could see Dawn wandering lost and alone on a Houston street. Lying in a downtown alley, discarded like old clothes, she was abandoned, forgotten, kicked away. She began invading my dreams.

In a dream, I am on the first floor of Auntie's house. I hear the water running upstairs, and I go to check. In the bathroom, the water is about to overflow the tub. It is a dirty brown, a greasy scum floating on top. Suddenly, my mother rises out of the water.

Every day that passed, I feared that my mother was getting worse—and no one was there to help her. No one else—not her sisters, not any of the professionals who had ever worked with her—could give her the care and attention that I could give.

So I thought. I worked myself into a panic just brooding about it. Of course, I was the real needy one, although I didn't want to admit it, even to myself. Although I didn't realize it at the time, I felt the need to give to others—particularly to my mother—what I lacked. I had to go home.

I decided to visit the one friend who was sure to offer sensible advice. I waited for the trolley that would take me into downtown Rotterdam and then out to my friend Janice's house. A horse-drawn dairy wagon rolled by.

Downtown, I caught the outbound Metro that would take me to the suburbs. The train streaked past stands of trees, through geometric fields of green-and-yellow farmland as flat as playing fields. It whipped past two-hundred-year-old farmhouses and windmills, paused at tiny villages of slate-roofed houses, churches and weather vanes, cobblestoned streets.

Among my fellow passengers were villagers from outlying areas. The men wore their black Calvinist hats, the women their starched lace hoods. Some wore *clompen*, wooden shoes. Subtle distinctions in their costumes signified the village where they lived.

What a beautiful, civilized place, I was thinking. Why would I even think of leaving? Why would I want to leave people like Janice Walker?

Aside from Sammy and Arlene, Janice had become my best friend. An Ohio native, in her early thirties, tall and slender with something of a school librarian look about her, she was a violinist with the Rotterdam Philharmonic. Under the direction of Edo de Waart, the Rotterdam Philharmonic was becoming one of the noted orchestras of Europe, touring the Continent and North America regularly. When she wasn't touring, she lived with her five Abyssinian cats in a three-story town house in the countryside, just outside Rotterdam.

Janice had been instrumental in persuading me that the Rhodos, despite the adventure and the tawdry romance of it all, was a dangerous place for a young, single American girl. It was also Janice who had introduced me to many of the musicians who had become my friends, most of them English or Dutch, a few American, and arranged for me to work part-time cleaning their houses. They were people in positions to help me find my musical niche on the Continent. It hadn't been that long ago that they too had been struggling young musicians. They were happy to be in a position to help.

That Saturday morning after Mama's death, Janice offered yet another suggestion. "Why don't you go home for a while, see your family, get your mother situated, and then come back?"

We were sitting on the couch in the living room. A bobtailed brown cat, Nefertiti, sprang into Janice's lap. "You realize, don't you, that you have a place here?" she said, stroking the sleek cat. "You can finish school, make a career for yourself. You and I both know that you are very talented. I don't want you to waste that talent."

We sat in silence for a while, sipping tea, thinking. Nef sprang off the couch, glided gracefully to the door, reached up with her paws, and turned the knob. She slipped silently out.

"In a way," Janice said, smiling at the cat's little trick, "we are your family now. We want you to stay. I think you *should* stay."

What Janice said made sense, as usual. I told her I would think about it, and I did—for three days. On Wednesday, having just about made up my mind to fly to Houston for an extended visit, nothing more, I came home to find another *telegraafantoor Rotterdam*. This one said: DAWN MISSING GONE FOR ONE WEEK. LOVE SISTER.

My nagging fears, my bad dreams, had become reality. My mother had slipped away from them. Who knew where? I felt frustrated, helpless. I knew I had to go home.

"What else can I do?" I said to Janice the next day as we stood outside the concert hall. "Leave her to fend for herself? Let her be lost?"

"Leave your things here," Janice said. "We'll look after them. Just go take care of your mother." She gave me a hug. "See you in three or four weeks," she said.

A few days later, I rode the train to Brussels for a voice lesson with Barbara Thornton of the early music group Sequentia. Walking down a cold, wet street, I was visited by the women I had come to call my three muses. They were frequent presences in my life.

"Tara, darling," my grandmother said in her lilting, ethereal way, "a talented artist like you doesn't have to study in Europe to truly learn her craft. You're better off at home."

Auntie quickly butted in. "You have no business studying music at all, unless you plan to be an elementary school music teacher," she said. "That's the only respectable occupation for you, if in fact you're talented and disciplined enough."

"You are neither talented enough nor beautiful enough," my mother observed. "And besides, who will take care of me?"

I realized that I was incapable of making a decision on my own. These three women, my muses, were always there with me, always talking at me. As usual, they prevailed. It would be three years before I returned to Europe.

Spring had broken out in Houston. The Texas coastal plain was green and lush, semitropical. Riding into town on the airport bus, I watched lazy moisture-laden Gulf clouds drift inland; by noon, I knew, they would give way to a hot blue sky. The city looked, and felt, like a greenhouse.

I felt assaulted by the messy sprawl, the smog, the gritty traffic pounding by us on the expressway. Huge, garish billboards bombarded the eyes. Every car that passed us seemed to be on a collision course with death. I kept noticing pickup trucks on the road with gun racks in the rear window. I remembered the *Time* story about Houston motorists shooting each other on the freeways. I had been embarrassed to admit I was a Texan.

Tara Elgin Holley with Joe Holley

226

After cozy, pristine Holland, Houston was loud, smelly, and ugly. Culture shock was setting in with a vengeance. I worried that I had become a snob.

Exiting the frantic freeway, the bus lurched slowly along familiar downtown streets, now shadowy canyons between sleek ultramodern skyscrapers. I got off at the Greyhound terminal, lugging two heavy bags containing most of my earthly belongings. I was home again, for better or worse, in the dingy, exhaust-choked bus depot where the Houston part of my life had begun sixteen years earlier. Outside, the sun splintered off buildings and cars, off chrome and glass and polished steel. I climbed into a cab waiting at the curb and directed the driver to Sister's house.

Later that afternoon, I sat at the dining room table with Sister and Betty Lee and Sally. The four of us had gotten past the tears over Mama's passing and my anger over not being notified sooner. My aunts were talking about my mother.

Dawn and Mama had been living in the little house near Sister and Don's place that my aunts had bought for them a few years earlier, after Papa died. I knew how they lived. Neither had a particularly firm grip on reality. Neighbors got used to seeing them wandering the quiet, tree-lined streets, their heads inclined together in deep, animated conversations. It was not a good situation, although perhaps better than having Dawn institutionalized.

Mrs. March, the lady who lived behind them, on the next street, looked in regularly. "Your mother and your sister," she once told Sister, "are two of the sweetest people I have ever known."

"I wish I felt that way about them," Sister had remarked to Betty Lee.

During the two weeks Mama was in the hospital, my mother was left to fend for herself, although Sister or Betty Lee or Sally tried to go by every couple of days. Mrs. March also kept an eye on her. They wanted to make sure she was getting something to eat, that her clothes were passably clean.

It was Sister who told Dawn that their mother had died in the hospital. "She was quiet," Sister said, "almost as if she didn't hear me. She didn't cry, didn't ask me any questions."

Listening to Sister's account, I thought of little Harold's death and how Mama and Papa had kept it from Dawn for weeks. "My babies are always being taken from me," Dawn had said when she learned her little boy was dead.

After telling her the bad news about Mama, Sister decided they could leave Dawn in the house alone. The sisters had agreed that she didn't need to go to the funeral. They worried that she might make a scene.

They planned to talk in a couple of days about Dawn's future. They knew she couldn't stay by herself, but they also realized that they weren't up to taking her in. They all had families of their own. Dawn would be a handful. It would be hard to come up with a solution.

The morning after the funeral, Sister went by to check on Dawn but couldn't find her, even though the door was unlocked. Sister waited around, thinking maybe Dawn had gone for a walk, since the front door was almost always open. Dawn didn't show up.

Sister checked with the neighbors. She called Sally and Betty Lee, but they hadn't seen her. Late that evening, they reported Dawn missing to the police. She had been gone five days when Sister wired me.

"We've been beside ourselves," Betty Lee said, tears rimming her eyes. "I just don't want to think what could have happened to her. I'm afraid we'll find her lying in a ditch somewhere." She covered her face with her hands.

Tara Elgin Holley with Joe Holley

Along with the fear and worry we all felt, I was feeling the same old exasperation. If anything was going to get done, I would be the one to do it—as usual. Why me? I was asking myself. Why is everyone else so helpless?

"I'm going to find her," I announced. I had no doubt that I would.

I began playing Sherlock Holmes the next morning at that one place I couldn't seem to avoid—the Greyhound terminal. I had a feeling that my mother might have tried to make her way back to California. I was trying to think as she might have thought—not the easiest task, of course, but I knew my mother, knew her ways. Then again, when you are dealing with a schizophrenic, patterns, logic, and reason are not always useful behavioral predictors, even when the schizophrenic is your own mother.

Maybe she was thinking she would find Mama in California, in the house on Miller Drive. Or maybe she thought she would find herself, the youthful, happy Dawn she had been so long ago. I could not imagine what the voices might have told her to do.

The station manager directed me to a little glassed-in room next to the bus lanes, the room where drivers checked in and filled out their reports. I had Dawn's picture.

"You know, she looks awful familiar," a driver who made the run to L.A. told me. I watched his ruddy face as he studied the face in the picture. "I couldn't swear to it," he said, "but seems to me I took this woman at least part of the way to California one day last week. Course, I could be mistaken."

I thanked the driver and left the snapshot in the office. Maybe it would spark a memory, or maybe Dawn would wander in.

I drove over to the Checker cab office—and happened onto my first clue. "Our records show we picked her up on the after-

My Mother's Keeper
229

noon of April second," the dispatcher told me. "Elgin," he said. "Dawn Elgin. That's right. Took her to the Greyhound station."

I felt motivated by this small accomplishment. Yet, what if Dawn had gone to California? How would I ever find her? I tried to think of someone I knew in Los Angeles who could do some checking.

My old friend and former employer Ari, who had friends on the Houston police force, suggested I try the police station. "Yes ma'am, she's on our missing-persons bulletin," a sergeant sitting at a desk told me. "It goes statewide, but less'n we hear something, there's not a whole lot we can do. We're not actively looking or anything. I'm sorry, but you know how it is."

The sergeant suggested that I go over to the county jail a couple of blocks away. "No offense, ma'am, but we pick up people like your mother all the time," he said. "She might be there."

A jail matron, a large, tough-looking woman in a short, too-tight navy-blue skirt and a light-blue blouse escorted me through clanging doors and down long, dim corridors to the holding cells. In each cell, women in gray prison shifts with buttons down the front and short, tight sleeves sat on bunks or slouched against the bars. They were drunks, prostitutes, street people. The place stank of sweat, stale cigarettes, and Lysol.

I scanned each cell, peering into dim corners and the shadows of the lower bunks, looking for a familiar face. I desperately wanted to find my mother, but it made me sick to think I might find her here. I thought about how helpless she would have been if a cellmate began abusing her, began having a little fun with the crazy lady.

I didn't find her in the jail, although I kept up the routine for a couple of weeks—bus station, hospitals, county jail, the police station. Meanwhile, I was working at Ari's Grenouille again. It was good to see the old gang after being gone for two years, good to take my mind off my mother. Each day before work, I would swing by her house, hoping that she had slipped back in.

Then the letter came. It was from the Austin State Hospital. "Dawn Elgin is a patient in our Harris County unit," the letter said.

She had been there the whole time. The hospital even had the missing-persons report, but no one had made the connection between the report and the disoriented new patient who called herself Dawn. How she had gotten to Austin, nearly two hundred miles from Houston, no one could say.

I was on a plane to Austin the day the letter arrived.

CHAPTER ELEVEN

I've seen crimson roses growing through a chain-link fence/I've seen crystal visions, sometimes they don't make sense.
—Jimmie Dale Gilmore

The buildings I saw when I stepped off the city bus didn't fit the image I had carried with me since childhood. I had always imagined my mother locked away in a medieval castle, in a tower all alone, like the castle in the movie *Jane Eyre*, which I had watched with Auntie. The Austin State Hospital, from the street at least, reminded me of a college campus. Through a high chain-link fence braided with climbing red rose bushes, I could see rolling, grass-covered grounds and yellow-brick buildings shaded by pecan trees and gnarled old live oaks.

The guard at the gate directed me to an old limestone three-story building capped with a dome, a miniature replica of the state capitol's. At the entrance, I noticed an official state plaque commemorating the building's historic significance. It had been erected in 1860, according to the plaque, when the Texas Legislature established the State Lunatic Asylum.

Inside, the building smelled dank and old. The hardwood floors squeaked as I walked toward a grim-faced woman behind a desk whose mouth reminded me of a slit in a coin purse. Once I had identified myself to her satisfaction, she sent me to the records office down the hall where a clerk produced my mother's files and showed me to a chair. With a sigh, I sat down to read the latest entry in the official account of my mother's nightmare, now more than two decades long.

"The first attack occurred in December, 1951," I read from a court transcript.

> The cause was believed to have resulted from a love affair. She was given no treatment, and the pattern of behavior gradually became set.
>
> The patient will not express any hallucinations, though it is my impression that these are present. She does admit to illusions concerning a small statue that was in her hospital room at the time of the birth of her daughter. These illusions are in the nature of some divine relations between the patient and God. She will not specifically explain these beliefs to anyone. She will go so far as to say that at times she is "rising up the steps to heaven with her soul."

I read on:

> The patient stated "she felt her soul rising from her body and going into heaven"; became hostile and suspicious of close ones without realistic cause. . . . She was a good student and learned easily. She was popular with other students and thought to be a leader. She completed high school.

Tara Elgin Holley with Joe Holley

234

From an entry in the summer of 1956:

In so far as the onset of this patient's illness and other pertinent details of this nature, she is unable at this time to give them. However, it seems that her present illness revolves in a large part around a five-year-old daughter. As nearly as can be obtained from the patient, she was unmarried at the time of the conception of this child and has not been married since. In addition to this, the patient has a great deal of confusion in the religious sphere where she seems to have a number of guilt feelings over her behavior. Especially with respect to smoking and drinking, as being uncompatable with ideas of a virtuous woman.

With each succeeding page, the years of my mother's troubled life passed by. Halfway through the records, I began to make appearances. According to the transcript:

The patient has been disturbed, has not been eating or sleeping well, and her daughter has been concerned about her physical and mental condition. Her daughter said that the water bill last month was about $78.00 because the patient let the water run all the time. The daughter stated that the patient's mother could not understand the patient's condition and made the patient worse.

The patient is rather confused, knows she is in Austin, but does not know or does not want to say why she was brought back to Austin. She is very inappropriate and at times irrational, and is unable to give information about herself; mostly answers, "I want to go back to Houston," laughs inappropriately and says that she believes in "Christian Science." The patient has her mouth full of tissue paper and little by little she takes the tissue paper from her mouth and places it in a paper cup she has in her hand; inside the paper cup she has a picture of a little girl about 5 or 6 years old; she showed the picture to the interviewer and mumbled to herself. At times she says that the girl in the picture is her daughter.

Maybe it is her daughter, I said to myself, or maybe it's a picture of Dawn, a little girl who has just lost her own mother. The more I read, the angrier I became—at the doctor whose at times muddled syntax suggested muddled thinking, at my mother, at the world, at myself for being angry. The preposterous words that presumed to explain my mother, blurred. Where is she in all this, I asked myself. Where is the talent, the joy, and the passion? Where is the fear and grief she still feels? Where is the mother's love for her child? I realized that it made no sense to be upset by a dry medical report, but I couldn't make the feelings go away simply by being sensible.

I continued reading:

This is a middle-aged white female, untidy, hair uncombed for several days; her finger nails are long and dirty. Her dress is untidy and shabby looking; has her mouth full of tissue paper, looks like she is chewing tobacco.

Under a section called "Personal History," a nurse noted:

It does appear that she has at some time been in California where she has worked for various and sundry persons and agencies in the capacity of a performer of some sort, possibly a singer.

Tara Elgin Holley with Joe Holley
236

Under the heading "Stream of Mental Activity," I read:

> Speaks in low voices many times. She mumbles to herself unintelligible. Most of the time, incoherent and irrelevant. Psychomotor activity increased.

Under "Special Preoccupations":

> Patient admits auditory hallucinations. "I heard voices from England the Christian Sciences" but she is unable to verbalize her experiences. No paranoid ideas elicited.

Under "Chief Complaint": "I want my baby."

I returned the records and left the administration building. I almost felt like laughing at the bleak absurdity of it all. It did no good to cry. I knew that for sure. I walked back outside and down a curving, tree-lined drive to Building 10, the Harris County unit. Most of the hospital patients were grouped in geographical units.

My mother's ward was in a newer one-story building with yellow brick and more glass than the others; it resembled a modern elementary school. I found Dr. Salazar*, the psychiatric resident for the Harris County unit and the man who had written the entries I had just read. He was in a tiny, cluttered office just off the dayroom of the Harris County ward. A large window in his office allowed him to observe his patients.

"Ah, yes!" he said. "Dawn has been expecting you." Salazar was short and fat, perhaps in his mid-fifties, with a goofy grin on his face. The longer we talked, the more I realized that he never stopped grinning, no matter what the gravity of the conversation. His was not a countenance to inspire confidence.

Salazar explained that my mother had been a patient for two

weeks, that hers was a ninety-day commitment and that she was, in effect, a volunteer patient. Any time she wanted to, she could request her release, in writing. Within three days, he explained, hospital officials either had to release her or, if they believed her a threat to herself or to others, they had to seek a court order to keep her.

I nodded. "But what if *I* want her to stay?"

"Then you have to get a court order as well," the doctor said.

Salazar reviewed my mother's records, noting her previous stays, and explained her medication. He had her on 200 milligrams of Moban daily, he said. I knew from past experience with her medications that Moban was a relatively new antipsychotic drug and that 200 milligrams was a fairly high dose.

He knew she had a long history of "decompensating," he said, deteriorating to a psychotic condition. He was hoping to avoid that.

"Good luck," I was thinking. I remembered all the antipsychotics, the antidepressants, the antimanic drugs that had helped my mother over acute episodes, but had stabilized her only for a while.

As the doctor rambled on, his explanation studded with empty psychiatric jargon, I could see through the office picture window. Men and women, young and old, were pacing back and forth in that pathetic, drug-induced shuffle characteristic of medicated mental patients. Others sat in front of a TV; a game show was on. Others talked to themselves, or to phantom voices. Occasionally, they laughed. One red-faced young man sat hunched against a wall, frantically masturbating. No one paid him any attention.

I spotted my mother. She was sitting in an orange plastic chair rocking back and forth and mumbling to herself. I felt a desperate urge to go to her, to hold and comfort her, but I had to sit while this grinning man in a white jacket rambled on about treatment resistance, psychotic episodes, and flight of ideas.

I could tell by looking that my mother had deteriorated in the year and a half since I had seen her. Her body looked worn out, misshapen. She was heavier and had lost more of her teeth. Her eyebrows were bushy and grown out, and the vacant look in her eyes suggested that she had retreated even further into her own frightening world.

Her appearance probably had something to do with her medication. As far as I knew, she had not been on any medication for the last ten years or more. I also was grimly aware that hospitals typically kept patients heavily sedated. They were easier to control that way.

My mother wore a pink voile dress I recognized. It had been Mama's.

At last, Salazar ushered me onto the ward. "Dawn, you have a visitor," he said, still grinning. My mother stared at me, and for a brief moment I wondered if she recognized her own daughter. "Mommy, it's me, Tara," I said nervously, and she stood up quickly and threw her arms around me. We held on to each other, laughing and crying at the same time. Other patients gathered in a circle around us.

My mother held me at arms' length and looked at me. "Oh, darling," she said in a breathy voice, "I've been so worried about you. But look at you; you're so beautiful. I'm so glad you're here. I've been so worried about you."

She held me tightly again, and then she whispered in my ear. "Darling," she said, "you've got to get me out of here. I don't belong here."

"Don't cry, Mommy," I told her over and over, tears streaming down my face. "Things will be better now. I'm going to be here for you. I'm going to help you."

We wandered down the hall to the ward where she slept. It was like a military barrack with narrow windows, a hard tile floor, and lines of single beds on each side of the room, separated by metal lockers. The men slept on the other side of the building, separated from the women's area by the dayroom, the doctor's small office, and the nurses' station. Although it was a large, open room, it felt crowded and close. The sour smell of unwashed bodies, urine, stale cigarettes, cooking smells, and disinfectant— the smell of an institution—pervaded the place.

Outside in the fresh air, I followed my mother to the hospital canteen, a little building with snacks and coffee and soft drinks. We sat at an outdoor table under one of the craggy, old live oaks and had coffee in Styrofoam cups.

My mother, though obviously sedated, was coherent. "My brain feels like lead," she said. "I feel like I'm walking under water."

She was able to explain something of what had happened. As she talked, it became obvious to me that she was grieving, that she was in shock at Mama's death. It seemed perfectly natural.

"It just broke me," she said over and over. "Mama's dying just broke me." She sipped her coffee, her hands trembling. I noticed the old scars on her wrists.

Not only did she understand that her mother had died, she understood that she was alone. She probably feared that her sisters would put her away. It was a reasonable fear. There was no way she could stay alone—or with her sisters.

"I caught the bus up here the day after Mama died," she explained.

Why she made her way to Austin, she couldn't, or wouldn't, say. Perhaps she was hallucinating; maybe voices compelled her to go. Perhaps in a flash of lucidity she thought that if confinement was inevitable, she would go to Austin, where she had been in the state hospital fifteen years earlier.

Tara Elgin Holley with Joe Holley
240

That night I took her to Sid's, a restaurant near the hospital that was popular with the college crowd. The hospital food was so starchy and unappealing, I wanted her to have a good meal. Over chicken-fried steak, a green salad, and iced tea, we talked about how things would be different, how we would be spending time together. She didn't talk nonsense at all; she wanted to discuss getting out of the hospital.

I could feel people at other tables stealing glances at us; I could hear their murmured remarks. I couldn't count the times it had happened over the years. By now though, I could think, To hell with you; if you don't like the way my mother looks, that's your problem, not mine. My mother didn't seem to notice.

"I'll come up every week," I promised. "We'll sing together, we'll go places. You never know, maybe we can get you singing again, once we get your voice back in shape. I hear there are a lot of little clubs around Austin. We'll get you in shape, get you out of the hospital. We'll find you a good place to stay."

"Oh, honey, that would be swell," my mother said, enthusiastically chewing ragged bites of her chicken-fried steak. She looked around the restaurant with a little smile on her face, apparently savoring her freedom. Then she looked back at me. "But, baby," she said, "you've got to get me out of that hospital. You know I don't belong there with those crazy people."

I smiled. Although I was enormously relieved to have found my mother, finally to be with her after all those months apart, a nagging little feeling was beginning to creep in. I had felt it before, though it wasn't clear to me what it meant. It was that my mother, despite her illness, was crafty, that she was using me, that she was more aware than she let on. I had no doubt that my mother was sick, but I wondered if she had ways of using her illness to get her way, the way Mama used her hearing loss as an excuse to pick up only what she wanted to hear.

My mother, I had heard, could be a masterful manipulator. Sally had told me stories about how Dawn as a youngster would always figure out—by hook or crook, Sally said—a way to get what she wanted. Not only was she single-minded, she said, the young Dawn always knew how to work the angles. Prisoners, of course, learned to use the system, to con their keepers. It's how they survive. No doubt about it: My mother was a prisoner—of the system and, most of all, of her illness.

I looked across the table at the middle-aged woman still busily eating, her chestnut-colored hair long and stringy, her nails bitten to the quick, her once lovely mouth now gapped with missing teeth. That's my mother, I reminded myself. A feeling that's difficult to describe—of disbelief, of love and sadness—washed over me. I wanted to take her in my arms and comfort her like a baby. I felt an overwhelming need to protect her—from the world, from her illness, from the people sitting around us who just didn't understand.

I knew my mother could be sweet and loving, but I also knew, even when I refused to admit it to myself, that I could never quite break through to her. In her sickness, she was focused inward, on herself. It seemed to be the nature of the illness. In fact, I had read that for schizophrenics, the range of awareness narrows to a tiny zone around them; they are oblivious to their own bodies, not to mention a wider world.

For my mother, it was the illness that mattered, even more than her own daughter. The illness, the monster, the odious thing that ruled her brain was the driving force. But none of that mattered when she looked across the table and pleaded, "You've got to get me out of that place." I stared into her eyes, and my heart broke. I would do anything it took to rescue her—not just from "that place," but from her prison.

The next morning, I met Victor Gomez*, my mother's social worker. A slender, handsome Mexican American in his late twenties, Gomez was courteous and friendly. He seemed genuinely to care about my mother. I felt better about him than I did about Dr. Salazar.

"Your mother's doing just fine," he said. "Dr. Salazar must have told you, we've got her on Thorazine, and we're working on her social skills. We believe in a couple of months, she'll be a prime candidate for one of our halfway houses."

Gomez told me about the grooming regimen my mother was expected to follow; she had to wash her hair, take a bath, brush her teeth daily. She was taking a battery of math and intelligence tests, learning to live with her fellow patients. If she continued to progress, Gomez said, she could go on occasional camp-outs with the group during the summer. Eventually, she would be able to hold down a job, on the hospital grounds at first, maybe later in the real world.

I felt good about what I was hearing. Victor Gomez actually seemed to have hope, maybe because he was young, energetic, and idealistic. I liked him, and I found it hard to believe that in this depressing, dreary place, someone actually had a plan for helping my mother recover. For the first time in a long time, maybe ever, I felt I had an ally in my mother's care.

I explained to Victor that I intended to be actively involved with my mother's recovery, in ways that had been impossible while I had been in Europe. "I'll be spending a lot of time with her," I said. "I really believe I can make a difference."

He listened, a polite smile on his face. He nodded occasionally, made notes on a yellow legal pad. He assured me that my mother was indeed fortunate to have her daughter back in her life. He told me that the involvement of family members was vital if the patient was to find a way of coping with the illness. Most family members, he said, rarely visited; they found it too painful.

"But Miss Elgin," he said, "a word of advice, please? I know you love your mother. I know you would do anything for her. But the truth is, you have to live your own life. There's only so much you can do for Dawn. The danger is that your mother's dependence on her mother will transfer to you. I'm telling you, that's a burden you don't want to live with."

I listened to what he said, and it troubled me. In my mind's eye, I saw Mama and my mother strolling along the sidewalk near their little Bellaire house, wrapped up in each other, in a world of their own. My mother, now that I thought about it, was like a little girl, like me with Auntie when the two of us strolled through the Village together fifteen years earlier.

Immediately, I heard the voice of Don Gautney, the psychologist back in Houston. "Give it up," he had said, not unkindly. "Go to Europe. Have adventures."

"You have to call the stops," Victor said. Call the shots, he meant.

I tried to summon convincing arguments to refute what Victor was saying. He was young and inexperienced. I was stronger and more determined than he realized. My mother was not as troubled as she seemed.

I kept the objections to myself. I would start to say something, and then I would realize that I just didn't want to argue. "I appreciate what you're telling me," I said at last, "but what I'm telling you is that I honestly think I can make a difference." I looked through the window at my mother, who was looking in and smiling. Probably, she was thinking that I was making arrangements to get her out.

"I will not let her become dependent on me," I told Victor. "You can count on that."

Riding back to Houston on the bus that afternoon, looking out the window at rolling green pastures and rippling sheets of bluebonnets, I planned my future—and my mother's. It was clear what I had to do. For fifteen years, I had waited for someone to rescue my mother, to climb the briar-covered tower, break the spell, and bring her back into the security and warmth of our family. No one had managed to accomplish the feat; everyone who tried had disappointed me.

Now it was up to me. For the first time ever, no one stood in the way—not Auntie, not my aunts, not Mama. Especially not Mama. As much as I loved and adored my grandmother, I held her responsible for my mother's condition—not totally, of course, but Mama certainly could have done things differently.

How would I accomplish this feat? Not with prayer and Christian Science practitioners; that was for sure. Not with medication and mental hospitals. Although the irony escaped me at the time, I presumed—with a faith and trust that rivaled Mama's—to rely on the power of love.

While I believed that my mother deserved the best professional care available, my basic trust was in myself. I would rely on devotion and care and perseverance; a daughter's love, not a doctor's expertise, would at last save Dawn. I didn't realize that a daughter's love and a daughter's need were often one and the same.

I would start by treating her like a human being. By lavishing care and attention on this bewildered, neglected soul, I would lead her back to a normal life.

The Greyhound approached the suburban sprawl and clotted traffic of Houston, and I found myself trying to imagine the long, slow process. My mother would gradually emerge from the forest of fear and confusion to which she had retreated. There would be setbacks, I knew; I could be patient, and persistent.

As for Europe? Well, it would always be there. I could postpone my plans—for a year, two years, however long it took. I would move to Austin. I would go to school at the University of Texas. I would rescue my mother.

As spring turned into a long, hot Texas summer, I plunged into my new routine. I returned to Houston, moved back in with Sister and Don for the time being, into the room I had shared with Donna. I took my old job as hostess at Ari's Grenouille.

I worked from noon to midnight Thursday through Sundays. On good weekends, I made $350. By the end of the summer, I had saved $1,000 toward tuition.

On Monday mornings, I took the 7:30 bus to Austin. From Monday through Thursday, I supervised my mother's recovery, staying in a Victorian-era boarding house where Bernie's old high-school friend, Jimmy, had a room. The house was only a few blocks from the hospital; most of the tenants were either college students or former mental patients.

I met with Dr. Salazar and with Victor Gomez and tried to chart my mother's progress. I got to know my mother's medications—Thorazine or Mellaril or Stelazine or Haldol—and made sure she didn't "cheek" them.

I was soon acquainted with everyone on the ward—both the

"chronics," the people who had been on the ward for years and would be until they died and the men and women who were there for ninety-day commitments. I got to know their own tragic stories. I came to recognize the characteristic symptoms of the various antipsychotic drugs my mother and the other patients were taking. A person on Thorazine, for instance, looked like a zombie, the face a frozen mask, the person's gait slow and unsteady. Lithium made the mouth dry, and people walked around with their mouths open, trying to swallow.

I was comfortable on the ward, probably because I had been with my mother so much, and I had no trouble relating to the patients as individuals, as fellow human beings. They seemed happy to see me. I was happy to be their friend.

They were scary and odd only for a little while. After I got to know them, I thought of them as sad and sweet. I watched them test visitors. Like children in a nursery school, they approached warily, reaching out tentatively to touch, to talk. If the visitor pulled back in shock or disgust or fear, the patients perceived it. If the visitor treated them as fellow human beings, they knew that, too.

Many had not seen family or friends for years. They were starved for companionship, for attention. I came to feel real affection for the people on the ward, although many nights I went back to Jimmy's house crying. These people had no lives. They—and their families—had given in to their illness, to their circumscribed existence. I would not let that happen to my mother.

Sometimes, on hot summer evenings, I watched the attendants in their white pants and T-shirts good-naturedly herd their charges outside for an after-dinner game of volleyball. The attendants clapped their hands and skipped about. They cheered the patients out the door into the early evening sunlight, trying to generate a little competitive spirit, a little enthusiasm. The patients were bewildered, like dazed sheep. Loss of affect, the psychiatrists called it. Watching them, I felt deeply sad.

I took my mother off the hospital grounds as often as I could. One night we heard Ella Fitzgerald sing at the university; another night we enjoyed a dinner dance sponsored by the Austin Symphony, with the Dorsey band as the headliner.

Some afternoons we took in a movie. Dawn loved reminiscing about her life in Hollywood, telling about the stars she had known.

"Did I tell you about the night at Ciro's when Lana Turner and Stevie Crane walked in?" she would ask. "I almost forgot my lyrics. She was so beautiful! You know they had a baby?"

Occasionally, I helped her get dressed up, and we would take a cab to the Driskill, Austin's lovely old downtown hotel. The two of us would sit at the piano bar and listen to Joyce, a black jazz singer with a jovial, husky voice. We would have a couple of drinks, though I worried about mixing alcohol with my mother's medication.

"Wow! This is fabulous," she would say. "I love this! Let's do this more often."

She was thinking of me as a sister, a chum, it seemed. "Isn't this swell?" she would say, as if she were sitting at Ciro's with Sally or Betty Lee back in the 1940s. It made me uncomfortable. It was a mom I wanted, not a sister. I wanted a mother to depend on, the way my cousins Carol and Donna depended on Sister. I wanted a mother who would offer guidance, who would help me construct an image of myself as a young woman. I wanted someone to tell me, "Honey, you're doing fine." My mother, of course, couldn't offer those things, but that didn't keep me from longing for them.

I wrote in my journal one night:

Mommy and I spent much of the day outside. Went to the canteen for coffee. She napped. Also talked about old school chums and how much I would have liked them. She told me often she loved me, and I *felt* that she loves me. Said she didn't like the hospital because she had always been the outdoor type and always enjoyed a good game of tennis.

My cousin Donna, a student at Southwest Texas State University in nearby San Marcos, came to Austin one weekend. "My teeth make me look like a hag," Dawn told her niece. "I know I look terrible. Maybe this exercise [she was walking daily] will get some of this weight off. It jiggles."

Once that summer, I took a razor to the hospital and shaved my mother's legs. "Honey, you don't have to do that," she said, as I got down on my knees at my mother's feet.

That was strange, I remember thinking later. She could not have cared less about her legs looking nice. I was the one who cared. I was shaving her legs, not for her sake, but for my own.

One weekend that spring, I bought her three new dresses, a slip, and a nightgown and gave her two dollars from Sister. We went to see the movie *Class of '42*. I thought she might relate. At dinner that evening, she took the two dollars out of her slip and tried to pay. I wouldn't let her, of course. On Tuesday night, I got a call from Victor Gomez. I hadn't heard from him in a while. I had been giving him piano lessons until I realized he was more interested in positioning his hand on my knee than on the keyboard.

He was calling to tell me that my mother had escaped, using

the two dollars. She had gotten as far as San Marcos on the bus and had been picked up by the police. She had been looking for Donna, she said. The police took her back to Austin.

I wrote in my journal after my visit the next weekend:

> Bernie and I took her to see *Fiddler on the Roof*, which I think she enjoyed very much.
>
> Withdrawn this weekend—only spoke clearly and coherently when I left. "I love you so much, baby. You're all I have left in the world now that Mama and Papa are gone. Bernie, now you take good care of my baby, okay?"
>
> Said not to worry—she wouldn't be running off any-place.

Occasionally, I got letters from Janice and Arlene and my other friends in Holland. They wished me well, said they were thinking of me. In June, Arlene sent three boxes of belongings I had left in Holland. Ari loaned me his big white Cadillac, so I could drive down to the Port of Houston to pick them up. There was something a little sad about those boxes, especially when I opened up one and saw all the beautiful heavy sweaters I wouldn't be needing in Houston. Those boxes, those sweaters, symbolized my last tie with a life I had turned my back on. I hoped I was doing the right thing.

In July, I got my letter of acceptance from the University of Texas. I began making plans to move to Austin. I scheduled an appointment to sing for the music faculty so I could be accepted as a voice student.

"Why don't we live together, save a little money?" my cousin Greg suggested. He had just gotten his discharge after a three-year Navy hitch, and he wanted to use his GI Bill benefits to study for his degree in child psychology at the university. He only had a year of work to do. We found a little house for $200 a month in a quiet neighborhood between the state hospital and the university. The two of us, along with Harley, Greg's floppy-footed Irish setter pup, moved to Austin in August.

In a month, I would be twenty-one, almost the age my mother was when I was born, almost her age when she got sick.

Tara and Dawn, 1986.

CHAPTER TWELVE

It has stripped her of everything—her mind, her career, her family, her daughter, everything. And now it's taking her body—her teeth, her skin, and now her hair. She always had beautiful hair. I know, I've washed and brushed it plenty of times. And now, goddamn it, the illness is taking that.
—Journal entry, 1973

The University of Texas was a crowded, busy city within a city. In the fall of 1973, it was a raucous, angry city. Almost every day, I walked to class past crowds of students gathered around loud, fist-shaking speakers on the campus's West Mall. Sometimes I would pause to listen to speakers railing against Tricky Dick and the war he had promised to end. At least once a week, hundreds of chanting marchers with large hand-lettered signs bobbing above their heads snaked their way from the tower at the center of campus—the tower Charles Whitman had made infamous a few years earlier—to the capitol six blocks away.

Kent State was still a raw wound, as it was on campuses

around the country. Watergate continued to build, and the headlines every morning sought to answer the question, What did Nixon know and when did he know it? Walking through the sprawling Student Union building, I couldn't help but notice that the typical smells of pizza, burgers, and beer were spiced with the acrid odor of pot.

On "the Drag," the busy street that ran parallel to the campus, long-haired students passed out IMPEACH NIXON handbills. Others sold tie-dyed T-shirts and handmade leather jewelry from little stands on the sidewalk.

The music building, only a hundred yards or so from the West Mall, was an island of quiet. Most UT students studying music were not politically inclined, and even those who were found that time constraints made it difficult to get involved. Typical college life, whether Longhorn football games and beer-drenched frat parties or marches and demonstrations, was a luxury for us. If we weren't sitting in class, we were stuck on the third floor of the music building, in practice rooms or listening labs.

We joked about it. We knew we were music nerds, but music was our life. We could not imagine any other.

I was no exception. In addition to looking after my mother and holding down a job, I was taking a full load of demanding courses. My mind felt close to bursting. It was a rich and daunting jumble of music theory, harmony, piano, private voice, and choir, as well as English literature and foreign languages. It was a ridiculously heavy load, even for someone who wasn't working to support herself.

Voice, choir, and piano demanded daily practice—voice for at least an hour a day, piano for at least two hours. I had a dozen pieces to prepare each semester—Bach, Beethoven, Mozart, Schumann, Ives, Barber, baroque, classical, and twentieth century. At least three of the arias had to be performed flawlessly; I would offer them to a jury of professors at the end of each semester.

On weekday mornings, I would leave the house at five and bicycle the mile or so to the music building so I could practice. Some mornings, I got to school before the janitor arrived to unlock the building.

When I wasn't in class or practicing, I was hurrying to a specified number of concerts every week, as required by the music department. I loved the concerts, but they cut into the precious little time I had to deal with my obligations.

On Friday evenings for the first couple of months of the semester, I still took the bus or rode with Greg to Houston, two hundred miles away, so I could work at Ari's Grenouille. Later in the semester, I got a job tending bar and waitressing at a place near the university called the Veranda. From six in the evening until two in the morning, every Thursday, Friday, and Saturday, I would be fending off the gross familiarities of pin-striped lobbyists and lawmakers from the nearby capitol, and serving round after round of Coors and Lone Star to the clean-cut, obnoxious, and invariably cheap tippers from the UT fraternities. Such fun it was.

At two-thirty in the morning, exhausted, my clothes reeking of beer and cigarette smoke, I slowly pedaled my bike through the dark, quiet Austin neighborhoods to the little house Greg and I shared. I saw Harley more than I saw Greg; the monster pup was destroying everything in the house he could get his teeth around. Greg had taken a job working a night shift at Austin State Hospital, so we managed to mumble a good morning to each other just as he was getting home from work and I was leaving the house. It was still good to have a housemate for a change.

Since nights on the ward were relatively quiet, Greg had time to read and study in the small pool of light at the nurses' station.

My Mother's Keeper
255

He told me that most nights all he had to do was sit and talk with patients who had trouble sleeping, maybe help someone find their way to the bathroom. Occasionally, when patients got into some kind of altercation, Greg calmed things down. He had the same effect on me.

Usually, he sat and tried to stay awake reading his psychology assignments—unlike some of the other college students working on the wards. They took advantage of their access to the medicine cabinet. Mood enhancers were the drugs of choice, for their own use or to sell to their friends. Skimming off the medication they were supposed to be administering to the patients was relatively simple to do.

On the second floor of the music building was a big, beautiful lecture hall with a high ceiling, floor-length windows, and French doors that opened onto a balcony. I have wonderful memories of the classes in twentieth-century music and medieval and Renaissance music I took in that room. I remember how Ken Jacobs, our music theory professor, would come to class excited about some new discovery and so eager to share it with us. I remember my friend George Cisneros, brother of the man who is now Secretary of Housing and Urban Development, standing up and saying something outrageously radical while all his female classmates marveled at how handsome he was.

On the second-floor balcony of that lecture hall, I could look across the street to the Drag—to "the real world" where I flipped hamburgers at Hamburgers by Gourmet every day at lunch and where my mother was a fixture. I would step out on the balcony, the music of the Renaissance still filling my soul, and there would be my mother standing at the corner bus stop. She would be shuffling her feet back and forth the way I've seen elephants do, shifting her weight from one foot to the next over and over and over. She would have something in her hand, usually a scrap of newspaper that she would be rolling and unrolling, worrying it into shreds. As she shuffled back and forth, she would lean her head back and stare at the sky. I could almost hear the nervous little chuckle that was also part of her neurotic routine.

She was in and out of the hospital. Since she wasn't judged a danger to herself or to others, she was in the hospital sporadically, and then only for brief periods. I tried to spend time with my mother at least twice a week, usually more often during those times when she was a patient. We would have lunch together on Wednesday, maybe dinner on Thursday evening. On weekends, once I started staying in Austin, we would do laundry together, or I would take her to get her hair fixed at the little beauty shop across the street from the hospital.

Like my mother, many of the other patients were in and out of the hospital sporadically for years, others were permanent residents. As usual, I was soon acquainted with everyone on the ward. One morning I was talking to Creature*, a gentle middle-aged man with long, black slick-backed hair and sideburns. His nickname had been Preacher when he first arrived—he had been a Pentecostal evangelist on the outside—but someone had misunderstood and thought his name was Creature. The name stuck. Creature no longer took the trouble to object.

"You know," he said in a conspiratorial whisper, one eyebrow cocked, "aliens from outer space are controlling my mind."

Dawn, who was standing nearby, heard Creature's comment. "And Creature, they're not doing a very good job, are they?" she said. The three of us laughed.

Creature would have been a short-timer if he had family willing to take him in. Apparently he had no one.

Often the short-timers were young people who had flipped

out from a drug overdose or who had been diagnosed as manic-depressive. People like Fred*, a hyperactive on the ward. I recognized him as a fellow student from four years earlier at the University of Houston. He had been a victim of police brutality, he told me. "I just flipped," he said, "and here I am."

I got to know Carol*, a young woman about my age. Like Dawn, like most schizophrenics, Carol had gotten sick in late adolescence. Her parents had her committed, but as far as I knew they never came to visit, even though their daughter's illness did not seem to be chronic. She was frequently able to carry on rational conversations. I liked her a lot.

One afternoon I was in the nurses' area when I heard a woman screaming. It was my friend Carol, I realized, begging Dr. Salazar not to give her such a high dosage. She hated the tremors, she sobbed over and over. I tried to go to her, but the doctor had her in a locked room.

Later that week, walking down the hall toward the laundry room, I heard a banging sound behind a door I passed. This, I knew, was the "seclusion room," though I had never seen it used. It was small, maybe eight feet by ten feet, with a metal door and a small plastic viewing panel.

I looked through the panel and, to my horror, saw Carol. She was naked. The only object in the room was a thin, gray mattress on the floor. The walls were padded, but the metal door was not.

The young woman was throwing herself against the door. *Bamm!* She would smash into the door, back up a few steps and— *Bamm!*—hit the door again. Over and over. Her face was red, and angry red welts stained her arms and shoulders. Her body glistened with sweat. The sound of flesh hitting the unyielding door was sickening. I ran down the hall to Dr. Salazar's office. "You've got to do something!" I shouted. I was in tears.

Salazar was not particularly concerned. "We gave her a heavy

Tara Elgin Holley with Joe Holley
258

injection of Thorazine, Miss Elgin," he said, shrugging his shoulders. "Everything's under control. She'll settle down in a little while." He was smiling, as usual.

The sound of my friend banging into the door, the sound of her muffled screams, stayed with me for weeks. So did the frustration. There was nothing I could do.

I met Brett*. "Do you remember me?" he asked in a soft voice one afternoon as Dawn and I sat at a table at the canteen. I looked up at the young man, about my age. He was tall, handsome in sort of an ethereal way, with blue eyes behind rimless glasses. He had silky blond hair that hung down to his shoulders. With two fingers, he constantly flicked it back.

I had seen that face, and that hair. Then I remembered. We had been at Lamar High School together. I vaguely remembered him as one of the brains who was always acing tests and winning science fairs.

Though we had hardly known each other in high school, we gradually became good friends that first semester in Austin. We talked almost every time I saw my mother.

He had gotten a scholarship to the university, and things had been going well, Brett explained. "But then, I don't know, something happened," he said, drumming his fingers on the table where we were sitting. "It got to where I just couldn't make myself do the work. I'd spend days, weeks, in my dorm room."

"Doing what?" I asked.

"I don't know," he said. "Sleeping, sitting at my desk smoking. I remember staring out the window a lot. I was diagnosed as manic-depressive. Mom and Dad would come up. We'd talk, they'd ask me what was wrong. I didn't know what to tell them. Finally, they brought me here."

The doctors said he was manic-depressive, but he felt he had it under control. He would be leaving the hospital in a couple of months, he hoped in time for school. He intended to switch majors, he said, from math to computer science. He had plans.

I was tempted to spend all my time with patients like Brett, but I tried to pay attention to the needier people as well. I got to know the patients who had physical disabilities as well as mental. I ate with people who wolfed down their food and made strange noises. I helped incontinent old ladies try to get to the bathroom on time.

I read to those who couldn't move their jaws because of the medication they were given to keep the voices and the hallucinations at bay. They would smack their lips and roll their tongues around in their mouths and then touch their lower lip with their tongue, over and over and over again. These were symptoms, I knew, of tardive dyskinesia, a side effect that some patients developed from prolonged use of antipsychotic drugs. I dreaded detecting the symptoms in my mother.

I tried to pay special attention to patients whose families had abandoned them or given up on them. There was Claire*, who looked about twelve years old, but was actually close to twenty. Like Brett, Claire was bright and attractive and possibly manic-depressive. She and her parents couldn't get along, she caused trouble at school; she ran away from home. Her parents took her to psychologists and therapists, but nothing helped. Finally, they had her committed.

Her parents hadn't abandoned her; they just didn't know how to help her. Occasionally, I would see them when they visited. Prosperous, nice-looking people, they would be sitting in the day-room, trying to carry on some sort of conversation with their child. Claire would be on downers, barely interacting.

How can people put their kids here, I wondered. How can they be so desperate? It seemed like a death sentence. Whatever the problems at home, there must be a better way to deal with them.

I thought of my own mother and how she had been only a bit older than Claire when she had gotten sick. What if she had been handled differently? Could she have been rescued?

I looked over at the small, blond girl sitting in an orange plastic chair, staring down at her hands in her lap, her mother and father trying to make small talk with her. I could see the years unfolding. I could see the visits growing less and less frequent, the girl becoming a woman, still sitting there in that orange plastic chair.

Get her out of here, I wanted to tell them. Take her home and love her.

Once I brought my kitten on the ward. The people came alive; there was no other way to describe their response. An old woman, her hairy, wrinkled face usually a blank mask, giggled as she stroked the tiny, black creature nestled in her arms. Watching the old lady toy with the kitten, I again felt the frustration with what passed for treatment here.

What we're doing is not the way to help them, I kept thinking. It's not the way to make these people well. They were people trapped in a nightmare, and we are not ingenious enough or caring enough to get them out.

Waiting for the bus after having lunch with my mother, the thought would suddenly hit me—God! I've really got it together! I'm normal. What in the world do I have to complain about? I can do anything! I didn't know whether to laugh or cry.

My mother's rehabilitation efforts continued. I met regularly with Dr. Salazar and Victor Gomez to monitor her progress. One week we might discuss her hygiene or her social skills. Like most mentally disturbed people, my mother had annoying little habits that the social workers tried to change so she could function in the real world without making people uncomfortable. Not many employers are interested in an employee who obsessively tears pieces of paper into little strips and chews them, or someone who carries around a piece of cellophane and constantly crinkles it.

I came to realize that my mother and others who are mentally disturbed have reasons for their habits, reasons that make perfect sense to them. Maybe they've made a deal with the voices that torment them. "Chew that paper for me, and I'll leave you alone," the voice might have said one night as Dawn lay sleepless in her bed. Perhaps the voice is afraid of the sound of cellophane, or the sound drowns out the voice. There are reasons, but they are not always reasonable or tolerable to the outside world.

Another week, Victor might report on Dawn's vocational aptitude—whether she worked well with her hands, whether she was good with figures. Occasionally, she would take a test—of her math skills, or her reading and writing skills.

Dawn was the child, it seemed; I was her keeper. We both found it humiliating. We would be sitting at a table in the canteen drinking coffee, with my mother's fellow patients sitting at tables around us, carrying on conversations, mumbling to themselves, indulging their strange little habits.

"I don't belong here," my mother would say, looking around the room and shaking her head. "This is not my crowd."

One afternoon after class, I walked onto the ward and didn't see her. "Anybody know where Dawn is?" I asked several people. No one did.

Slightly apprehensive, remembering her escape effort earlier in the year, I walked over to the canteen. "She was here a while ago," a man who called himself Oz* told me. "She probably

Tara Elgin Holley with Joe Holley

walked up the street to the alcoholic unit. Building Eleven. You been up there?"

The alcoholics, I knew, were short-timers. They weren't crazy, and they had more generous off-grounds privileges than the other patients. My mother had mentioned that a couple of them were her friends.

Walking up the street to Building 11, I spotted them lounging on the front steps, my mother and five men. They were smoking cigarettes, carrying on a conversation. As I walked up, my mother was talking. She was telling the men about California. She sounded just as sensible as anyone else.

"Hi, honey," she said brightly, stubbing out her cigarette on the concrete step.

"How're you doin', little girl?" one of the men greeted me. He wore khaki pants and a plaid sport shirt, and as he lounged back against the top step, his long legs reached to the sidewalk. "Dawn, you didn't tell us what a beautiful little girl you had. The name's Maurice*," he said, "but everybody calls me Slim*." He held out his big, long-fingered hand for me to shake.

"This is my beautiful daughter, Tara," my mother said proudly, her arm around my shoulders. "She's a music major at the university." My mother introduced each of her friends, and I shook their hands.

From then on, whenever I couldn't find her, I knew where to look. It was all very confusing. With her alcoholic friends, she seemed to have no symptoms. With her daughter or when she was back on the ward, she acted like a crazy person. Who was fooling whom?

In my diary that first fall in Austin, I wrote: "Here I was running around trying to straighten out her life, and with me, she acted like a sick, needy person. But with these other people, she had a different relationship."

My Mother's Keeper

If my mother was involved in some kind of charade, so was I, engaged in my own mission. I believed I had to deny the validity of her complaints. Unlike Mama, who had encouraged her rebelliousness, who took her off her medication and abetted her escapes, I was determined she would stick with the regimen. I steeled myself against her entreaties.

"Honey, can't you get me out of here?" she would beg. "It's so horrible here."

I would not concede it was so, though I knew as well as she did that it was horrible. Sitting at the dining table with her, I would look down at the starchy, unimaginative food plopped on plastic trays, at the imitation mashed potatoes, the dry gray patty of ground meat.

"Mmm, it looks good today, doesn't it?" I would say. I could hear myself. I sounded as if I were speaking to a three-year-old who wouldn't eat her spinach. All around us, patients played with their food or drooled and slobbered. Some could not handle a knife and fork, so they shoveled in the food with their hands or waited for an aide to help them. Some let it dribble into their laps. Others were so dejected they ate little or nothing; they just sat and stared.

My mother wasn't fooled by my forced enthusiasm. "Here, honey," she would say, "why don't you have these mashed potatoes?" She would pick up her tray and start to slide the heavy mound onto my tray. I could feel my mouth twisting into a smile.

On other occasions, she would show me the clothes she had picked out at the hospital clothes closet—cast-off items donated by churches and charitable organizations. "That's a nice color," I would say, desperately searching for something positive to say about the tired, faded, mismatched articles she had chosen. The stylish young woman she had been twenty-five years earlier, the well-groomed woman with impeccable taste, would flash through my mind.

We were engaged in a farce, and at one level or another, we both knew it. I felt compelled to deny the cruel fact that my mother had lost twenty-five years of her life. As for Dawn, I couldn't say with certainty what she understood. Were her pretenses a desperate effort to please me? Were they a way to get what she wanted by pretending to play the game that I seemed to be playing? I never knew for sure.

So I would say, "Mmm, it looks good today!"—isn't that what parents say?—but all the while I was thinking, That meal is revolting. It's horrible. It's crazy. If I had to live this way, I would not want to live. I could not bear the thought that my mother would go on living without ever again enjoying the warmth of friends, the arms of a gentle man holding her, long hours of reading her beloved Shakespeare, the ecstasy of music, the beauty of dawn itself. I could not bear it.

At lunch one day, I looked around for my friend Brett

"I'm sorry to have to tell you this," Victor Gomez explained. He took a deep breath and looked at the wall behind me. "But Saturday night, we missed him; I thought maybe he had left the grounds. But then one of the orderlies went into the laundry room. And there he was. He had tied a couple of sheets together and tossed them over the water pipes near the ceiling. We were too late."

Victor rubbed his eyes with his hands. "Tara," he said, "he was going home in a week or so. It happens. Just when they're doing better, getting ready to leave. I just don't know."

I worried about my mother doing something desperate. She had tried, on more than one occasion. Yet, despite her grumbling and her discontent, she seemed to be making progress. Maybe it was part of our mutual charade, but as the days passed into weeks, she was talking more sensibly, and she had put aside many of her annoying little habits. She seemed to be putting more of an effort into her appearance, her hygiene. She was even following the rules.

"It won't be long," Victor would say every week or so. "We'll get her into Transitional Services, and she'll be in a board-and-care before you know it."

I hung on his every word, listening for the vaguest sliver of encouragement. Surely I was being proved right—that all it took was someone willing to take the time to set her on the right track, to make sure she took her medication, to love her.

In October, Victor announced that my mother was ready for a job on the hospital grounds. She would work behind the desk in the arts and crafts room, checking off names and checking out equipment. She smiled when Victor called her in to his office to give her the good news. She would be making fifty cents an hour, enough to have a little spending money for cigarettes. Maybe she could even save a little for when she got out.

On those days that I strolled into the activity center and saw her behind the counter, interacting with her "customers," I felt a great rush of pride—pride mixed with hope. It was a sign. A sign that my plan was working. It was agonizingly slow, but she was coming back. As long as she stayed on her medication, she really could make progress. All the effort was worth it.

"Oh, honey, I really am trying," she would say. "I know this is important to you. I really want to do well. I want to have my own apartment. And I would love to have a real job."

Then she would slip. "Had a little trouble with Dawn this week," Victor would say. He would be sitting at his desk consulting my mother's chart.

Tara Elgin Holley with Joe Holley

266

"Three mornings this week we couldn't get her out of bed," he would read. "And when we get her to go to class, she's disruptive. Doesn't care a thing about it. Just sits there, refuses to participate."

Like a concerned parent called in for a conference with the principal, I would be upset. I would sit at Victor's desk fuming, so many angry little lectures in my mind competing to get out. After the first half-dozen occasions, my lecture got to be a litany: "We know you don't want to be here. And that's fine. We don't want you to be here. But the only way you can leave is to prove to us that you can be responsible. You have to show us that you can take care of yourself. That's not an unreasonable request, is it?"

My mother, sitting quietly in a chair, head down, her hands in her lap, would nod. "No, that's not unreasonable," she would murmur.

"Why don't we draw up a contract?" Victor would suggest. "Dawn, see how this sounds," he would say. "If you agree to get up on time every morning for a week, if you agree to do your chores, take your baths when you're supposed to and get to work on time, we will agree to increase your cigarette allowance from one pack a week to two. And if you can stay on the routine for a month, we'll increase your off-campus privileges. Is that a deal?"

My mother would listen politely and nod her head. Victor would write out the contractual agreement on a piece of notebook paper. He and my mother would sign their names. And for a while, she would be on track.

Whatever problems my mother had adjusting to life on the ward, the two of us had music to share. At least once a week, I would sing for her the songs I was working on for my classes.

Invariably, she was familiar with the composer and usually with the song itself. Often, the piece that I had spent hours learning, she would know by heart. Music was still a part of her life.

She sang too, maybe a piece from her old jazz repertoire or a pop song she had heard on the radio that week. Listening to her sing as she accompanied herself on the tinny piano in the rec room, I would try to analyze her gift.

She responded viscerally to music, it seemed, even though she had studied music since childhood. Mama had her playing violin and piano before she was old enough to go to school. She read music almost before she read words. She played in the school orchestra in high school. She had studied with voice teachers, taken classes at UCLA.

Yet, the training wasn't the source of her musical gift. It was something natural, something intuitive that set her apart from those musicians who had *only* the craft. It was what set Sinatra apart from other good singers, Hemingway from writers who were merely talented. She sang, and the words took flight. Riding on a wave of rhythm and feeling, set free from the structure of the music, the lyrics swooped and soared and celebrated. What my mother had, even after she had lost everything else, was this gift.

She may have bequeathed the gift to her child, and yet it wasn't the same. I wasn't as free and easy in my music-making as my mother was. Auntie may have had something to do with it.

To Auntie, Dawn's musical gift was something mysterious and disturbing, something magical, something from deep inside that ought to be kept under control. But Dawn didn't keep it under control; she welcomed it, encouraged it, embraced it. As far as Auntie was concerned, that eagerness to embrace the magic may have had something to do with her illness.

Auntie was determined that I would not be seduced by the dangerous gift my mother had bequeathed me. It was acceptable that I would be a singer, but only if I sang classical music, like a good little girl, like Daisy Elgin, Papa's Houston cousin. Daisy had sung at Carnegie Hall; she was regularly written up in the society pages of the *Houston Chronicle*. That was the kind of career little Tara would have.

Certainly I would not sing jazz. I would not hang out in smoky bars, with boozing, disreputable people. I would not sing in clubs. I would not pursue the illicit, the enticing, the dangerous. Auntie sensed that Dawn's music, her rhythms, came from the gut, the thighs, the belly. That earthiness would never do for me.

My mother was aware of the distinction between these two particular kinds of music—classical and jazz, popular and formal. She was both in awe of her classically trained daughter and, it seemed to me, slightly scornful. Music had to be felt, not understood. Music had to come from the heart, not the head. Studying so hard in school, I ran the risk of denying the heart.

Most of the time, though, singing for my mother at the hospital, I felt only her joy. I would hurry onto the ward, music books in my arms, and we would stroll over to the rec room.

"Let me sing my jury song for you," I would say. "This is the Schumann piece I was telling you about."

"Oh, I'd love to hear it!" my mother would say.

I can transport myself back to those afternoons in the rec room. I can see myself position the songbook before me and scan the text. I glance at my mother and begin to sing. It is one of those days when my breathing is natural, the diction precise. My voice seems to soar so easily. Everything is working, and I am transported by the music that is such a part of me. My mother listens intently. She is mouthing the words as I sing them. Others in the room stop what they are doing to listen.

The last note fades with the hint of an echo. The people in the room start to applaud. "God, honey, that's beautiful!" Dawn

My Mother's Keeper

murmurs. "I can't believe that's my very own daughter singing like that!"

I felt so happy. Only in our music-making, I realized years later, were we functioning as mother and daughter. I wasn't trying to fix my mother; I was offering what any daughter would offer—myself and a gift we both loved. For her part, my mother wasn't being needy. She was giving her daughter the approval I needed.

I couldn't hold on to the happiness, though. It would give way to sadness. Was I stealing from her? I could sing, because of my mother. I could pursue a musical career, because of my mother. Meanwhile, my mother, the truly talented one, could have neither. Somehow, my own success tore at the heart of my mother's loss.

I would try to visualize myself standing before an audience singing the pieces I had known all my life, and the person I would visualize was Dawn. Though my feelings didn't make sense, they fed the guilt I felt.

One night, after singing for her, I tried to record in my journal how I felt: "I am very proud, and I desperately want my mother's approval. But I also feel guilty. This is *her* life, and I'm taking it away. I've already taken everything else. I have my health, my family. Now I'm taking her music. I can't do it. I feel blocked. I've left her with nothing."

Tara Elgin Holley with Joe Holley

CHAPTER THIRTEEN

It is the spring of 1975, 9:55 in the morning, and I am dodging through the crowds along the Drag, trying to get to class on time. Clothes and hair smelling of bacon grease, I have just finished up my four-hour breakfast shift at Hamburgers by Gourmet.

I was always rushing that year. I'd get home from school in the afternoon, change clothes, and immediately hop on my bike and ride to Steak Island, a couple of miles from my apartment. At Steak Island, I would change into my hostess gown, smile and seat customers until closing time at eleven, spend an hour balancing cash-register receipts, and then bike back home through the dark streets of Austin. For some reason, I had moved into an apartment at the top of a steep hill. I may have been exhausted much of the time, but at least I was thin and fit. At five the next morning, I'd stagger out of bed and bike to Hamburgers by Gourmet to start the breakfast prep.

During the first part of the school year, I was still spending much of every weekend with my mother; I'd usually take her out on a pass, and she would spend the weekend at my apartment.

With a full schedule of classes, I had to work in voice and piano practice whenever I could.

On one particular morning that spring, Dr. Epstein fell into step beside me. Jeremiah Epstein was my cultural anthropology professor, and since it was his class I was rushing to get to, I could slow down and enjoy the conversation.

We had become friends over the course of the semester. At lunchtime on warm days, we occasionally drove over to the old state cemetery with its Civil War tombstones and monuments to Texas heroes, and we would sit on the soft grass and talk or have a picnic. I confessed to having spent a lot of time in cemeteries as a child.

A wiry, white-haired man with children my age, Dr. Epstein was just a friend, nothing more. We enjoyed each other's company. He was an amateur sculptor, he had lived in France where he studied the cave paintings at Lascaux, and he loved music; we had a lot to talk about. He was interested in how I had made my way in the red-light district of Rotterdam, during my nights bartending at the Rhodos Bar. He thought the experience might make a good research topic.

His mother, he told me, had been a circus performer, so he had lived a vagabond existence as a child. I never told him about my mother.

On the Drag that morning, I was asking him about a paper due later in the week when I noticed my mother coming toward us. She had been out of the hospital and on the street for months ("not a danger to herself or others"). People on the crowded sidewalk parted to let her pass. A few stopped and stared. As she got closer, I could smell her urine-soaked clothes. Just as I had with my friend Hallie Welborn on the streets of the Village years before, I panicked. I simply could not face my mother. Making some flimsy excuse to Dr. Epstein about having to go to the Co-Op, I ducked into the store before she noticed me. I'd get flustered every time it happened; I'm sure people wondered about me.

I stood in the doorway and watched as she shuffled slowly past, talking to herself all the while. She wore stained polyester pants, a torn flannel shirt, a ragged brown misbuttoned sweater, and some kind of beat-up baseball cap. I noticed her fingernails. They were bitten off to the quick; blood had dried around the cuticles. As she passed where I was standing without noticing me, I dashed across the street to class.

My mother's latest decline had begun soon after the move into Windsor House*, the halfway house that Victor Gomez had helped me locate when we thought she was doing so well, when we both had such high hopes. She was still on her medication, still working at Goodwill Industries—a job Victor had arranged for her—and still checking in regularly at the hospital for outpatient care. I was as optimistic as I had been in the twenty years or so I had been trying to rehabilitate my mother.

Windsor House was a two-story frame house in a pleasant residential neighborhood not far from the university. It was clean enough, and the meals were decent, but after my mother had been there several weeks, I began to sense something strange and unsettling about the place. It wasn't the fact that mentally ill people lived at Windsor House. I had been around mental patients and the mentally ill my whole adult life, so I certainly wasn't bothered by their presence. I couldn't put my finger on it, but for some reason, the people at Windsor House didn't seem settled or comfortable. Heads down, they moved from room to room restlessly, like animals in a cage. When they spoke to anyone, they stared at the floor.

I gradually came to realize that they were afraid of Mabel

Bolton*, the proprietor. Mrs. Bolton, a former nurse, was a small, heavyset woman, probably in her early sixties, who rarely stirred from a worn, overstuffed chair in the parlor at Windsor House. She must have suffered from arthritis; her hands were twisted. From that threadbare old chair, she ruled the house like a potentate. I don't think she physically abused her tenants, but she certainly had them emotionally cowed.

Mrs. Bolton had an assistant named Virgil* who slavishly did her bidding. Virgil was the house manager, but it didn't take me long to see that he was as troubled as my mother was. Tall and pale, with a high forehead, either mildly retarded or heavily sedated, he reminded me of Lurch from the Addams family.

The residents may have been disturbed, but they weren't too disturbed to know that Mrs. Bolton could send them back to the hospital on a whim. She often reminded them of that fact.

My mother had quit her job at Goodwill Industries. She said it drove her crazy to clean electrical cords all day long. It would have driven me crazy. Fortunately, the hospital had helped her find another job with the Flower People of Austin, a business run by Gabe and Joy, two former hippies who were husband and wife. They had come to the university from somewhere in the Midwest and had stayed on. They hired recovering alcoholics and the mentally ill to sell flowers on street corners around town.

Gabe and Joy were saints. They cared about their employees, looked after them. Dawn thought they were great. "I just love being outside," my mother told me more than once. "I love talking to people and the flowers smell so good. It's just the perfect job."

Several days a week, she'd stop by my house on the way back to her room at Mrs. Bolton's. Just to talk, she said. She had sold her quota of flowers for the day, she had a little money in her pocket, and she was happy. I was happy to see her—until she started shuffling her feet and rocking back and forth, probably because of the medication. It drove me nuts to see her act like a crazy person. "Stop it!" I would yell, and she would duck her head like a naughty child.

Once, Betty Lee, Sally, and Sister were visiting. We had made a doctor's appointment for my mother, so my aunts and I went to her street corner to pick her up. "But I can't just leave," she reminded us. "I can't leave my flowers."

My aunts looked down at their hands, stared out the car window, and waited for someone to break down and volunteer to do what had to be done. My mother watched them with a smile on her face. Finally, Betty Lee, fashionably dressed and striking as always, climbed out of the car. She tied the money apron around her Neiman Marcus frock, took Dawn's bouquet of roses, and glanced up at the red light that would stop her potential customers. Dawn climbed into the car, and the four of us drove away, giggling at the sight of elegant Dr. Elgin peddling flowers on an Austin street corner.

I talked to Joy or Gabe every few weeks to see how my mother was doing. Sometimes before school, I would ride over to the flower warehouse to see her before she and the other vendors were loaded onto wonderfully intoxicating, flower-filled vans and dropped at street corners around town.

The only trouble Dawn had gotten into was minor. Something, or someone, prompted her to attend to her filthy clothes, so she walked into a Laundromat, stripped off everything, and tossed it all into a washer. While she stood there in the nude waiting for her clothes to wash, someone called the police. The police called the flower people, who called me, and I drove downtown to the police station. A medical staff person had identified her as mentally disturbed, so the police had no intention of filing charges. They were willing to release her into my custody.

Dawn began telling me that Mrs. Bolton was taking her

money. The flower people began telling me that Dawn was taking *their* money. For months, she had been one of their most conscientious salespeople, but suddenly she seemed confused about how much she had sold and how much money she had made.

Mrs. Bolton began threatening to send Dawn back to the hospital. "People who live in my house contribute to their upkeep," Mrs. Bolton told my mother. "If you can't contribute, we'll just have to send you back."

"But Mommy," I would say, "she's getting your Social Security check at the first of every month. She gets all of it. You don't owe her anything."

It was hard for Dawn and the other tenants to understand. Mrs. Bolton was the woman who fed them, who provided them with a clean place to sleep, and a roof over their heads. Didn't they owe her their measly allowances?

Mrs. Bolton always denied to me that she asked for their money. She would tell me, "I'm concerned about Dawn. She is not really up to the level of the other people here. We have to work with her much more than we have time for. I'm just not sure she's ready for a halfway-house arrangement."

I couldn't understand what she was complaining about; several of the residents were worse off than my mother. Since I didn't want to jeopardize my mother's situation, I tried not to make trouble. I assured Mrs. Bolton my mother would "try harder." Despite the sarcasm she couldn't help hearing in my voice, she agreed to let Dawn stay, but not in the main house. She moved her to a ramshackle little cottage out back. It was dirty, and no one was around to supervise her medication. Because of her late hours selling flowers, she often missed meals. But at least it was better than the street.

I woke up one morning several months later and read in the newspaper that Mrs. Bolton had been arrested. She had been embezzling money from the state and from the residents of Windsor House. Thousands of dollars in small bills were found in and around the chair she always sat in. Windsor House was closed. Like birds flushed from a nest, the frightened, helpless residents scattered, most to the streets.

Dawn fled one afternoon shortly after we got the notice that Windsor House was closing. Despite her addled state, she was determined not to go back to the hospital. Though I could hardly blame her, I wanted her in the hospital. I thought she belonged there. These were the days of deinstitutionalization, however. All over the country, mental hospitals were being emptied, their staffs cut—all in the name of civil rights for the mentally ill. Courts were ruling that the ravings and mumblings of people like my mother were constitutionally protected free speech.

I certainly believed the mentally ill had rights, but many of them, including my mother, were simply not capable of making rational decisions about what was best for them. It would be like entrusting a five-year-old with basic life decisions.

The plan throughout the 1960s and '70s was to replace large state hospitals with small, community-based facilities—halfway houses, drop-in clinics, foster homes, community psychiatric centers. With new drugs and drug therapies available, the mentally ill could reenter society.

It was a great idea, a humane idea, but many states, including Texas, never got around to funding the community-based facilities. Low-income housing programs disappeared. It was a cruel joke that both Washington and Austin played on people like my mother. They emptied out the hospitals and consigned the patients to the streets. My mother was one of them.

I investigated other living arrangements for her. While I

looked for something permanent, I paid rent for her weekly at the Bluebonnet Courts across the street from the mental hospital.

The Bluebonnet was originally a tourist court, one of several seedy little dumps that had been built in the 1930s on what was then the main highway through Austin. Tiny rooms with kitchenettes, each unit separated by a carport built for Model Ts, they were clean enough and adequate for my mother, who was rarely there.

To walk along the gravel area separating the two rows of cabins was like walking into a bizarre twilight zone inhabited by people the world had left behind. They were transients, down-on-their-luck alcoholics, sad-faced single women without teeth, hospital outpatients. I would see them sitting at metal picnic tables, smoking and drinking beer late into the night by the light of a naked bulb over the door of one of the cabins. The world had washed them up on a desolate shore, and they had been left behind in these sad little cells.

I was mildly surprised that the people behind the desk, who were about as down-at-the-heels as their tenants, never hesitated to rent a room to my mother. I always told them she was an outpatient from the hospital across the street and that I needed a place for her to stay while I looked for a long-term housing arrangement for her. As long as I paid her bill, they didn't care who the two of us were, but I always felt as if they wondered about the earnest college kid with the long, dark hair, the gold hoop earrings, and the stylish clothes. What did she have to do with the befuddled bag lady?

For me the juxtaposition of our very different lives would throw me into bouts of depression and long crying spells. It was wrong. It was confusing, and I felt helpless to change things, even though I continued to try. I felt as if I was doing everything I could, and it wasn't good enough.

Tara Elgin Holley with Joe Holley

I would pay for two weeks and then go by to check on my mother. The room would be filthy, but she wouldn't be there. "Seen Dawn?" I'd ask the people sitting at the picnic table. "Haven't seen her in about a week," they would say. She preferred the street.

Sometimes I wouldn't see her for several weeks, though I could sometimes track her down through Gabe and Joy, the flower people. I never knew exactly where she spent her nights. In my own warm, comfortable apartment, I lay awake wondering where she could be at that very moment. It was torture to lie there and wonder. I would think about getting up, throwing on some clothes, and wandering out into the dark to look for her. But what could I do if I found her—that night and the next night and all the nights to come?

From not seeing my mother for weeks, I would go to seeing her daily. For long stretches, I would track her down wherever she was, either in the tourist court or on the street, just to make sure she took her medication. Usually, I would have to watch her swallow the tablet, because I knew she would smile sweetly, then try to cheek it, and spit it out as soon as I turned my back.

This is what it had come to. After all we had been through together over the past couple of years, after the hospitalization and the therapy and the effort to impose a routine, after all the weekends we had spent together, all the efforts to find a half-way house that would accept her, after all my pathetic obsessive efforts to rescue her, and after all the hope and the hard-won signs of progress, my mother had decided that she preferred the street.

Decided, I suppose, is not the word. Maybe I should say that she had succumbed to the street. She spent her days wandering the crowded sidewalks, with no place to rest, no place to get in out of the weather, at the mercy of muggers or cruel, uncaring passersby or the police. Roaming is common among the severely mentally ill. I don't know why.

She spent her nights curled up on a flattened cardboard box behind a trash bin or beneath a railroad bridge near downtown. Her skin toughened, her hair became straw, she wore every article of clothing she owned. This life—unimaginable to most of us, unimaginable to the person she had been—was the life she now preferred. The street, with its dirt and danger, was preferable to the death-in-life of a mental hospital or the routine and responsibilities of a halfway house. My mother was a street person.

Dozens of other street people made the Drag their home. They lay sprawled on the sidewalk, they panhandled, they sat in entryways and talked among themselves. They're not "socialized"; that's the biggest problem with them, a friend once remarked. I had never thought of it like that. The problem with them, it seemed to me, is that they are very sick. Nor do we know what to do with them. The administration in Washington at the time didn't even want to acknowledge their existence.

Of all the street people on the Drag, my mother was the most grotesque. The multiple layers of clothes she wore were filthy. She walked stooped over, with little, mincing steps, usually mumbling to herself. Her lank, stringy hair stuck to her head. During the long, hot Austin summers, her face, already reddened and rough from the sun and wind, blistered deeply. She would pick the scabs off her blistered nose, and her skin would bleed. As the dry prose of the medical records noted: "She is able to take care of herself to a minimum degree when she is on her medication; however, when she gets off of her medication, she becomes confused, bizarre, she dresses herself in Laundromats, she sleeps in Laundromats."

Her antics made her stand out. Stationing herself across the

Tara Elgin Holley with Joe Holley

street from the crowded main entrance to the university, she would pace back and forth talking to herself, waving her arms and laughing every now and then. Some days, I would look at her from across the street, and she would be wearing a bra over her blouse. With thousands of students making their way to and from class, waiting for buses, shopping, or just hanging out on the Drag, my mother always had an audience.

Maybe that's why she had chosen the Drag. It was her stage. Some people who saw her every day called her the Princess, because the Drag seemed to be her kingdom. The Stinky Lady, a local poet called her, "in her urine-stained polyester pants." Others called her Piss Lady.

Maybe she was on the Drag because all the noise and activity in the area helped to drown out the voices in her head. Since she refused to take her medicine, the voices must have been loud and insistent.

Perhaps, as a psychologist friend once suggested, she liked to imagine herself being a college student. As soon as he said it, I remembered sensing my mother's envy about my own classes, about my college life in general. I remembered that she had studied jazz piano and harmony at UCLA, just as her career was taking off; maybe that's where her mind was.

My mother had a right to be on the Drag, of course. The only problem was that the Drag was my place, too. I was making a life for myself at the university, but hardly a day passed that I didn't run into her. Once, on a busy morning at Hamburgers by Gourmet, I looked up from preparing breakfast and there she was in line. I smelled her before I saw her. It was startling, upsetting, and so very depressing.

I lived in dread of being exposed, of someone finding out that the strange woman on the street corner was my mother. I don't know what I thought might happen, but to me it seemed my world would fall apart if a boyfriend or a professor or someone I cared about found out about my mother.

Then there would be times when I would say to myself, To hell with what they think. I'd walk down the street defiantly, my arm around my mother, leaning in to her to ask if she needed money, to ask where she was sleeping, whether she was getting enough to eat. Other women I knew had mothers who called on the weekends, wrote letters, sent boxes of cookies. My mother was mentally ill. My mother was crazy. Acting as if I didn't care what everyone else thought gave me strength and helped me ignore the pain.

On the street, the odor of urine and filth always preceded her. It was noticeable half a block away. Shop owners regularly called the police to have her removed from the sidewalk in front of their businesses; she was keeping customers away, they complained. Whenever we met, I would try to steel myself against the smell; after a while, I got to where I didn't really notice it. Breathe through your mouth, I'd remind myself.

How can this be, I'd ask myself over and over. Riding my bike to work at night, smiling at Steak Island customers, doing my vocal exercises in the practice room, lying in my bed late at night unable to sleep despite my exhaustion, I would torture myself with questions. The rawness of it all, the demand that I be sensitive, aware of what my mother was experiencing, then and there, was at times unbearable. There was no running away. It was like a wound that demands your attention. It made me feel weak, vulnerable, spent, sometimes even nauseated. Why me, I wondered. Why me?

One afternoon, at a time my mother was in the hospital for a fourteen-day commitment, I decided to take a break and see the latest Bergman movie, *Cries and Whispers,* at the Varsity Theater on the Drag. I had been looking forward to it. I went alone. In my youthful and impressionable state and with my tendency to interpret film literally, *Cries and Whispers* seemed to make a clear statement about our family relations regarding my mother. Like the ill sister in the film, she was outcast and unacceptable. Until these three sisters acknowledged their sister—what she had been, what they had shared—she would continue to decay in the back bedroom. She would not die, she would not go away. She reminded them of their own inability to be whole. In fact, in their attempts to live out their lives in denial of her, they each suffered differently. Their desperately ill sister represented not only their past together but a time of hope and intimacy that the four of them had experienced with one another.

I was shaken by the movie. As soon as it was over, I walked out into the gathering darkness and hurried up Guadalupe Street to the hospital. "Are you all right?" an attendant asked, noticing my red eyes.

"I just want to see Dawn," I said.

I was doing good work, intense and satisfying work, but I could not let go and give myself to it. I would be busy, active, involved, and suddenly the image of my mother on the street would assault me. It was no easier for me to ignore my obsessive thoughts than it was for my mother to ignore her insistent voices. How can this be my mother? How can it be that my mother lives on the street?

Is this what our society's shame does to sick people? I wondered. We treat them the way people afflicted with leprosy have been treated down through the centuries. They are outcasts, because they frighten us. We must keep our distance. We seem to have this need for "the other"—those poor unfortunates who carry our shame, our guilt, our fears. They are our scapegoats. My mother, the woman who had brought me into this world, who had given me life, was one of them.

I tried to make sense of my mother's fate and mine, but no theory ever seemed plausible. My aunts had their theories about their sister's plight:

It was her drinking just before I was born.
It was her pregnancy. (They meant me, of course.)
It was her high-strung nature.
It was her artistic temperament.
It was Mama and Papa and their neglect.
Something just snapped.

Since all the theories fell short, since nothing seemed to make sense, I reverted to doing what I had been doing for most of my life—trying to concoct yet another plan that might combat the horror of my mother's life.

My own life, despite my penchant for overload, was going relatively well. I had a new job, waitressing in a pre–New Age place where my mother would have been right at home, even accepted, had she ever wandered in. It was a vegetarian restaurant near campus called A Movable Feast: Natural Food Restaurant*, and it was run by two brothers in their mid-twenties who had drifted into Austin from Hollywood. They called themselves Christian* and Poseidon*, and they were members of a Topanga Canyon commune called the Brotherhood of the Source.

The commune allegedly adhered to the teachings of Gurdjieff, although it was difficult to discern any core beliefs beyond peace, love, and vegetarianism in Christian and Poseidon or in several of their Austin cousins who helped run the restaurant. Christian, a tall, blond California surfer type, occasionally mentioned that all the women in the Brotherhood gladly slept with the cult leader as part of their discipline. He himself, Christian modestly claimed, had learned from the leader at least fifty ways to please a woman. His wife back in California, the daughter of one of the stars of the TV show *I Dream of Jeannie*, never came to Austin to testify to her husband's talents, although Christian was ever eager to share them with Austin girls, particularly at the end of the evening shift when we were all encouraged to stay after work for massages, back-walking, and religious instruction.

It was Christian, I think, who decided that my friend Andy, one of the waiters, had to have a more exotic name, so Andy became Siddhartha. My friend Sherie became Haze, as in Purple Haze. Tara was exotic enough, as was Marie, the name of another waitress who had just moved to Austin from Hawaii, where she had slept on banana leaves and watched UFOs fly in and out of a volcano.

Tall, muscular Poseidon was, shall I say, less cerebral than his brother. A former state wrestling champion in California, he had been a black belt karate instructor for the cult. He seemed more interested in the other family venture, a car-towing business that made thousands of dollars a year removing cars from the lot next door and collecting impoundment fees.

My friend Cas, who's now a physicist, was also a waiter at A Movable Feast. He remembers several occasions when diners would happen to glance out the window and see their car drifting by on the tail end of a truck. The no-parking sign was deliberately obscure. The lucrative scam worked, Cas reminded me recently, until a tow-truck driver made the mistake of hauling off the mayor's car.

Despite the goofy management, the food was good, and the

restaurant soon began to attract an interesting university clientele. I enjoyed the place; it was a respite from the pressures of my life. Each day after class, I'd slip into my filmy muslin belly-dancer pants and my bikini top and short jacket and serve up the house specialty—a hearty peasant's meal of vegetable soup, salad, and thick sandwich topped with bean sprouts, and a choice of fruit smoothies. Although I lost track of Christian and Poseidon as soon as possible after leaving the restaurant, I made lifelong friendships among my fellow waitpeople.

I was also singing with a couple of Renaissance and medieval groups and doing some solo work. I was becoming a good student again, though I had a hard time being consistent and an even harder time juggling work, school, my mother's needs, and my own mental and emotional well-being. I would make D's and A's in the same semester because I couldn't keep my focus on so many things at once.

My mother was on my mind, even when I didn't realize it. I went through musical infatuations with one composer after another, and invariably my composer of the moment was one who had suffered some tragedy. We would be discussing Mahler, and I would focus on his hauntingly beautiful *Kindertotenlieder*, a song cycle written in memory of two of his children, who had died young.

A professor would be discussing Schumann, my hero at the time, and I would feel compelled to raise my hand and recall for the class that Schumann suffered from syphilis, and that his brain had been ravaged by the copper treatment that was standard for the time. Schumann's mind, I would mention, finally snapped in 1854, when, on the night of February 10, he could not sleep because of an insistent high A that sounded in his inner ear. The sound tortured him for a week until it at last resolved itself into a lovely melody. He tried to write down the melody, the sound of angels singing to him, but the sound became the voices of howling demons. Confined to an institution, Schumann lingered for two years before death itself set him free.

My obsession with my mother affected my other classes as well. To satisfy my science requirement, I took courses on the brain. I couldn't read enough Jean Genet, and for German class, I would sit for hours beside a flowing outdoor fountain reading Kafka. In art history, I wrote papers on Edvard Munch's mental demise and on Van Gogh's tortured family relationships. I never missed a Bergman movie at the student union.

I also discovered the *Mignon Lieder*, a set of songs based on poetry by Goethe and set to music by a handful of classical and romantic composers including Beethoven, Liszt, and Wolf as well as Schumann and Schubert. Mignon was a changeling, an other-worldly lost child in search of her father, who is forced to become attached to a group of traveling circus-like acrobats. She is not aware that she is the result of an incestuous union between a brother and sister who knew nothing about their own origins. After their blood relationship was revealed, her mother left her to be raised by strangers. She is not long for this world and longs to go to another place, whether it be her unknown homeland or simply a death wish. This music and poetry continued to haunt me and to evoke many dreams. It imbedded inself into my daily life and I couldn't get to the core of the grip it had on me.

I was unaware of my morbid streak. Didn't all twenty-somethings feel a certain fascination with tragedy and the romance of death? Finally, a voice teacher demanded that I bring in vocal music in a major key. "Enough of the minor," she said. "Bring me Mozart! Bring me Bach!"

Another music teacher, Ken Jacobs, saved my life. I was probably at the point of physical and emotional exhaustion, and his theory and harmony class was giving me fits. We were studying complicated twentieth-century rhythms, and I just couldn't get it. I was failing the course. Finally, he called me into his office.

"What's the matter?" he asked. "You're one of the brightest, most unique students in the class. You're not afraid of hard work, so why can't you get this?"

The kindness of this tall, slender man with glasses and disheveled brown hair disarmed me. He was twenty-eight that year and working on his Ph.D. in composition. His wife was pregnant, and he was always telling us how the pregnancy was going. He was a wonderful teacher, with an enthusiasm for new music. Sometimes he would get choked up about the music he was introducing us to, and he would be hurt if we didn't share his enthusiasm. "Listen, open your ears!" he was always telling us. I was indiscriminate; I loved everything he so eagerly shared with us.

Sitting in his office that morning, I began to cry and to spill out my tale of woe—taking eighteen credits, holding down two jobs, trying to look after my mother. Neither he nor anyone else in the music department knew about my mother. I sat there in his office and told him everything.

It came in a rush, and suddenly I was embarrassed about my tears and my hard luck story. I didn't want him to think I was feeling sorry for myself.

He sat there looking at me, slowly shaking his head. I noticed that his eyes were red, and my own tears began to flow again.

"I can't believe you've gone through this whole year without telling anyone," he said. "I don't understand why you didn't let some of us know. We get together and talk about our students all the time. I know we could have helped."

I couldn't explain why I had never told him. I couldn't really explain it to myself. On some level, after all these years, I still must have believed that if people knew my secret they would reject me the way people rejected my mother. They would think

Tara Elgin Holley with Joe Holley

288

I was crazy, too. Or they would say to themselves, Oh, that explains why she's so strange.

"I'll tell you one thing," Ken Jacobs said, smiling. He leaned across the desk and shook his finger at me. "You're not going to fail this class; I'm not going to let you. I'm going to meet you here at seven-thirty every morning of the week until you get it."

He kept his promise, and one morning, a few weeks later, it happened. These particular musical problems that had tormented me for so long were finally tamed. Asymmetrical rhythms never seemed threatening again.

I found yet another boarding house for my mother. Hampton House, it was called, a two-story frame residence down the street from the Bluebonnet Courts and across the street from the hospital. The house was probably a century old and had been tastefully restored.

I leased a room for her by the month. It was a nice room at the front of the house, light and airy, with access to the second-story front porch. Dawn said she liked it, and as I walked down the stairs and out the front door, I could feel the weight of worry lift. If she insisted on spending her days on the street, at least she should have a roof over her head at night and a bed to sleep in.

We met weekly, either at the house or at the corner where she was still selling flowers. Our meetings always were awkward. I was the mother, demanding that she take her medicine, that she take care of her bleeding nose or a cut on her hand, insisting that she tell me when she had last eaten. Although now past forty, she was the recalcitrant child, shifting her weight from one foot to the other, fidgeting, singing snatches of tunes she had heard somewhere. "What's it all about, Alfie?" she would croon, cocking her head and smiling at the end of the phrase, as if waiting for an answer to the musical question. She would break into "If You Could Read My Mind," the Gordon Lightfoot piece. Or she would do her Ethel Merman rendition of "Hooray for Hollywood!" and that would prompt a stream-of-consciousness parade of *Gone With the Wind*, Humphrey Bogart, Betty Grable, Cornel Wilde, and Darryl Zanuck mementos out of her threadbare Hollywood grab bag. "Humphrey Bogart, now there's a father for you," she once said. "I liked him a whole lot."

Our encounters continued to be a strain on both of us, but they allowed me to keep track of my mother. I knew about it when her small suitcase full of all the clothes she owned was stolen. I knew when someone stole her money, which happened fairly often. I knew when the bus driver stood in the door with his arms folded, shaking his head, when she tried to board; he and his passengers could not tolerate her odor.

Like a parent, I felt I could at least have some effect, however small, on her life, but I was reluctantly beginning to realize that I couldn't do everything. I wanted to be able to seek her out and try to help, and then withdraw. It was when she began turning up unexpectedly in my life that I began to feel vulnerable and unsettled.

All schizophrenics go through cycles. A few months after moving into Hampton House, my mother began moving into a period of deterioration. She was off her medication, which only made things worse. She was detached from her body; she was unaware when she wet herself. She never bathed or changed her clothes, and eating meant consuming a few candy bars to still the pangs of an empty stomach. She was losing weight rapidly.

She had lost her job with the flower people. Gabe was apologetic and kept her employed probably longer than anyone should have expected. "I wish I could keep her," he told me, "but

Tara Elgin Holley with Joe Holley
290

I can never tell what she's going to do. I hate to say it, but people won't buy from her. They're repelled by her."

She would take the twenty-dollar bills I gave her, and go to pawn shops and buy transistor radios or watches or jewelry. Then she would make deals with other street people.

She seemed happy, even euphoric. She was elated when the world allowed her to just be crazy. But I couldn't let her just be crazy. One cold, rainy December night when she was especially euphoric, I decided I had to do something. I called the state hospital and talked to the social worker who was assigned to my mother, but the social worker refused to recommend commitment. She knew my mother was gentle, docile, wouldn't hurt a flea. "And she's just not a danger to herself," the social worker said, "even if we don't approve of the choices she makes."

The next day, I set up an appointment at an outpatient clinic, borrowed a friend's car—I had only a bike—and went out to collect my mother. The clinic would prescribe Prolixin, a drug she would have to take only twice a month. I got her into the car, but when she realized what I had in mind, she opened the door and jumped out at a busy intersection. She disappeared before I could stop the car and chase after her. Again, I was at a loss.

The day after, I went to her room at Hampton House to talk to her again about the new medication. She didn't answer my knock, but the door was unlocked, so I walked in. I gagged. The smell was overpowering, the room stifling. In a corner, I noticed a little white space heater, the restless blue flame turned up full blast. Breathing through my mouth, I looked around the disaster of a room. My mother had turned it into a hovel.

An open-burner hot plate on a card table was burning a hot and gaseous flame. Near the hot plate were open jars of instant coffee filled with water. Scattered about the room were half-empty cans of beans and SpaghettiOs, gray-green mold growing on what was left in the cans.

Hands over my nose and mouth, I walked over to the bed near the window. The wood floor was sticky and coated with dried food, coffee stains, and mud. I stripped off the dingy sheet wadded up on the bed and discovered that the mattress my mother slept on had been so thoroughly soaked that the covering had rotted away; in several places, the springs were exposed. Near the bed were cans of urine and rags clotted with dried feces. I couldn't stand it. I rushed out of the room, trying not to be sick.

I paced back and forth on the front porch, taking deep breaths of fresh air, desperately trying to decide what to do. I went back upstairs and frantically began straightening up the room; I was afraid my mother would be kicked out. Then I realized that was exactly what I wanted. Maybe now someone would believe me when I told them she was a danger to herself, if not to others.

I hurried back to my comfortable—and very clean—duplex apartment a few blocks away and called John Holmes, a county constable who had helped me with my mother in the past.

Even when he couldn't help me, he had at least been sympathetic. "Look, I know what you're going through," he had told me a few months earlier. "But I can't pick her up. I don't have the authority."

This time, I begged. "Please, John," I said, "just go to the boarding house on Guadalupe; it's across from the hospital. Dawn's room faces the porch on the second floor. Please, just go see for yourself."

He called me two hours later. "I'll pick her up immediately," he said. He hesitated. "Tara," he said, "you were right. I've never seen anything like that room."

I changed clothes, gathered up mops, brooms, paper bags, and disinfectant and went back to the room. Several hours later, the place was in slightly better shape than it had been. I fled to my apartment and threw away the clothes I was wearing. I took a long, long shower. Later, a few weeks after my mother left, the room had to be demolished—the walls replaced, the floor boards taken up, everything in the room disposed of before anyone could live in it again.

My mother was behind the tall fence across the street, back in the state hospital for a 90–120 day commitment. Winter was coming on. At least she would be out of the cold.

Dawn at the microphone, Hollywood Bowl, 1948.
Photograph defaced by Dawn at a later date.

CHAPTER FOURTEEN

The simplest way of restoring a lost parent [is] to become one yourself . . . to succor the abandoned child within, there was no better way than having children of your own to love.
—Ian McEwan, *Black Dogs*

At the start of the new year, a new decade, 1980, I set myself the task of getting my own house in order. My mother, for a while, was being taken care of; she was still in the hospital on a ninety-day commitment. As usual, her confinement was a relief to me. When she was in the hospital, I could sleep at night, knowing she was in a safe place. I would go see her every day, and since she was on her medication, she would be clean, calm, and relatively clear about who and where she was. I could talk to her and enjoyed being around her. That's the way it always was, whether she was confined for ninety days or fourteen.

This time, she had been confined for ninety days—a three-month vacation for me, in a way—but when the ninety days were up, she was out again, on the street, and as much as I hated it, I was out of ideas. My mother was fifty. For more than half of her life—and for all of mine—she had lived in the company of strangers, in thrall to disembodied voices, insistent and demanding. For her, the year was 1951, not 1980, and she was in Hollywood, not Austin. She could see, unfurled like a red carpet at her feet, a life of grandiose accomplishment and acclaim. At least I hoped that's where she lived.

Once the ninety-day commitment was up, Dawn and I settled back to our old pattern. I would meet her on the street at least once a week, ask whether she was taking her meds, and give her some money. "I'll meet you at noon on the corner by the candy store," I'd tell her, and if I had a nine o'clock class, I would see her standing on the corner, talking to herself and shuffling her feet, waiting for me. Meeting me was her focus for the day.

I hated having her on the street, but I couldn't think of anything else to do. I had tried how many times—twenty-five? thirty?—to find some other arrangement. The law would not allow me to confine her, even if I was able to, and I certainly couldn't control her. I couldn't invite her into my own house; I would have been evicted. I couldn't spend my days—and nights— forcing her to eat, to bathe, to control her urine, to clothe herself, to take her medicine. I could not have remained a student, held a job. I had tried everything I could think of to keep her off the street: temporary confinement in a hospital, halfway houses, motel rooms I paid for out of my own pocket. Nothing was ever settled; never could I tell myself, "At last, I've found the place." Looking back, I suppose I could have bought her a bus ticket to Houston and turned her over to my aunts, but at the time, the thought never crossed my mind. I suppose my aunts and I could have found a private hospital, although it would have been unaffordable for any of us.

Tara Elgin Holley with Joe Holley
296

Nothing ever worked, so I fell back on my last resort—giving her money and with it the freedom of the streets. I didn't tell her where I lived. I was trying to live my own life, and that involved making some changes.

First, I extricated myself from a three-year marriage I had spent the entire three years trying to escape. Doug had been my unofficial music-history tutor. A graduate student in musicology with medieval and Renaissance music as his emphasis, he was a disciplined, analytic music intellectual; I was an emotional, inexperienced singer with a voice made for early music. He loved being the tutor, and he had much to teach me, but in the long run, the only reason we were together was the music.

When the marriage ended, I felt relief, mainly, and some regret. The regret had more to do with the five years of hard work I had invested with an early-music group Doug had founded as much as it did with the end of the marriage. Leaving the marriage meant that I would be on my own as a musician. We still had to finish out the concert season because of our contractual obligations, but as soon as we came back from a series of concerts in Mexico, I looked forward to striking out on my own.

I was deeply involved with music composed between the ninth and fifteenth centuries. From Doug and a handful of extraordinary European teachers, I learned that I had the perfect voice for the pure, nonvibrato sound characteristic of early music. I discovered that when the straight pitch of a vocalist blends with the straight pitch of a string instrument or a wind instrument, when the pure sound that results is teamed with exquisite poetry and resonates in the sanctuary at Cluny or some other sacred space a thousand years old, it's an exquisite experience, both spiritual and physical. When every voice and every instrument is in tune, the sounds lock together and produce a series of pitches, or overtones, above the pitch being sung or played. The sound is heavenly, the experience euphoric.

Singing in France, in Belgium, in Holland, performing medieval plays in the churches where they had originated, I could imagine the monks and nuns centuries earlier who had given their lives to nothing else. I remember singing fifteenth-century Sephardic music in Mexico, in churches around Monterrey. In a tiny church outside town, our audience was a gaggle of Mexican children. Eyes shining, mouths open, mesmerized by every note that filled the high-ceilinged chapel, they didn't want the music to end, and neither did we.

I wanted to sing forever, but I also wanted to learn, and that required at least a meager income to stay in graduate school. Singing for weddings and occasional concerts, performing at Renaissance fairs and in folk bars was not the most lucrative calling I could have chosen, so I took a job in a newly opened bookstore whose owner hoped to bring to Austin a literary sensibility and a personal touch that chain bookstores couldn't provide. Watson and Company Books quickly became a meeting place for Austinites who loved to spend their Sunday mornings lingering over coffee and *The New York Times* at the patio café next door and then strolling over to talk books and scan our well-stocked shelves. The store was ten years ahead of its time. With my friend and boss Ella Watson, I helped arrange book-signing parties and poetry readings, welcomed visiting writers, organized concerts on the patio outside the store, and thoroughly enjoyed myself. My biggest problem was trying to resist allowing my employee's discount on books to eat up my salary every week. Eventually, Watson and Company would succumb to those chain stores it desperately tried not to be, but for a few years, the store was an Austin Mecca.

I began taking graduate courses in ethnomusicology and folklore and rented a room in a wonderfully funky three-story house—a proud, old dowager of a place, built for an Austin mayor in 1867. A few years before I moved in, the house had sheltered Janis Joplin. After her death, she had appeared to a black jazz singer who was then living in the house. Twice the woman had seen Janis at the top of the stairs.

I moved into a turreted, high-ceilinged room on the first floor, crowded the built-in mahogany shelves with wonderful books, sprinkled potpourri under my sheets, filled my photo books, stacked my Beethoven and Mahler books atop the piano and filled my journal with the dense and fascinating dreams this new phase of my life seemed to inspire. Unconsciously, I suppose, I was attempting to re-create the home that Auntie had made for me, perhaps even the life. It was a good time, a time of replenishment.

I thought about Auntie a lot. She had died two years earlier while I was in Europe for a second extended period. At the end, she was in a Catholic nursing home in Houston, pretty much unaware of where or who she was. While I was in Europe, one of her wealthy nephews took charge of her affairs and had her will changed. He made sure that her estate, which had been left to me in an earlier version, went to him and his two equally prosperous cousins. When she died, he sold the house and auctioned off all the antique furniture, the artwork, the family heirlooms, all the bits and pieces of our lives together that had meant so much to me. Even so, much of it was eaten up by lawyer's fees. He allowed me only a few keepsakes.

Although I sometimes wished I could have stayed with Auntie as long as she needed me, I realized during more rational moments that I had done all I could. Toward the end and before she went into a nursing home, we mended our relationship. I would go over and sing German lieder for her, songs I was studying in school; I would enlist my cousins to help me clean the house and put food in her refrigerator. I'd give her a bath, cut her toenails, change her bedclothes and linens.

Although Auntie and our life together were often on my mind, I was getting on with my new life. My housemates were Jim Whitaker and Jim Wood, two bookish eccentrics who quickly became my friends and confidants. Jim Whitaker, tall and thin, almost a hermit, was a gifted poet who worked in the classics department at the university. He read voraciously, making notes in the margins and typing long, thoughtful responses to works that moved him and mailing them to the author. His letters, written in a tiny, precise hand—to writers and critics, to me, to hundreds of other correspondents—were smart, witty, impassioned, the eloquent outpourings of a man who found it difficult to connect with people in person. To Jim and me and to others who shared his literary interests, he talked passionately about Joyce and Pound and the uncanny power of words to create reality.

One afternoon, Jim screwed up his courage, picked up the phone, and called one of his favorite writers, the novelist Walker Percy. They talked for a couple of hours. "You know," Percy told him in his soft Mississippi Delta accent, "I have to have five shots of bourbon every afternoon just to stand the twentieth century."

Occasionally, when Jim was writing, I would stroll into his room and sit quietly beside his antique mahogany table where he kept his manual typewriter, and I would read the poems and letters he ripped from his typewriter and allowed to float into a big magazine basket beside his desk. I retrieved one called "Anxiety Attack": "It is the dry click of bone/on metal drain that puts one off,/the quick monkeyhouse clatter,/'Eleanor Rigby' from cafeteria strings,/trays of gray gristle and lime jello. . . ."

Like Emily Dickinson, Jim wrote hundreds of poems and squirreled them away in his room, too shy to deal with editors or to face rejection. Finally, an exasperated friend of his, an editor at *Texas Monthly*, wrangled book-review assignments for him and helped to get him a six-month writing fellowship. Even though Jim would seem the ideal fellowship recipient, since it gave him the opportunity to live alone on a ranch in the Texas hill country just west of Austin, the setting reminded him of his grim childhood on a ranch in West Texas, and he couldn't write a word. He was happy to return to the house.

I lived on the first floor. Both Jims had rooms of their own in the attic. A woman the Jims called "the screamer" lived on the second floor, directly below Jim Whitaker's turreted attic window. Her enthusiastic, high-pitched lovemaking resounded throughout the whole house, but particularly with the shy attic writer laboring over his lines. Whenever the screaming started up, a sound not unlike the bleating ululations of a European ambulance, Jim swore his turret rotated like a gyroscope.

As for Jim Wood, in his plaid flannel shirt, sleeves rolled up over muscular forearms, in his jeans and his work boots, he reminded me of a lumberjack. As a university student a decade earlier, he had been a young Marlon Brando, slender and so handsome he was almost pretty. In college, he wrote novels and poems and made short films with titles like "Pygmies Riding a Vespa in a World Gone Mad" and "Dreams of an Aging Mousketeer." His novel, *The Memoirs of Lord Halifax*, won a Texas Institute of Letters award.

However, his writing days were past. Jim now worked as a chef at a university-area restaurant and no longer wrote, although he collected rare books. Within the carefully tended Wernicke book cases crowding his room, he kept a first edition of every Walker Percy book published, first editions of the mystery writers James Lee Burke and James Ellroy, a first edition of James Agee's *A Death in the Family*, first editions of Nabokov, Bukowski, Faulkner, and many others. Every inch of wall in his room was covered with rare film-noir movie posters, prints by Edward Gorey and the Pre-Raphaelites, Julia Margaret Cameron photographs and Jim's own hand-tinted photographic work. He was particularly fond of Joyce and the modernists, and he yearned to find a woman who shared his literary enthusiasms. I suggested that he might have more luck if he changed the faded yellow Raggedy Ann and Raggedy Andy sheets he had on his bed.

Next door was an old woman who hated the classical music that wafted out of the apartments in our house. "Turn down that damn opera!" she would yell. Once she sneaked into the house and cut the wires to the Jims' stereo systems. She also hated the nubile young graduate students who frequented the place. Many a morning, she stood in her front yard yelling "You little whore!" to any young woman leaving the house. Once a group of us were sprawled around Jim Whitaker's attic room talking about Janis Joplin. "I think this was her room," Jim said. "Yes, she did live there," a voice from the yard next door yelled, "and let me tell you, she was no lady, either." We howled.

The two Jims loved to bring people into their house and to open their minds to new cultural and literary enthusiasms. I was an enthusiastic member of their salon but far from the only one. Friends of theirs and friends of friends were constantly trudging up the narrow stairs to talk books. Some nights, the two Jims and I never went to sleep. We talked about Joyce, about Percy, about film noir. We listened to recordings of Ezra Pound reading the *Cantos*. Jim Whitaker was writing every day, so he would read his poetry to us, and we would respond.

I remember staying up half the night arguing about whether Kafka's *Metamorphosis* had been correctly translated. Fueled by shots of Wild Turkey, Jim Wood argued passionately that the commonly accepted cockroach in the story was actually a winged beetle that could have righted itself at any moment.

Tara Elgin Holley with Joe Holley
302

"Don't you see what that means?" Jim shouted, almost spilling his shot of whiskey as he slapped the table. "It implies free will, and that completely changes the structural significance of the story! Surely you two can see that." Jim Whitaker and I disagreed, mainly for the sake of a good argument.

Jim and Jim were literary esthetes, gentleman scholars in the southern Gothic tradition. All they lacked was money. They were wonderful friends, and I loved being with them.

When I wasn't spending time with them, I was with my closest female friends. Rebecca, a painter and philosophy major from Iowa, was pretty and political and bright about all things except men. Against my advice, she was involved with one of her professors, a man twenty-five years her senior who was separated from his wife of many years.

Our mutual friend Sherie was my fellow waitress at A Movable Feast. An aspiring writer who worked as a producer for the *Austin City Limits* TV show, Sherie was a good friend to both of us, but when it came to men, she was no help whatsoever. Beautiful, with blond hair and porcelain-blue eyes and a vulnerable, childlike face, she went through men like potato chips: the Yugoslav filmmaker we met on one of our several trips to Paris; Harry, the Austin street magician who would later became a big TV star; Andy, the international-business major (known as Siddhartha at the restaurant); Igi, the Italian filmmaker and friend of Bertolucci's; the brass-bed salesman; the male model—they and all the others were characters and experiences to be packed into all the many novels she seemed destined to produce. I loved her like the sister I never had.

With Sherie and Rebecca, as with Bernie and his pot-smoking friends a decade earlier, I was the counselor, the sober, practical voice of reason. But then, suddenly, unexpectedly, it was my turn to be sent spinning, to need sound advice. As my twenty-ninth birthday approached in the fall of 1980, I was reveling in my independence. I had my share of male admirers—four bouquets, a dozen cards, and several calls arrived on my birthday—but I was free, unencumbered, and the last thing I needed was a serious relationship.

"There's this guy I just met; he's unlike anyone I've ever gone out with," I told Sherie one afternoon over coffee. Unlike the tousled, troubled rebels, the obsessed artists, the exotic foreigners with whom I'd been involved over the years, Joe was clean-cut handsome, an athlete, about as straight-looking as they come. "Sure, he reads," I told Sherie, "and he writes. I love being with him, but I'm not sure what I'm getting into. And besides, he's got kids."

He had strolled into the bookstore one Sunday morning with two adorable little girls in tow, and I had waited on them. The next weekend, the three of them had happened onto one of my concerts. Joe and I had lunch a few days later, and then he came over to the house one night when Rebecca and her official boyfriend, a rancher/philosophy major from Abilene, were visiting. When Rebecca and her friend left, Joe and I explored the old house. The two Jims were out, although a few days earlier Jim Whitaker had left me a peevish note about "the Italian Stallion" who was taking up all my time. Climbing the creaky stairs, we lingered in the dark on the vacant second floor. (The screamer had moved out.) We talked and talked, and then, leaning out of adjacent open windows into the soft autumn night and holding on to the window frame to keep from falling out, we kissed.

How needy we were. Neither of us was aware of the depth of our need. Joe had moved to Austin under the illusion that he had a new lease on life, that his divorce was an opportunity to start all over again. He wore what a friend calls the glow of the newly divorced, but with two small daughters to care for and a conflicted marriage breakup with an unresolved twist to it, his start could hardly be a fresh one. Although he would be reluctant to admit it, he was trying to have it all. With me, he had someone who loved being with his children, someone who by her very presence helped him re-create the domestic arrangement he had known his whole life. While he was still interested in playing the field when we met, he was intrigued by the kind of nontraditional woman I symbolized. I was a musician, an artist. I had lived abroad. In Joe's eyes, I was different. He would soon discover just how different.

But Joe wasn't the only needy one in this relationship. I thought I wanted my time alone, but give me a needy man, especially one who's smart, funny, handsome, and a good father, and I quickly thought otherwise. Now, add two small children who needed mothering, and what chance did I have? Other men had wanted to get married and have a family, but I had run like the wind. Maybe the proverbial biological clock had something to do with it, maybe it was Joe, but in any case, I was ensnared.

At the time, I didn't realize that I wanted a family. Since leaving Auntie's, I had been able to convince myself that my free-wheeling independence was a choice, that if marriage and family were offered to me as potential prizes, along with independence, I would proudly, defiantly choose independence. I had been trying to create "family" for most of my life. Bernie and the guys in high school, my musicians' circle in Europe, my extended Greek family at Ari's Grenouille—those were my families, but they weren't enough.

Within weeks, Joe and I were spending most of our days and many of our evenings together. We couldn't stay away from each other. I remember Heather and Rachel, nine and ten at the time, sitting in the backseat on one of our trips to some out-of-the-way Texas curiosity and Heather pulling on my arm impatiently. "All you and Dad do is talk, talk, talk," she complained. She was right, and for the rest of that trip, the girls and I sang every song we could think of, laughing uproarously at "Sardines and Pork 'n' Beans," and "I Knew a Little Dutch Boy," and every other little ditty we'd learned at church camp or with the Camp Fire girls.

Their father and I had lives to share, elusive hopes and dreams we yearned to make reality. We couldn't wait to share the writers we were always discovering, everyone from Carl Jung to Walker Percy, James Agee to Toni Morrison. Since Joe was working for the state humanities committee, dinner-table conversation often revolved around teaching the humanities in the public schools or preserving Texas folklore or investigating the Texas-Mexican border culture—all the yeasty issues that the humanities committee and my graduate work were exploring in those days.

Joe knew the nooks and crannies of the vast state of Texas, so he always had some obscure little café in San Antonio or a country inn in a little Alsatian community in south Texas that he couldn't wait to share. He tried—with little success—to explain to me the lure of sports, which had been such a big part of his life growing up in Waco; I tried to share with him the mysteries of music. (Since he was taking voice lessons when I met him, I had something of a head start.) He was extremely charming. Certainly too good to be true.

At first I introduced Joe to a few of my friends, but he seemed uncomfortable with the male ones. Gradually, those friendships seemed to recede as more and more of my time was taken up with family activities and the needs of two darling little girls. We talked endlessly about families and children, about the future. We were earnest and hopeful, if slightly unrealistic, about our lives together.

Joe was writing magazine articles about Texas politics and about cultural issues; not long after we met he was offered the editorship of *The Texas Observer*, a feisty political journal that had nurtured the journalism careers of Willie Morris, Molly Ivins, and several of Joe's literary heroes. "But they can only pay me twelve thousand dollars a year," he said. "But you can't turn it down," I said. He didn't.

Still juggling school, work, and music, I set for myself the scary task of making the transition from an early-music singer to a jazz singer. One night, Joe and I were having drinks at the Driskill Hotel piano bar, listening to a local jazz pianist, when suddenly I started singing along. Joe and everybody else sitting at the bar were shocked, and so was the pianist, but I couldn't help myself. The music I had known my whole life just over-flowed. I began regular long evening rehearsals with a very good young North Texas State jazz guitarist who wanted the experience of working one-on-one with a vocalist. We ended up doing a lot of weddings and a few jazz gigs.

Afternoons, I would drop by a local bar where a jazz pianist would let me run through some tunes. Some nights I sang at open mikes in little clubs around town, although it was never easy trying to live up to the woman in my life who still sang so well, even when she was living on the street.

Improvisation was particularly challenging. Both my ear and my vocal technique were up to it, but improvisation also requires a knowledge of the melody so deep and thorough that you can dare to depart from it. An improvisational singer like Ella Fitzgerald is like a tightrope artist who has no doubt that she can dance on the wire because she trusts implicitly that it will be there when her feet touch back down. While I had studied and performed hundreds of difficult pieces in a half-dozen languages, the depth of trust I needed for improvising was elusive. For someone whose life epitomized the old Chinese curse—May you live in interesting times—perhaps my lack of trust was metaphorical.

Our blended lives were full. I was helping the girls with their piano lessons, occasionally coming over to prepare meals for the four of us, meeting Joe's extended family, and seeing less and less of my old pals.

"Joe seems like a nice man, but I hope you realize, Tara, that good looks are not to be trusted," Sally commented one weekend when I took Joe home to Houston. "He does not have your best interests in mind." I imagined I knew what she was thinking. Perhaps she was talking about Mike, her devilishly handsome radio-personality first husband.

I could hear Elvis warbling about fools rushing in. No doubt about it, Joe and I were fools—happy, euphoric fools in love. We were in deep and, like the song says, we had our hearts above our heads. Pop psychologists would call us codependent. We were in love, in transition, and both were looking to the other to fulfill some kind of impossible dream. A counselor advised us to see less of each other for a while. We tried, for a couple of days.

I told Joe about my mother from the very beginning, although I didn't go into details until we had known each other a few weeks. I told him she was schizophrenic. Like almost everyone else who hears the word, he assumed I meant that her personality was split down the middle: one minute she was Dawn and the next Lauren Bacall. I suppose I had no right to blame him, since the word is so often misused. However, for anyone who has seen the delusions, hallucinations, impaired thinking, and radical changes in behavior that characterizes actual schizophrenia, the pervasive public ignorance gets to be tiresome.

Gradually, for Joe, I wove the pieces of Dawn's life into a cohesive story. Often in the evenings, after work, after school, after the girls' piano lessons and homework, after dinner, we sat in the wooden swing on the front porch of his house, and I would tell him about my mother and our lives together. He was curious, but it seemed to me that it was the curiosity of an objective reporter, not a caring, empathetic friend. It made me feel uncomfortable, the way a grieving family member must feel when a reporter sticks a microphone in her face and asks her how it feels now that her child has perished in a car wreck.

When I told him one night that he had actually seen her without knowing who she was, he got quiet. It was getting dark, and I could hear mourning doves in the live oaks in the backyard. "She's been on the Drag off and on for years," I said.

Journalist that he was, Joe went looking, and one afternoon that same week, he found her. He didn't tell me that's what he had done; he didn't have to. I could tell that encountering Dawn, knowing she was the mother of the woman he loved, had shaken him. I could see the distracted look on his face, feel him withdraw from me emotionally.

I was disappointed. I was thinking of my friend Sherie, who helped me keep track of Dawn when she was on the street, and of Rebecca, who was always available to drive Dawn to the clinic. My gentle, sensitive friend Greg Jones, from an African-American family of twelve children, had grown up with a schizophrenic brother. I could always talk to him, and he to me. What was interesting about these special friends is that they came from every walk of life. We understood that neither color nor money nor social class barred this kind of illness. We understood each other and depended on each other for some sense of perspective.

I might run into my old boyfriend Bernie, who now lived in Austin. "Talked to your mother on the Drag yesterday," he would say. "She was eating a bag of chocolates. I gave her some money, and we talked for a while. I tried to find out where she's been staying since the weather turned cold."

I don't know if there's an easy way to be introduced to a person suffering from schizophrenia, but my friends, because they knew me, seemed to have no trouble accepting Dawn. That was all the more reason that Joe's reaction confounded me. What did I expect him to do? Maybe if he had introduced himself, had taken the time to talk to my mother, it would have been okay. Wasn't he enlightened, caring, educated?

I remember thinking during the first dozen years or so of my life that the world was divided into two camps—the normal and the rest of us. Schoolmates like Hallie Welborn—whose mothers weren't crazy, whose great-aunts weren't senile—were the normal ones. The rest of us, the lonely few, could only stand on the outside and wistfully observe the carefree, well-adjusted people we could never be.

I think it was *Catcher in the Rye* that helped me begin to realize that human beings are much more complex than that, and much more interesting. Nobody was normal, not Holden Caulfield, not me. We all had our idiosyncrasies, our differences, and those were the very qualities that made us interesting. Everything I read, from *King Lear* to *Jane Eyre* to *Ballad of the Sad Café* reinforced my insight. I liked the way Sherwood Anderson put it in *Winesburg, Ohio*, when he wrote about the twisted, deformed apples that the pickers have rejected. "One runs from tree to tree over the frosted ground," he writes, "picking the gnarled, twisted apples and filling his pockets with them. Only the few knew the sweetness of the twisted apples."

Joe read as much as I did, probably more. Why couldn't he accept my mother? Why couldn't he say, "That must have been hard on you. What can I do to help?" Why couldn't he walk up to her on the street and with arms open wide proclaim, "I'm in love with your daughter and I'm going to marry her, and you're

Tara Elgin Holley with Joe Holley
310

going to be my mother-in-law"? But he didn't do that. Instead, he observed her from a distance, as if she were some kind of dangerous, disgusting animal.

I had seen it too many times before. There had been times when I'd been in a car with people, and as we drove past my mother, I would hide my eyes, cringing inside for the taunts, the jokes about the bag lady, the freak. I remembered being fifteen years old and waiting for the bus after choir practice in front of Foley's in downtown Houston. Usually, a mentally disturbed street person or two hung out at the bus stop. I would talk to them, even though my friends preferred to look the other way.

I thought I knew what Joe was thinking: If Tara's mother is crazy, maybe Tara is, too. Maybe I can spot the subtle signs—a certain look in the eye, a temper tantrum, a wild-eyed obsession. Maybe she'll rise from our bed one night and murder our children. If I marry this woman, how do I know that madness won't take her where it took her mother, leaving me stuck with caring for a crazy person the rest of my life? He could feel pity for my mother, it seemed, but not empathy.

What was to keep my family history from becoming Joe's new family future? Certainly, I could offer no guarantees, because the fact is, schizophrenia sometimes runs in families. Not always, but sometimes.

The question of how the disease is transmitted is but one manifestation of the many scary questions about mental illness that lurk in most people's minds. Our deep fear of mental illness has to do with our fear of losing the self, of falling victim to an affliction not unlike a slow death. The person afflicted with schizophrenia is no longer the same person; she's lost control of her mind, her very being. Most of us would rather run away than confront something so awful.

To his credit, the man I loved did not run away. He stayed until he understood. Gradually, I learned that I could trust him to stand with me in the effort common to all family members of the mentally ill. He became my mother's friend and champion, and he encouraged me when I felt overwhelmed. For her part, Dawn, who always had an eye for handsome men, liked Joe and approved of my choice. Joe and I married in 1982.

After my mother discovered where I lived and broke in—trying, it seemed, to reclaim my attention—I decided I had to make yet another effort at rehabilitation, if that's the word. Or rescue. Was I trying to entice her back into the world the rest of us live in? Make her respectable, for my sake as much as hers?

I found her on the Drag one afternoon, and we strolled along the sidewalk together. I placed my arm over her shoulders as we walked. "Is this really the way you want to live?" I asked in a gentle voice. "Wearing these awful clothes, sleeping God knows where. Wouldn't you rather be in a nice, clean place?"

"I like my freedom," she said. "I like being able to go where I want to. I have my friends." I looked into the beautiful brown eyes set in her weathered face. They still sparkled with life and spirit and stubbornness.

"But Mommy," I said, backing her gently into the wall of a drugstore, out of the flow of pedestrian traffic, "wouldn't you like to have your own place, have a piano to play?" Earlier in the day, I had talked to Donna Payne, a social worker at the state hospital who knew Dawn. If we could keep Dawn on her medication, Donna said, we could get her into a halfway house, into vocational training, and eventually into some kind of assisted living in an apartment of her own.

Donna's plan sounded hopeful to me, and Dawn agreed, reluctantly, to give it a try. I went to a pay phone and called Donna, eyeing my mother as I talked to make sure she didn't scurry away. We drove up the street to the state hospital, and all the way I was assuring Dawn that I wasn't about to commit her.

At the hospital, Donna carefully explained the terms of the agreement to Dawn and me. "Oh, thank you!" Dawn burbled. "I'm going to do my very best."

Maybe she will, I said to myself. Maybe this time, she will.

The house where Dawn would live was on a busy street up the hill from Deep Eddy, a cold spring-fed swimming pool that's been an Austin institution for years, and next door to the Deep Eddy Cabaret, a neighborhood pub and pool hall. The house was run by a middle-aged woman named Judy Anjoorian, a single mother. Judy, along with her three young children, was being paid by the state to care for a severely retarded elderly woman and two other former state hospital residents. She reminded me of a strong, patient earth mother.

Dawn was happy enough to move in, but, as usual, she was the most troublesome resident. The others were docile, but Dawn questioned everything Judy tried to do. Like a balky teenager, she had to be told to do her chores, get to bed on time, go outside to smoke, be courteous to her housemates. But Judy was willing to work with her. She was interested in Dawn's music background, and she believed she could help her.

She put my mother on a nutritious regular diet and got her to exercise regularly, quite a change for a woman who existed for years on candy, soft drinks, and soggy pizzas scavenged from trash bins. Gradually, she got her to do her chores around the house. Dawn began taking voice lessons from an Austin jazz artist named Tina Marsh; I let myself imagine her dropping in at the Deep Eddy Cabaret one evening and singing old standards. She was staying on her medication, and Donna Payne had arranged for her to begin working for her former employer, Goodwill Industries.

I dropped by at least once a week, happily surprised by the transformation I could see taking place, and cautiously hoping against hope that we could keep it going. The weeks became months, and still she stayed with the regimen. For the first time in years, I wasn't waking up at night, imagining something dreadful happening to my mother as she lay in an alley behind some convenience store, imagining the stench of Dumpsters, the hard pavement on which she curled up every night to get some rest. It was as if I could now relax, after holding my breath or clenching my teeth for years without realizing it.

Gradually, my energy, my focus, began shifting from my mother to the new people in my life. The challenges of coping what with what society would come to call the "blended family" were more difficult than either Joe or I imagined. Heather and Rachel were becoming teenagers, and I was trying to adapt to the difficult role of stepmother. Their mother was back in their lives, which was good for them but brought to the foreground all the unresolved issues in their parents' marriage.

As much as I loved the girls, I had no idea how to be a good stepmother. I found it much easier to be a mother. I was thirty when Pete was born. My whole life changed when this strong, handsome, loving little boy came into my life. That was to be expected, but his arrival also transformed my relationship with my mother in ways I did not anticipate.

Motherless daughters fear what will happen when they reach the ages their mothers were when they disappeared. When I was twenty-one, the age my mother was when she got sick, I wasn't unduly worried about what would happen to me. I was aware that schizophrenia can run in families, and I worried about it occasionally, but by the time I was seventeen or eighteen, I realized I was pretty solid. I never heard voices, didn't feel disoriented or paranoid; I just could not imagine suddenly coming unraveled. My sessions with Don Gautney, the Houston psychologist, affirmed what I was feeling. I felt I had such a grip on my own senses that it was hard to imagine my mind falling prey to the insidious disease.

"Every daughter's experience," I have read, "is one of identifying with and differentiating from the mother, and both processes are equally important." As much as I identified with my mother, living beyond twenty-one without getting sick was a reminder of our essential separateness. Whatever genetic roulette is involved in schizophrenia, I knew I was not going to repeat my mother's fate. Auntie often assured me that what happened to my mother—due, in her mind, to Mama and Papa's negligence—would never happen to me, because she would not allow it. Even though I wanted to be like my mother in many ways, my relatives never said, "She's just like Dawn." Usually, they would laugh and say, "You're just like Auntie, so determined and disciplined." They meant it as a compliment, I think.

So I was surprised when the fear of losing my mind to disease crept back into my consciousness a few years later, when I was pregnant with Pete. Pregnancy, of course, means relinquishing control over your body, just as mental illness represents a loss of control over your mind, so perhaps it wasn't all that irrational to be afraid. I recognized that the trauma of an unexpected pregnancy may have been a factor in triggering my mother's illness. Even though I knew it was irrational to fear the same thing happening to me, I was afraid.

Although nothing was triggered by the stress of pregnancy— with Pete or with my daughter Kate six years later—I found that as the responsibilities and duties of motherhood began to occupy most of my time and energy, my compulsion to rescue my mother began slowly to recede. Immediately following Pete's birth, the endorphins kicked in, and combined with the nursing experience, sent me into a euphoric state I have not experienced since. I was calm and happy and, perhaps for the first time in my life, thought less about my mother.

Actually, I had begun to consciously withdraw from my mother when I was pregnant. Like most first moms, I was determined to shield my unborn infant from anything negative; I knew how upset my mother could make me. I made a point of eating healthily and gave up my drug of choice: strong, freshly brewed, black coffee. Once I found out I was carrying a little boy, I withdrew into a deep and intimate relationship with him. I talked and sang to him, told him how much I loved him, and assured him how wonderful our lives would be together. Over lunch each week, I shared the vicissitudes of pregnancy with my friend Bob Sweeney, a caring man who had considered the priesthood and worked in his spare time as a hospice volunteer.

I also shared my pregnancy with my old friend Sherie and my new friend Penny, both also pregnant at the time. Our three boys—Peter, Vincent, and Benjamin—were born within three weeks of each other. The three of us began a tradition of comparing notes that continues to this day.

With Pete, I think I began to understand the meaning of the word love for the first time. I realized that it was bigger than all of us and that motherhood was at its heart. I imagined that my mother had experienced the same emotion.

When I finally introduced them, Dawn was ecstatic about Pete. I would drop by Judy's with my wonderful baby boy, and Dawn would hold him and rock him, twisting his blond curls around her finger; she was in rapture over him. I couldn't help but think of her holding her own little Harold for those first ten months, even if it was only on the weekends, and then, suddenly, without explanation, he was gone, just as I was gone.

The day before my mother was to begin her job sorting clothes at Goodwill, I got a call from Judy. "Tara," she said, "is Dawn with you? I haven't seen her all day."

Neither had I. As the day turned to night and then another day, I realized that once again, my mother had disappeared. She was gone—afraid of being tied down to routine, responding to insistent voices, seduced by old friends on the street—who knew what was driving her? She would be back when she ran out of money, I consoled myself. She would show up at the Salvation Army looking for "three hots and a squat." In a day or so, I'd run into her on the Drag. Still, I immediately called the police and gave them the information they needed to set up a statewide missing-persons alert.

This time, though, it was different. For months, we heard nothing. An Austin detective called occasionally to report that no one had seen her. I tried to get used to the idea that she was dead. She had been hit by a car, mugged, or beaten. She had fallen off a cliff in the dark. She had walked into Town Lake. I hoped desperately that she hadn't suffered. But no bodies turned up, either.

From thinking about my mother, my obsessive thoughts wound their way back to myself. In a way, of course, I had lost my mother years before, but now, I felt a new emptiness that I would never fill. I had lost my role in life. I was no longer my mother's keeper.

I had been "mothering" so long, the role came naturally. As

Sally has said, "You were always for the underdog." She meant that literally. "Even as a child," she says, "when our puppies were born in Galveston, you wanted the littlest, ugliest one, the runt, the one no one else wanted."

I seemed to have opportunities for nurturing everywhere I turned. When I went to Auntie, she was unusually strong and healthy for someone in her seventies, but from the beginning, she let me know that she needed me. "Honey, will you thread this needle for me?" "Let me lean on your shoulder, dearie, to get down these three steps." "Tara is my eyes and my ears," she would say. "Beauty before age," she joked, turning the phrase on its head as she encouraged me to walk ahead of her so she could lean on me. From pushing grocery carts to reading fine print on medicine bottles, I felt useful and essential.

It was a bit ironic, because Auntie, this woman who needed me, was also my model for strength and self-sufficiency. She was always advising, cajoling, reprimanding; people sought her out for counsel. In the years I was with her, she was passing along that role to me—the role of spinster daughter who cares for her elderly mother, the role of matriarch who serves and provides and functions as a family anchor.

She told me often that she was preparing me to care for Dawn, but what she didn't tell me was the cost of that role. She never told me what she gave up to be the family matriarch— always to be giving, to be the one who had to give.

From being Auntie's girl Friday, it was a natural progression to begin caring for my mother. By the time I was twenty, the pattern was established. Aunts, mothers, boyfriends—if they were needy, I could surely help. If they wanted to do things for me, I resisted. A power struggle ensued. I felt they were trying to control me or tell me what to do. Auntie never told me that I would have trouble getting along with men who weren't needy—who were strong and self-sufficient, who had plans and strong opinions. I had to mother: I had to be in control.

Now, the person who most needed me was gone. I would continue giving to others what I lacked; I would continue "mothering" Joe, Heather and Rachel, and Pete, but I knew deep down inside it wasn't enough. My own incessant mothering was a way to deny—to myself and others—that I would be unmothered for the rest of my life.

I was angry. I knew my mother didn't voluntarily contract a mental illness. I knew she didn't choose to leave me, and that she longed to see her little girl grow up. But she didn't. She went away, we were left to cope with what she had left behind. Then I would remember what others had said when they realized that her condition was irrevocable: Perhaps it would have been better if she had died long ago.

I can't deny that I also felt relief. My mother and the burden she represented were out of my life. I could imagine that we were just taking a break from each other, like when I was in Holland, and only now and then would it hit me that this time it was forever. I could live with that. With a new baby, a new marriage, a blended family, I could get on with my life. Or so I told myself. It was a strange, in-between place to be imagining her dead, trying to fathom what could possibly have happened and realizing that there was almost nothing to be done.

But my mother wasn't dead. In the middle of winter, eighteen months after she had disappeared, a policeman found her on a street in downtown Dallas, two hundred miles from Austin. She was dehydrated, anemic, and bleeding internally.

Still, she was tough. She would survive, although it took several days for the people caring for her at Parkland Memorial-

Hospital to banish the lice from her body. When I walked into her hospital room, I was shocked to see her debilitated condition. Her skin, chapped and red against the white sheets, covered what looked like a bag of bones. I bent down to hug her. She put her sticklike arms around my neck. We both were crying. How could I ever have imagined that I didn't miss my mommy?

"How did you get here?" I asked her over and over, amazed and even a little proud at her ability to survive. "Where have you been all this time? Where have you been staying?"

"I don't know," she murmured, her voice raspy and weak. "I was just—I was just out there. I wanted to be in the city."

I never did find out how she got to Dallas, or how she survived all those months. I couldn't believe it when I found out that the hospital, after making sure she was no longer in danger, was prepared to put her back on the street in fourteen days. Of course, that's been the story all along: The better my mother does, the worse it is for her in the end.

Fortunately, a social worker at a state mental hospital in the small town of Terrell, thirty miles east of Dallas, intervened and got her transferred to the Terrell facility. The social worker knew it would be outrageous to release my mother back to the streets. She had seen it happen all too often, and she took it upon herself to call around on my mother's behalf. Finally, she found a place willing to take her in, a board-and-care facility for the mentally ill called Putnam Home near the small East Texas town of Athens.

When all the arrangements were made, I checked Dawn out of the hospital at Terrell, and we drove east to Athens. There was nothing fancy about the converted nursing home next to the highway. Despite what the owner had told me over the phone, there was no rehabilitation, no therapy, no pleasant private room—just bed and board and bare-bones maintenance. This dingy cinder-block barrack surrounded by cattle pasture would be my mother's home. It was a long, long way from Hollywood.

CHAPTER FIFTEEN

Every woman extends backward into her mother and forward into her daughter.

—Carl Jung, *The Archetypes and the Collective Unconscious*

On a sunny February morning, Joe and I, with our two kids in the backseat, drove into the small town of Athens, self-proclaimed "black-eyed pea capital of Texas." The square was deserted on this Sunday morning as we took a left at the old courthouse and headed into the rolling East Texas countryside. I got the same, slightly nauseous feeling that always came each time I visited my mother. It was not unlike performance anxiety, just before I went onstage to sing; I felt I had to prepare myself to visit with this sixty-year old schizophrenic woman who for so many years had been the focus of my existence.

Just as when I'm singing, the anxiety subsides when the performance begins. Within minutes, we turned into the sandy lane that leads to Putnam Home, the board-and-care facility for the mentally incapacitated that was operated by a man named Virgil Putnam. My anxiety became anticipation.

The rambling, one-story building, its cement blocks painted a faded yellow, was a dreary-looking place. Several of the sixty or so residents sauntered out the front door to see who had arrived. Others on this winter day were enjoying the sun on a bench at the side of the building. They clambered to their feet when they saw the car and ambled toward the driveway. They walked slowly, a bit unsteadily, almost zombielike. They gathered around us as if in a stupor.

They were black and white, old and young, male and female. They were former drug addicts and alcoholics, paranoid schizophrenics, people with organic brain diseases or brain injuries. Like my mother, many were street people before finding their way to Putnam Home. By this time, for nearly six years, they had been my mother's companions, her neighbors.

Like Dawn, the people who lived at Putnam Home didn't belong in hospitals, but neither could they function on their own. In a state where deinstitutionalization had emptied out the hospitals and where available community facilities couldn't meet the need, social workers were desperate to find a Putnam Home. Young people who'd blown out their brains with drugs, the borderline mentally ill who, with a little help, could have had a life outside an institution—all desperately needed places to live. Virgil Putnam—the residents call him Daddy Put—took them in.

Dawn was wearing a shapeless brown sweater over a dowdy rayon blouse, baggy blue slacks, and scuffed red pumps. A knit cap that Sister had sent her covered her thick, uncombed hair. She reached out her arms to me, then hugged Pete and Joe. She took Kate in her arms. I did my usual quick assessment. She hadn't showered recently and her nails were chewed down to the quick, but she seemed calm and symptomless, in good health.

Tara Elgin Holley with Joe Holley

Carrying Kate, she led us inside for a tour of the place she called home. Half a dozen other residents trailed along with us. The air was close and stale, the ceiling low. I made a point of taking shallow breaths. I never ceased to be stunned by the lack of the most basic amenities—fresh air, sunshine, flowers—at so many facilities for the mentally ill, but it only increased my resolve to be stoic. If my mother could live that way, I could at least be respectful of the situation.

In Dawn's small room, which she shared with four other women, an older woman was lying on one of the beds. She was fully dressed and wearing shoes. Her tongue, swollen from the medication she took, protruded from her mouth. Another roommate, a woman named Mary, talked to Pete and gave Kate a dingy little teddy bear to hold.

In the dim hallway outside Dawn's room, most of the other residents were lining up at the dispensary window to receive their medication. A staff person was allowed to make the medication available, in little paper cups, but it had to be the patient's choice to take it. A team of five doctors in nearby Athens looked after the residents' medical needs.

Later in the morning, a minister from a little country church came by to conduct services. The residents seemed happy to see him. I was pleased to see that he was relaxed and easy with them. Few of them, he told me, ever have visitors. Their fellow residents, most of whom had been here for years, were their only family.

Just before lunch, Dawn and I ambled down a grassy hill to a stock pond, where Dawn's friend Mary fed bread to the ducks and snakes—or so Mary said. My two-year-old daughter Kate was with us, and we walked slowly so she could keep up. Nodding my head while Mary talked to me, I watched my mother and her granddaughter walking together ahead of me, and I thought about what might have been, and what was.

My daughter insists we call her Kate, or Katie, although her name is Kathryn Theresa Elgin Holley—Kathryn for Joe's grandmother, Theresa for my great-grandmother. Her arrival in 1989 led me into uncharted territory.

I had been a mother of sorts to Heather and Rachel, but they headed into bumpy, unsettling adolescence not long after we met. I had missed those earlier, miraculous years with them. With Kate, I was a mommy from the beginning. I became much more aware of the psychic cord that connects mothers and daughters through the generations of a family. Once I became mother to a daughter, I no longer felt the need to continue my desperate, relentless search for my own mommy.

I remember Kate toddling into the kitchen one morning, and when I lifted her up, she noticed a snapshot on the refrigerator. In the photo, the year is 1953, and Dawn is holding me in her arms. I am fair-haired, smiling, and happy, just as Kate is today.

"How old am I there, Mommy?" she asked, looking over my shoulder at the photograph.

"That's not you, honey," I said. "That's me, and that's *my* mommy. That's Dawnie."

"No, Mommy, you're wrong," she said, shaking her blond head. "That's me."

She wasn't right exactly, but I didn't argue. Kate is the reincarnation of Dawn, Sally says. She has the same gregarious, joyful enthusiasm. She's funny. She loves people. When we go to restaurants, Kate is the family member who flits from table to table greeting acquaintances. After school each day, she makes a point of shouting good-bye to each of her kindergarten classmates by name. She's strong-willed and outspoken—just as Dawn was.

I know that Joe has been concerned about a genetic factor,

Tara Elgin Holley with Joe Holley

and I have shared his concern—and his pleasure—when family members troop out the usual old saws: "She looks just like Dawn at that age." or "Tara, your hair was just like that when you were three." "Oh, honey, I'm so glad she's taking piano. Is she musical like Dawn?" In fact she looks no more like Dawn than other members of the blond set in our family, and some have been bold enough to say that she looks nothing like the Elgins at all. Although she likes music, she is not overtly musical, but I've learned through teaching that most children will grow to be so after enough exposure. Because of her physicality and the pleasure she takes in movement, she may be happier in ballet or gymnastics. She is noticeably artistic, but as her kindergarten teacher says, "Give them materials and they will create!" I used to think I was destined to model myself after my mother until one of my aunts reminded me that I was stronger and more determined than many in my family, more like Auntie—also not wholly true.

As far as genetics go, I feel strongly after watching Dawn for so many years that there are so many other factors involved as well. This is not to say I dispute the environmental factors or the in-utero viral theory or the twin studies or any of the other important research directed at this baffling illness. I believe we will know much more soon, and that the findings will be complex and will change our ways of thinking. I believe we may discover a number of illnesses with related symptoms, and I hope we will change what we call them and the way we talk about them for the sake of those who must live with them.

I remember one night Joe was watching his little girl as she giggled and played with her big brother when she was supposed to be going to bed. "I cannot imagine losing her the way your grandparents lost their daughter," he murmured. "I could not bear it. I would rather kill myself."

My Mother's Keeper
327

"You couldn't," I told him. "You would have to be there for her."

I have no doubt he would be. I watched him grow and change when his younger brother died of AIDS. I think of Mama and Papa, and how they must have done everything they could to try to rescue their daughter. What we hope, of course, is that medical advances will preclude the terrible possibility that either of our children—or anyone else's children—will drift into the dreadful house of mirrors my mother has known for most of her life.

Kate has been a healing presence for me. How easily she fits into me, her arms around my neck, her legs encircling my waist. Just as with Pete, to feel her little body wrapped into mine is to feel at peace, to be deeply, completely relaxed. I feel the tension drop away. I don't remember when it first began to happen, but I gradually became aware that what I was feeling with Kate in my arms were the same feelings of connectedness and euphoria that I experienced with my mother when I was Kate's age. I remembered the visceral delight of simply being with my mother. The strength of my emotions confirmed that I had once had a mommy, not just a mother, but a mommy who loved me.

It's a feeling that comes back, as evocative as a remembered fragrance, and I am calm and happy. I'm no longer desperately seeking. It's not so much memories of particular moments or experiences, but memories of familiar feelings. Singing to Kate, holding her in my arms, I can be drawn into a time warp. I feel what it's like to be a three-year-old, when my mother was my whole life, what it was like to want her, to have her, and to be delighted with her presence.

I sometimes became Dawn singing to her daughter, and I was suddenly able to imagine how she must have been as terrified of losing me as she was of losing herself. I look down at the lovely little girl in my arms, and the lyrics followed: "The very thought

Tara Elgin Holley with Joe Holley

328

of you makes my heart sing/like an April breeze on the wings of spring/and you appear in all your splendor/my one and only love . . ."

During those times, I could hear Dawn; it was one of "her songs." I could feel her voice rising and falling, her chest against mine. I could feel her warmth, the warmth of her being, and I couldn't go on.

"Why do you call Dawn 'Mommy'?" Kate asks one night after I've talked to my mother on the phone.

"Because she is my mommy," I explain. "Remember I've told you that being a mommy is one of life's greatest pleasures? Dawn didn't get to be a mommy very long, because she got sick, but she still likes it when I call her Mommy."

Recalling those few years I had with my mother as a child, which were awakened by my connection to Kate, was enough to loosen the bonds of my over-identification with Dawn. My mother, I now understand, looks through my eyes when I look with love at my children; loving them, I now know how much she loved me.

Sometimes I imagine what would happen if Kate lost me. It's a way of working through the pain and remembering. She would have Joe to answer her questions, to comfort her, but would she eventually block out the memory of our parting? Would her memories fade? Given all the memories I've managed to retain about my mother, the one memory that eludes me is what it felt like for her suddenly and without warning to disappear. Auntie told me that I often asked Sister about her the first few weeks I was back in Houston, but then I stopped asking. At some point, I asked Sister, "Can I call you Mommy?" Auntie wouldn't allow it.

In fact, losing my mother is the excuse I give myself for my intense fears for people in my life. When I was in my twenties, I was obsessive about arriving at appointments on time, and when close friends or boyfriends weren't on time, I reacted irrationally. The anxiety would build as I waited for them; the longer I waited, the more convinced I was that something had gone wrong.

These days, my fear expresses itself in a preternatural concern about my children's safety. "You're just a mother," friends tell me, but I think, at times, my fears are irrational. When Pete was younger, I would have nightmares about leaving him at the mall. With Kate, the fears run to forgetting to pick her up at school or a stranger snatching her out of the front yard.

In my life, the connection between mothers and daughters, both biological and emotional, is clear and distinct; I am who I am because of my connection to my mother; Kate is who she is because of her connection to me. I acknowledge that connectedness and celebrate it, but at the same time, I want my daughter to maintain her independence. Ms. Gibson, Kate's kindergarten teacher, sent home a note asking that each member of the class bring a baby picture for the bulletin board. When I visited Kate's class a few days later, I saw that Ms. Gibson had festooned the board with phrases like—"Does she look like her father?" "Does she have her grandmother's eyes?" All of us, she wanted the children to know, are made up of a diversity of ingredients—as elderly aunts and other relatives frequently remind us—but out of those ingredients, a unique and precious self emerges. That's what I want for Kate; that's what I've accomplished for myself.

I feel I have emerged from my mother's shadow—from her ebullience, her talent and beauty, her despair—but it has taken me a long time. I want Kate to know that a daughter can be liberated from her mother. I love being with her because she's so unique, and I delight in not labeling her in any way. I take pleasure in standing back and watching her own strong personality emerge. As Ms. Gibson's bulletin board reminded me, Kate is very much her own little person.

Tara Elgin Holley with Joe Holley

Freed from a natural enough compulsion, I'm a more responsive daughter. I'm more comfortable doing what I can for Dawn, setting limits in ways I couldn't earlier.

Not long after Dawn had moved into Putnam Home, Joe and I and the children moved to California. Although my mother's need for me was a consideration for us, it was a relatively minor one; I believed at that point that I had done just about everything I could do. Joe had received an enticing job offer as editorial page editor at a big-city newspaper, his salary would be substantially higher, and both of us were eager to go. We had talked off and on for two years about what we would do if a good job elsewhere came along. As an Elgin, California was in my genes.

We offered Heather and Rachel the possibility of going with us, if that's what they wanted to do. I, for one, hoped that moving to California would help us as a family resolve parental strains that kept me as stepmother in the uncomfortable middle of everything from financial needs to whether the girls should be allowed to quit piano lessons. Resolving those strains was on my mind as much or more than my mother. In fact, she had begun to recede during the year and a half she was missing.

In that period, I went from daily imaginings of what she was suffering to profound relief when we found her—relief not only that she had survived but that someone else would have to care for her. I looked at her as she lay in her bed in the mental hospital at Terrell—her body emaciated, her skin weathered and peeling, her mind elsewhere—and I tried to visualize what she had experienced. I saw her in the cold canyons of downtown Dallas, huddled in a doorway as passersby hurried past. I grew short of breath, in a panic, as I imagined the days and nights she spent with no food, no clothing, no shelter, no connections to anyone.

At that moment I realized that we were at the bottom, and I had had it. How could I start all over with her? Dawn's social worker in Terrell must have recognized my frustration, because she had quickly offered Putnam Home as an alternative and arranged a visit for that same day. I immediately grasped at the opportunity to leave my mother in the hands of someone else; certainly Putnam Home was an improvement over the streets of Dallas. I wanted to head west with my husband and three-year-old Pete. I wanted a fresh start.

During the five years we were living in California, we saw Dawn once a year on average. Once we moved back to Austin, we made the four-hundred-mile round trip to Athens more often. Each time I saw her, I realized that she would never get better as long as she was at Putnam Home. She was simply being warehoused, left to bide away her time in an isolated facility where she would be fed, clothed, sheltered, and sedated—and nothing more. Each time I walked into the dreary confines of Putnam Home, it was all too obvious that she could live the rest of her life in a low-ceilinged country warehouse of broken human beings. I could see that whatever spirit she had left was ebbing away, though I still held out hope that, somehow, her condition could improve. I was ready to try again.

One morning, I walked into the small, cluttered office of the Putnam Home general manager, a woman named Mary Pediford. I wanted to find out about getting dental care for my mother. After we talked for a while, Mrs. Pediford summoned Dawn. My mother came in, we embraced and Mrs. Pediford smiled. "Now, Dawn," she said, smiling, "now that your daughter's here we're not going to do that crying anymore, are we?" Mrs. Pediford glanced at me. "Some days she goes off in her room and just cries her eyes out like a baby." My mother, staring at the floor and smiling like an embarrassed child, agreed not to cry anymore. No one had ever told me that she cried. "If she needs to cry, she should be able to cry," I told Mary Pediford.

While Dawn and I were sitting in her room talking that morning, an older woman out in the hall was yelling obscenities to the voices inside her head. I looked out the door. She was enraged, and as she yelled, she picked at large, open sores on her face and neck. Later, as Dawn and I walked down the hall to the cafeteria, a young woman ran up to us. She was crying. "Tell people outside what goes on here!" she told me. She was deeply agitated because she couldn't find anyone to light her cigarette.

Driving home that afternoon, I had a long time to think about the agitated young woman and my mother in tears in that little room. How had I come to assume over the years, without thinking, that a certain detachment and inability to communicate much indicated that she felt nothing? As I thought about it, I realized that surely she and the other Putnam Home residents were in pain, even though they weren't being abused. They were lonely and unhappy, and they longed to feel, to make connections with their fellow human beings. They had every reason in the world to cry.

On the other hand, I choose to assume that there are some things my mother and other chronic schizophrenics don't feel. I don't think she's aware every minute of what she has lost. I think about those times when we reminisce and how invariably she'll tell me something about Hollywood, about what it was like when she was a young woman, she never mentions anything about a hospital stay or a nurse or anything that's happened to her since the onset of her illness more than forty years ago. I think that in many ways she's still twenty-two, and for that I'm grateful.

My Mother's Keeper

Yet again, I resolved to do what I could to make sure my mother's life was as satisfying and free from difficulty as it could be—this time, with my eyes wide open and with a little help from friends and family. Back in Austin, Joe and I enrolled in a weekly class for families of schizophrenics, sponsored by a local mental health–mental retardation center. In all the years I'd been trying to understand my mother's illness, it was the first class on schizophrenia I'd ever taken, and it turned out to be tremendously useful. My only regret is not finding such a resource when I was a desperate twenty-year-old.

Many of us in the support group were eager to learn more about clozapine, a so-called miracle drug that we had just begun to hear about. Clozapine, the generic name for Clozaril, represented the first major step forward in drug treatment for schizophrenia since the development of Thorazine and other neuroleptic drugs in the early 1950s. We had heard that Clozaril alleviated the negative symptoms that afflicted schizophrenic patients—lack of motivation, inattention, emotional withdrawal. Most of the antipsychotic drugs that had been around for forty years generally failed to affect these negative symptoms and sometimes exacerbated them.

By blocking the brain receptor where the nerve transmitter called dopamine works in some parts of the brain, Clozaril also relieved the "positive symptoms"—delusions, hallucinations, and bizarre behavior. Earlier drugs had relieved these positive symptoms, but the side effects had been almost as debilitating and humiliating as the symptoms themselves. Clozaril, from what we had heard, did not cause such side effects.

"It's been around since the 1970s," our group leader Jerry Frampton explained, "but it wasn't an approved medication in this country until 1990. There's no doubt that it has helped people who were considered untreatable, but there's one little problem.

It can interfere with the body's production of white blood cells, a condition called agranulocytosis. It can be fatal."

Although one person in our class said her brother had tried Clozaril for six weeks and had been sleepy the whole time, with no sign of improvement, Jerry had seen it work more effectively with other patients. "I know one person who's improved dramatically after four or five months," he said. "I know others who have been discharged from the hospital. I've heard of people who were staring at hospital walls for forty years, and after getting on Clozaril, they're coming up to the nurse and saying, 'I'm bored, isn't there anything to do?'

"What we're seeing with Clozaril," Jerry added, "is the reemergence of personality."

Many of us in the class probably had the same reaction I had when he used that phrase. I thought of Robert De Niro, my favorite actor, in the movie *Awakenings*. Suffering from a debilitating brain disease that for decades has kept him and other patients in a kind of coma, the De Niro character and the others respond to a new medication administered by Dr. Oliver Sacks, played by Robin Williams. Gradually, the old personalities emerge, only to disappear again, forever, when the medication loses its effectiveness.

Joe and I were determined to get Dawn on Clozaril. Attempting to preserve my more realistic mode, I tried not to fantasize about my mother's own reemergence of personality, but I couldn't help myself. I could see her in a little apartment of her own in Houston, where family members could look in on her, where she could go shopping when she wanted to, go to the movies as she used to love to. We'd talk on the phone every couple of weeks, like sisters, and we'd be together with all the other relatives who crowded into my aunts' Houston homes on Thanksgiving and on Christmas Eve.

My Mother's Keeper

I used to bargain with my mother. "Just stay on your medication," I would beg, "and I'll help you get a job singing at a piano bar downtown." Now, I could see her in a recreation center for elderly people, singing and playing the piano. As I saw it, she had a good ten or fifteen years left of being physically able. I wanted to help her get a part of her life back and to live it to the fullest.

Reemergence of personality would also mean, of course, a dawning awareness of what had happened to her. What would it be like, I wondered, for her to wake up one morning, look in the mirror, and recognize, perhaps for the first time, that forty years of her life had been snatched away. She was twenty-two when she went away. Would she be the same age when she returned?

Clozaril had been most effective with younger people. Jerry Frampton said that doctors didn't have much experience with older people. I was afraid my mother would be refused.

At a Clozaril workshop sponsored by Austin State Hospital, Joe and I heard about a Cleveland hospital that had established a "Rip Van Winkle" unit to deal with the sense of loss invariably experienced by the patient who responds well to Clozaril. A rock band at the hospital played strictly 1960s music since that's what the musicians remembered before they lost contact. Our friend Michael, whose brother is schizophrenic, was amused to hear his brother's 1970s-era slang when his personality reemerged.

Another doctor told us about what he called "brief periods of appropriate depression." Patients recalled frightening events that had happened during their illness, and were deeply depressed as they came to realize all they had lost. "We may have to include some old-fashioned psychotherapy for these people," he said. Although psychotherapy is futile for treating schizophrenia itself, it would be necessary for someone coming back to life after years in the limbo of mental illness.

I had to take all these considerations into account, but still,

Joe and I agreed, we had to try. For her sake, we had to see how she responded.

At first, Clozaril was prohibitively expensive for most people—about $9,000 per patient when it was introduced—since the company that manufactured and marketed it, the Sandoz Pharmaceutical Corporation, required weekly blood tests to be administered by its own personnel. Eventually, the system was modified so that physicians and other prescribers were allowed to monitor the patient's blood, thus reducing the expense. Texas was one of several states that had recently approved Medicare payment for Clozaril.

At the state-hospital conference on the drug, we learned that at the end of 1992, more than thirty thousand people in the United States were on Clozaril. Sixty percent were showing improvement, and these were people who had not done well on other medications. Clozaril is "a significant advance," a psychopharmacologist from San Antonio told the conference.

"The medicines we had available to us were not doing the job," a physician at ASH admitted. "Thirty to forty percent were not improving enough under Clozaril's predecessors to leave the hospital. The treatment team at ASH sees its job as a way station, a launching pad, to get out of the hospital and into the community to live a more satisfying life. ASH deals with the hardest cases. You can play a lot more tunes if you've got more than one string on your fiddle."

The doctor reported that out of fifteen people at ASH on Clozaril, all but two had shown clear improvement. One, he said, had not been on it long enough. The other was doing neither worse nor better.

Two, he said, had been released from the hospital and two were about to be released.

Social worker Donna Payne, who had once worked with my

mother, told about her experiences with clients on Clozaril. "I was an early skeptic," she said, "but eight months after we started, I realized there was enough of a difference that people could get out of the hospital and stay in the community. Not only did they get out, they stayed out."

After her eight years at Putnam Home, I was determined to find a place closer to Austin for my mother. I turned for help to Beth Covey, Dawn's social worker twenty years earlier and, when I contacted her, head of patient outreach for the county. Beth remembered my mother. When I told her that Dawn had basically fallen through the cracks over and over again, she resolved to make amends.

"The system failed Dawn," she said. "I want to give it a chance to really provide for her."

As one of her last projects before retiring, this slight, matter-of-fact woman set about bending a resistant system to my mother's needs. She assembled a five-person team composed of a community health worker, three social workers, and a psychiatrist. She arranged the transfer of Dawn's medical information, set up a comprehensive physical exam, and began looking for a place in or near Austin where my mother could live. Her team examined Dawn's situation from numerous angles, explored resources available to her in Austin, and considered various options—everything from hospitalization to a board-and-care facility to assisted living in her own apartment. Austin and Houston offered the most resources for the mentally ill, Beth told us.

"We certainly are using Clozaril and have seen some encouraging results," Dr. Mark Longley, the psychiatrist on Dawn's team, told us. "If they're going to respond to Clozaril, if they clear, they don't feel angry. They just feel so much better. They don't have that cloudy, muddy feeling. We start with a gradual low dose and weekly blood draws." He asked whether Dawn had any health problems and whether she had caused any problems at Putnam Home. I could tell him that she hadn't.

A couple of weeks after I first talked to Beth, she called with good news. She had found a place willing to take Dawn, a personal-care facility called Oakwood in the little Czech farming town of Granger, forty miles outside Austin. It was a good place, she assured me, clean and responsive to its residents' needs. "And Tara," Beth said, "they've got a piano." It was September 1992, and a new chapter in my mother's life was about to begin.

Betty Lee flew up to Austin from her home in Houston, and for the last time, the two of us made the two-hundred-mile drive to Athens. I had called to tell Dawn we were coming, but I don't think she had believed me when I tried to explain that she would be leaving Putnam Home. When we drove up in front of the home, she was waiting for us on the porch. I could tell she was confused. She was both happy and frightened about leaving. We helped her pack her meager belongings, she said a few awkward good-byes to her friends, and we drove away.

As we drove through the Texas countryside, Betty Lee and I tried to be cheerful and upbeat. We sang and talked, listened to jazz tapes. We even stopped at a bakery in Corsicana for coffee and doughnuts. We tried to engage Dawn, but she was quiet and withdrawn, apprehensive about what was in store. She was also prone to carsickness; four times we had to stop.

I had reserved a room for us at the Stagecoach Inn, a beautiful hotel in a historic little town called Salado, ten miles from Granger. My friend Alana, a personal-care nurse who worked at Austin Hospice for Dawn's childhood friend Peg Orem McCuistion, was waiting for us at the hotel. Accustomed to helping AIDS patients and terminally ill cancer patients with their physical needs, she welcomed us and immediately set to work getting Dawn ready for her new home.

Our comfortable room at the Stagecoach Inn had a bathroom designed for the handicapped, so it was big enough to accommodate all three of us as we worked on my mother. We started by sliding her into a relaxing hot bath. Although my mother had been required to shower regularly at Putnam Home, I had seen how the institutionalized mentally ill often take showers. The water cascades down their shoulders while they just stand there. Most attendants are reluctant to go to the trouble of helping them. I'm sure it had been years since my mother had gotten really clean.

Alana shaved my mother's legs and shampooed her hair, and once again I was surprised to see that my mother's hair was still thick and luxuriant, with gold highlights and only a few strands of gray.

I watched as Alana gave my mother a massage with herbal oils. She was a godsend. She knew how to handle Dawn, how to cradle her head when she was washing her hair, how to be gentle and reassuring. I was in awe. I had never seen anyone perform a difficult task with such proficiency and good cheer. She had a miraculous ability to put people at ease. My mother was in heaven.

I gave her a facial, plucked her eyebrows, gave her a manicure and pedicure. "I don't know who's enjoying this more, you or Dawn," Betty Lee said as she watched while I set my mother's hair with my electric rollers.

We dressed Dawn in new slippers and a white nightgown with I LOVE YOU printed inside red hearts. I ordered a meal from room service, including two rounds of celebratory gin and tonics, and after we finished eating, we said good-bye to Alana. Betty Lee and I talked late into the night. "Thank you all," my mother told us over and over. "You don't know how good this makes me feel."

I slept fitfully that night, worried that my mother might decide to leave in the middle of the night. She slept better than I did and was in good spirits the next morning. Betty Lee helped her dress in the new clothes we had brought for her, and then we had breakfast in the coffee shop. After breakfast, we strolled past the antique stores and gift shops in Salado's old limestone buildings. Crossing a grassy, sloping meadow, we came to the little creek that flows through the bucolic village. We sat on a rock under a weeping willow, near a stone replica of Hans Christian Andersen's "Little Mermaid" kneeling in the stream. The sun was shining on the water, although the summer heat had broken and the air was cool. "I love this place," my mother said with a sigh. "I don't ever want to leave."

One morning several months later, Paulette, the young psychiatric nurse who worked with Oakwood residents, picked up my mother to take her to the clinic in the nearby town of Taylor. Kind, patient, and good-humored, Paulette had become my mother's friend. Not only did this pretty, fresh-faced woman monitor my mother's health, she talked with her as one human being to another. She asked her about her singing career and talked to her about her family. Dawn enjoyed being with her. Without Paulette, she probably would not have endured being stuck in the arm with a needle once a week just because I told her she had to. I remembered the time some years earlier when she jumped out of the car as I was taking her for a blood test. She hated needles.

My mother had been on Clozaril for six months. Although she had settled into her new home, her response to the drug had not been easy. For the first few weeks, all she wanted to do was sleep, and then she stopped eating. She lost fifty-eight pounds. "It's not working," the Oakwood staff told me each time I talked to them. "We believe she should be back on Thorazine."

I knew about Thorazine. On Thorazine, Dawn would be calm and sedated. She would be cooperative and easy to handle and out of it. Any "reemergence of personality" that Clozaril might prompt would never happen with Thorazine. "Just a little while longer," I begged. Paulette was my ally. "She's very much like a sixteen-year-old with an eating disorder," she told her colleagues. "We can work with her." Later, I saw my mother's records; she was described as "anorexic" during this period.

Dawn was sitting in the passenger seat while Paulette drove to the clinic. "She had a sweater in her lap," Paulette told me that afternoon, "and she leaned down and sniffed it. She said, 'Ooh, this smells. I need to get it cleaned.' What that meant to me," Paulette said, "was that she is aware of herself and her surroundings! It was the first time I had seen it!"

The Clozaril was working. I began to notice a difference as well. I called her one day from work. "How are you feeling?" I asked.

"I feel different," she said slowly, wonderingly. "I feel alive."

It was Christmas 1993. When we dropped by Oakwood to visit with Dawn and help her open her presents, we noticed the difference immediately. She was clear and focused, attentive. She gave Pete and Kate a hug. "What did Santa Claus bring you?" she asked. She told us, shyly, that she had a boyfriend. While we talked she glanced over her shoulder to see if he had joined the cafeteria line. Minutes later, a tall, white-haired man, probably in his seventies, walked over with his tray and shook hands.

"She's definitely different," Joe commented as we drove home that evening. "You can see it in her eyes."

I was talking to my mother on the phone one day a few weeks

later. "I definitely want to stay on these pills," she said. "I think they're making a difference."

Her psychiatrist agreed. He decided to increase her dosage to the maximum safe level and combine it with Prozac to combat depression. My mother's body rebelled. She was dizzy and disoriented. She fell in the hallway at Oakwood and broke her nose. The veins in her arms collapsed, and Paulette could no longer draw blood. She began to experience persistent internal bleeding, one of several health problems that hit all at once. She had to be hospitalized.

Although not all my mother's health problems were related to Clozaril, the experiment with the "miracle drug" was suddenly over, at least for a while. Like a stage set dismantled at the end of a performance, my fantasies about a new life for my mother were dismantled. We all returned to the old reality that I had become accustomed to.

Another year passes, and I am talking to my mother on the phone. "You've got to get me out of here," she tells me in a breathless whisper she often uses when she's agitated. "It's so boring here. There's never anything to do. I just can't stand being here."

"What do you have in mind?" I ask. I would be happy for her to leave Oakwood. I would love to find her a little apartment in Austin she could share with someone. Maybe she could move into a halfway house, get a part-time job.

That's not what my mother has in mind.

"I want to be free," she says. "I want to be outdoors."

"This is October," I remind her. "It's cool at night, and it's going to get cold. Where would you stay? Where would you keep your clothes. Where would you eat? Where would you cook?"

Whether she's on Clozaril or Risperdal or whatever medication comes next, my mother seems to become clear-headed enough to become aware of what has happened to her, and then she turns away from knowing. Tantalizing fragments of her personality reveal themselves, and she seems to have some clarity about her illness. She becomes more communicative, and then it all becomes too much for her. She surrenders to her illness, or seems to. If it is a choice she is making, who can blame her?

I ran into my psychologist friend Jerry Frampton at a neighborhood bakery recently. I gave him the latest report on my mother's condition. He filled me in on the latest in psychotropics and how they're being combined these days with antidepressants. We talked an insider's mental-illness jargon. "What you have to remember," Jerry said, "is that Dawn's story is to be continued." If there is progress in the coming years, he reminded me, it will be slow, with frequent setbacks.

He's right, of course. I can only look forward to the next drug breakthrough, the newest research insights, the next social worker who will connect with my mother.

I realize that what I want for my mother these days is not all that different from what many of us want for friends and relatives who are ill. I have friends battling cancer or AIDS. I know families trying to do what's best for aging parents, for relatives with Alzheimer's. We're all trying to cope. I would hope to offer them what I could have used during the most difficult years. I want to be there for conversation, for assistance, for advice.

In my hectic dual-career, blended-family, typical 1990s life, I revel in the simple pleasures of this family that is my own, one so different from the family I knew as a child. My days are full of the details that drive all mothers . . . well, not crazy, but to the brink of despair. Socks without mates on school mornings; "Mom! Mom!" yelled hundreds of times from morning to night; stand-up comedy routines

Tara Elgin Holley with Joe Holley
344

worthy of Jim Carrey performed by miniature comedians consigned to bed hours earlier, all going on exactly six hours before I have to get up to make lunches and breakfast and prepare for a 7:00 A.M. breakfast meeting, where I will sit across a table from an Austin executive and try to persuade him that he ought to contribute $100,000 toward a new downtown museum for the city.

But there are nights—it seems they are always cold nights—when I vaguely hear Pete wander up the stairs and into our bedroom, find a favorite blanket, and curl up on the Victorian couch at the foot of our bed. Kate follows, almost sleepwalking; like a long-legged puppy, she burrows under the covers between Joe and me. I'm more asleep than awake, but I am clearly aware of a deep feeling of ease, contentment. I am grateful beyond words for this grace and these gifts in my life.

On Dawn's sixty-fifth birthday not long ago, I got up early and drove to Oakwood to help her get ready for the party we had planned at our house in Austin. It was a Saturday, and as I drove through the Central Texas countryside, I had time to think about the long journey my mother and I have traveled, indeed continue to travel, together. I thought of so many things I would have done differently, had I known to. I would have relied on others much more extensively, and I would have been more willing to share the ordeal of coping with mental illness. I would have sought out others who were going through the same torment my mother and I were experiencing. "This is a disease!" we would shout to the world. "There's nothing to be ashamed of."

I thought about how I had finally come to accept my own limitations. I've had so many people say, "I just couldn't bear it," when I mention my mother's condition, and sometimes I can't, either.

Sometimes I leave my mother after a particularly good visit, and I resolve to see her at least once a week; other times, I walk away thinking that if this is what it takes to maintain a relationship with my mother, I'm just not up to it. I can never make things right, and it makes no difference to her, anyway. In years past, I would have felt intense guilt about not seeing Dawn regularly.

Now, I realize that the only way to balance my mother's needs with the needs of my own family and myself is to go away for a while. I go away, so that I can come back replenished.

As I drove, I thought about how well I know my mother, although not the way other daughters know theirs. Mothers and daughters prepare meals together. They share shoes and clothes and recipes. They sit at the kitchen table with cups of coffee, and they talk about men and relationships and life.

That's not the way I know my mother. I know the wave in her hair near her ear. I know the smell of her urine-soaked clothes. I have washed her body and shaved her legs and lavished lotion on her skin, desperately trying to make her acceptable to public view. I know the sag at her waist, the result of two births, both unexpected. I know the dirty scalp beneath a mass of beautiful honey-golden hair. I know the expressive and unmanicured brow, the heavy ankles and fleshy arms, the result of forty years of neglect and despair.

My mother is schizophrenic. What a clumsy and difficult word it is. It is meaningless. "Does Dawn know?" Sister has asked. "I hope to God she doesn't." But of course she knows. She knows that her life was taken from her.

I was pleased that Sister and Betty Lee would be with us later in the day for the celebration. As different as Sister and Betty Lee are from each other, I admire both of them for who they are. I understand in ways that I didn't understand when I was younger how much Dawn's illness had affected them. I wish they had taken me into their confidence much earlier. We could have been a good team—and perhaps still can be. We're trying.

I thought of Sally, the sister Dawn was closest to when the two were young. Of my three aunts, Sally is probably the one I'm closest to as well. In a way she's been a surrogate mother to me, and yet she cannot bear to see the condition her sister has been in all these years. She would not join us for Dawn's party. It's been years since she has seen Dawn.

I drove through the faded little farming town of Granger, crossed the creek, and turned on Alligator Road. My mother was waiting under the portico when I got to Oakwood. She waved as I drove up. I went inside with her and helped her get ready. I had called Oakwood the day before and requested that her hair be shampooed. I quickly heated up my hot rollers for her shoulder-length hair and set it the way I had seen it done in her Hollywood photos from the 1940s. I helped her put on the new clothes I had bought for her—a southwestern denim skirt, a white Gypsy blouse with ruffled sleeves, silver hoop earrings and necklace, and new white sandals. My mother always loves new things, especially if they are youthful looking and stylish. When someone gives her something that looks like an old lady would wear, she tries to be polite, but it's hard for her to conceal her distaste. "Well," she'll say, "it's not something I would have chosen," or "It's not really me."

I watched as she smiled at her image in the mirror. I thought of the spunk that still popped up unexpectedly, the spirit that still has not been totally broken. I thought of the dry humor, the sarcasm, the musicality, that are still part of the rich and complex fabric of my mother's personality. I thought of the insurgencies she still waged for scraps of independence.

That's my mother, I was thinking, the woman who loved me as best she could. Suddenly, I knew what I had to tell her on this, her sixty-fifth birthday. You are a hero to me, I wanted her to know. You're one of my models. I admire you more than you'll ever know.

That's what I wanted to say, but instead I launched into a series of housekeeping questions to fend off the emotions that are always with me, just below the surface. "Have you been going to the clubhouse?" I asked her as we drove back to Austin. Oakwood has a small, frame house in a nearby town where residents get together for classes, hobbies, envelope stuffing for good causes, and parties. I very much wanted Dawn to be taking part.

"I haven't been going," she said. "I don't like riding in a car, and it's usually a little boring for my tastes."

I smiled and bit my tongue.

"Car," my mother mumbled. "Car. Carnation. Car. Nation. United Nations."

Listening to her, I realized yet again that people who suffer from schizophrenia don't suffer from a dulling of the senses. They constantly deal with sensory overload. They don't have the subconscious censoring devices that most of use to block out the irrelevant stimuli that would otherwise overwhelm us.

Words and word play continue to intrigue her. Dawn was telling Joe one day about a trip she made to Boston, apparently when she was living in New York just before I was born. "I wanted to visit the Mother Church," she told Joe. "I had Mother on my mind." She smiled wryly. "Now, I don't have a mother or a mind."

"Have you seen your social worker lately?" I asked. She said she hadn't.

"It's important that you talk to your psychiatrist or social worker," I said.

She burst into song. "Hap, hap, happy talk, keep talkin' happy talk."

I answered, "Talk about things you like to do."

"You gotta have a dream, if you don't have a dream . . ."

Tara Elgin Holley with Joe Holley
348

"How're you gonna have a dream come true?" I sang, laughing. "I don't really like that song," I said as I pulled onto the interstate. "Of all the songs from *South Pacific*, that's not my favorite one."

"Which one do you like best?" Dawn asked.

" 'Younger than Springtime,' " I said. "I love the way you do that one."

When we got back to Austin just before noon, Joe welcomed my mother into our home, now filled with friends and relatives waiting to wish her a happy birthday. As I ushered her into the living room, Pete and Kate were waiting with presents. Sister and Betty Lee had driven up from Houston. They exclaimed about the outfit she was wearing and how nice she looked.

Peg Orem McCuistion and her twin sister, Ann, the childhood friends who listened to Dawn sing on the radio a half century ago, had come to wish their old friend a happy birthday. The three women hadn't seen each other since they were fifteen.

Alana, the wonderful woman who helped get Dawn ready for Oakwood, gave her a big hug and presents. Paulette, the psychiatric nurse, had driven in from Taylor with her husband. "So few of my patients have families, I wanted him to see how it should be," she said. Beth Covey, the social worker who had done so much to get the system to respond to Dawn's needs, had dropped by. Now retired, she and her husband were planning to move to their lake house in North Texas. As we visited, Rich Harney, a jazz pianist friend of mine, played old favorites from the 1940s. ("I remember Dawn on the Drag," Rich mentioned to Joe later. "I never knew she was Tara's mother.")

We trooped into the dining room, and Kate led us in singing "Happy Birthday." Dawn blew out the candles as everyone cheered. She was quiet, a bit embarrassed by all the attention, but she seemed pleased.

"Dawn, you've got to sing for us!" Peg McCuistion urged. "You can't imagine what a beautiful voice this woman has," she told Alana. Peg's sister Ann recounted the story of how she and Peg as children lay in bed and listened to Dawn on the radio.

Listening to the sisters, I realized how much I appreciate Peg, whom I've gotten to know over the past couple of years. Every day of her life, she works with terminally ill people and their families, and yet she may be the most upbeat and happy person I know—perhaps because of her work. She looks at Dawn and sees beneath the outward signs of illness the beautiful young woman she had known so many years earlier. So what if Dawn had changed since she had last seen her? We all change, Peg reminds us.

My mother is shy and reluctant to perform, but at last we get her to sit down at the piano. Immediately, she launches into "Malagueña." She is playing from memory, but as her hands range up and down the keyboard, the ornaments and lush embellishments fill the room with rich, rippling sound.

"It's the same old Dawn!" Peg exclaims, clapping her hands and smiling. "The same beautiful Dawn."

My mother finishes "Malagueña" and looks up at me. I slide in beside her on the piano bench and open sheet music to a song we both love. "Younger than springtime am I," she begins to sing as I play, "sweeter than music are you." Her voice is tentative at first, but when I join in—"angel and lover, heaven and earth, are you to me . . ."—her voice grows stronger. Shoulders touching, voices blending, we sing the song together.

It has been a good day, and my mother is tired as I drive her back to Granger. At Oakwood, I take her inside and help her get ready for bed. I go through my normal routine—checking the condition of her clothes, discussing her medication with a staff member, making sure she has spending money. "Now, don't you keep this in your bra," I remind her, handing her some bills. "You let the office keep it for you, okay?" She enjoys being a wheeler-dealer, selling cigarettes and swapping watches, and sometimes her money and her things have a way of disappearing.

I ask her what she wants, tell her what she needs. I ask myself whether I'm really listening to what she's telling me, whether I've complimented her on how well she did with everyone at her party. I hold her close and tight, for a long time.

"When can I see you again?" she asks like a forlorn lover, like a child being left at camp. "Two weeks? Three weeks? Ten days?" She laughs sheepishly.

"Soon," I assure her. "I'll see you as soon as I can, but I've got a lot of kid stuff to do during spring break."

A few days later, I am trailing along behind Kate while we shop for school clothes at a local mall. I watch her golden brown ringlets bouncing atop her perfect little shoulders as she skips along singing to herself. Kate, like most children, enjoys a rich interior life. She calls her language Chinese or Japanese, though much of it is borrowed from Jieun, Youngsuk, and Jiyoon, her three Korean kindergarten friends.

Her distance from me in the mall is a reminder that she is oblivious to my anxiety about losing her. She has no idea that a mother and daughter can be inseparable one day and torn apart the next. For that I am thankful. I catch up with her, touch her shoulder, and remind myself yet again not to squelch her sense of adventure and independence.

"I love you, Katie," I say, taking her by the hand. "More than anything."

She looks up and grins. "You are the best mommy," she says, "my only mommy, for ever and ever."

I know what she means.

My Mother's Keeper

Stars in her eyes—Dawn, 1946.

EPILOGUE
—Joe Holley

As for me, you must know I shouldn't precisely have chosen madness if there had been any choice. What consoles me is that I am beginning to consider madness as an illness like any other, and that I accept it as such.
  —Vincent van Gogh, from a letter to his brother Theo, 1889

The disease that took away the Dawn of so much hope and promise continues to devastate and mystify. In any given year, according to the National Institute of Mental Health, nearly 3 million Americans over age eighteen suffer from schizophrenia; 300,000 new cases are diagnosed each year. This madness in our midst is more common than either multiple sclerosis, muscular dystrophy, cystic fibrosis, or Alzheimer's disease. Despite efforts to encourage community living, 30 percent of the hospital beds in this country are occupied by schizophrenia patients.

Schizophrenia is also an equal-opportunity disease. It occurs in all cultures, all races, and all socioeconomic groups. It tends to affect men earlier in life than it does women and tends to be more destructive in men. About one in three women diagnosed as schizophrenic will return to something approaching normalcy, but only one in five males will.

An estimated 360,000 people with schizophrenia live in state hospitals, halfway houses, subsidized hotels, or group homes. Many thousands more—perhaps as many as 200,000—live on the streets or in homeless shelters.

The disease continues to mystify medical science as well. For example, recent studies suggest that the prevalence of schizophrenia in the United States has increased in recent years. No one can say for sure whether that's the case, or why.

Despite promising advances in understanding how it affects the mind, scientists still don't know what causes the disease. There's no clinical test for schizophrenia; it doesn't show up in the urine or the blood. It's diagnosed only by its symptoms. It could be a single disease, or it might be several related diseases. Some researchers theorize that it is some kind of brain deficit that might even be latent from gestation, to be activated years later.

At Cornell University Medical School, brain scan pictures taken while a patient is hallucinating show activity in specific areas of the brain, both on the surface and deep in the interior. When a patient "hears voices," an entire brain circuit seems to be activated that is fundamentally different from where and how normal thought processes take place. These findings, however tentative, could help researchers plan new medications and modes of treatment.

Could. May. Who knows? The conditional continues to prevail even in the highest reaches of brain research. "Psychiatry is still pretty much in the Dark Ages," Dr. David Curtis of the Institute of Psychiatry in London commented recently. "We have no idea about the basic biochemical abnormalities that occur in the course of the illness." (*NYT*, 10/31/95, B7)

Evidence for a genetic contribution to schizophrenia is compelling, although the connection between genes and the disease itself remains murky. Among identical twins, if one gets the disease, the other will not get it about 50 percent of the time. In about one in ten cases, the children of a schizophrenic parent will get the disease, but two thirds of the time, it afflicts people with no history of the disease.

Dr. Irving Gottesman, a geneticist at the University of Virginia, has suggested that in the cases of twins, the healthy twin may be carrying some predisposing genes for the disease, even if they're not activated. Gottesman has also proposed that some life experience triggers the illness in those genetically predisposed to get the disease.

Dr. E. Fuller Torrey, a senior psychiatrist at St. Elizabeth's Hospital in Washington, D.C., and a world-renowned expert on the viral theory of schizophrenia, believes that the illness is the result of the combination of a genetic predisposition and a viral trigger of some sort that injures the brain. He has compared it with breast cancer in women and bowel cancer in men, in the sense that some people are born with a predisposition to the disease. If they are exposed to a certain environmental factor, they get the disease; if not, they don't get it.

Factors such as lack of oxygen in the womb or head injuries later on also may contribute to the onset of schizophrenia. Torrey notes that a somewhat disproportionate number of schizophrenics are born in late winter, when viruses are more prevalent. He also notes that schizophrenia is more common among those who were in utero during influenza epidemics.

The latest research suggests that a gene on the upper arm of chromosome 6—out of the twenty-three pairs of chromosomes we all have—may play a role in some cases. The chain of evidence remains tantalizingly elusive, and scientists are still a long way from isolating a particular gene. Even if they isolate a gene and it proves to be a factor in some cases of schizophrenia, it will never be as clearly connected as the Huntington's gene is with Huntington's disease. Any one gene plays only a minor part in the cacophonous music of madness.

More people seem aware these days that schizophrenia is a biological disease of the brain, but that awareness still has not erased the stigma of mental illness. Most people, I would guess, know that the onset of schizophrenia has nothing to do with personality flaws or weaknesses of character, but if you have to tell people that someone in your family has been diagnosed as schizophrenic, it's still somehow vaguely shameful. Somehow, they—or their family—are to be blamed for the illness.

Too often, schizophrenia remains a family secret. At a time when family members are most in need of help and encouragement, they hold their terrifying secret close. They know the stigma is lasting. It will stain job applications and insurance coverage, friendships, and future relations. It will affect the way a person is perceived, perhaps for the rest of his or her life.

Studies conducted by the National Institute of Mental Health (NIMH) have found that most Americans think that the two worst things that can happen to a person are leprosy and insanity. In this country, ex-convicts are more readily accepted than former mental patients. Asked to rank twenty-one categories of disability,

Tara Elgin Holley with Joe Holley

respondents placed mental illness as the most offensive. According to one study, nearly everyone regards the mentally ill as "fundamentally tainted and degraded" (from "Plain Talk About the Stigma of Mental Illness," produced by the National Institute of Mental Health, office of Scientific Information, 1990).

Those with mental disorders are dangerous, many people believe, perhaps because they are perceived as unpredictable. We've all seen madmen, eyes glaring, brandishing knives on TV. The truth is that the behavior of former mental patients is, almost invariably, no different from that of the rest of society. The truth is that people who have experienced the storm of emotional and mental disturbances are usually anxious, passive, and fearful, not dangerous.

Misunderstanding mental illness—or refusing to face the facts—results in enormous costs to society, including lost work, reduced productivity, and prison recidivism. Although it's difficult to calculate the direct costs of schizophrenia, according to NIMH, the number of persons with mental illness among the homeless is an estimated 200,000 to 350,000 persons. A recent NIMH study found that more than 37,000 mentally ill men and women are in jails, most charged with simple misdemeanors such as loitering or trespassing. Nearly one third had not been charged with any crime; they had been arrested on "mercy bookings," because access to mental health care is restricted or denied.

The stigma also manifests in more subtle ways—in insurance coverage, for example. HMOs typically cover the costs of treatment for nonpsychiatric (or physical) illnesses in full, or with minimum patient contribution, but they exclude or limit coverage of the treatment of mental (or psychiatric) illnesses. In the words of a report from the National Alliance for the Mentally Ill

(NAMI): "Schizophrenia and severe depressive illness are essentially viewed by private industry and government as second-class illnesses in this country."

As NAMI points out, mandating health insurance coverage for the severe mental illnesses would slow the rapidly growing costs of Medicaid, Supplemental Security Income (SSI), and Supplemental Security Disability Income (SSDI), since the mentally ill are the largest single group among those now covered. It would also stem the tide of mentally ill persons who end up in jails, emergency rooms, and overcrowded homeless shelters.

Even though schizophrenia is still an illness that sweeps through a person's life like a devastating storm, there is some good news to report. Federal research funds for the disease have increased in recent years, and knowledge about how to treat brain-related disorders, including schizophrenia, has increased exponentially. Despite the increases, funds for research into schizophrenia still lag behind other areas of research.

We now know better how to cope than when Tara was trying to deal with her mother's illness as a teenager and young woman. For one thing, we've learned that some people, particularly young people, experience a single episode of schizophrenia; with close attention and appropriate medication, they can recover. They go to school, they hold down jobs, they marry and have children. According to NAMI, the treatment success rate for schizophrenia is 60 percent. Early detection and treatment are critical.

For another thing, a second generation of medications that act to balance nerve transmitters—among them Clozaril and Risperdal—are achieving remarkable results for many suffering from schizophrenia, particularly younger people. Even more effective medications are in the research pipeline. They're not cures, but they offer the hope of happier, more productive lives for people who have been battling a disease that robs them of their very being.

Support groups have become vital tools for combatting the stigma of mental illness and the misinformation that's still prevalent. To share one's experience is to invite others to share theirs. When people who have confronted mental illness, either personally or in a family member, come out of the shadows, they find strength and solace. They realize they don't have to bear their burden alone; by speaking about their experience, they can change public perception. People will come to know that mental illness is common and that no one is beyond help.

Support groups are an important resource for family members, not only for the emotional support they offer but also for exchanging useful information about dealing with legal matters, the service delivery system, and situations at home.

Support groups can be advocacy groups as well; they offer a vehicle for educating policymakers and the general public about employment opportunities, housing needs, and changes in the law that would make the difficulties of mental illness easier to bear. NAMI and its state and local affiliates, as well as the work of state and local groups of mental-health consumers, do immensely impressive work. Struggling with a cumbersome, bureaucratic mental health system, these groups tirelessly help the mentally ill move toward independence and recovery or, if not recovery, survival and dignity. They press public officials for funding that will lead to a cure, for public services that meet the needs of the mentally ill among us.

There is no question that those services are distressingly inadequate. "We are so used to the mediocre services," E. Fuller Torrey says, "that we forget how bad they are."

For Tara and me, the dawning awareness of the value of support groups came as we took part in a seminar sponsored by our local mental health–mental retardation agency for the families of schizophrenics. The leader of our seminar was a counselor in his mid-thirties named Jerry Frampton with a gift for focusing completely on the person he's talking to. He patiently answered our every question, helped us understand that we weren't the only ones bearing the burden of a mentally ill relative. He offered useful information about what it feels like to be schizophrenic, what family members can do when their schizophrenic loved one is angry or anxious or depressed, what services are available—information, in short, for making our lives and the difficult lives of our loved ones easier.

Two dozen of us gathered every Tuesday evening for two hours. The young woman with three children of her own told us about her efforts to obtain custody of her younger sister's three-year-old child. The sister, who had been diagnosed as schizophrenic as a teenager, had been estranged from her family for years, lived on the street in Kansas City, and didn't want to give up her child. We listened as an elderly couple told of all the years they had cared for their son, now forty, and their fear that when they were gone, he would be locked away in an institution. The young parents of a fourteen-year-old boy exhibiting schizoid symptoms told of their fears that he was getting into drugs, possibly as a way to escape the voices and delusions. One woman, reserved, well dressed, probably in her mid-fifties, calmly told of caring for her schizophrenic son and her schizophrenic father.

"Keep in mind that everything you're experiencing is legitimate," Jerry Frampton often reminded us. "You've been through hell. But also keep in mind that whatever you're experiencing pales in comparison to what the person with the disease is going through."

We sat in a large circle. As I looked around the room at these people, strangers who knew exactly what Tara had experienced, what her mother had suffered, I could feel the strength they were getting from the group. For people tired, angry, fed up with facing the unrelenting nightmare unleashed by a change in brain chemistry, Jerry's words and the presence of others were a balm.

We had stories and experiences to share with each other, and questions, hundreds of questions, for our leader and the experts he brought to the ten-week class. On other evenings, Jerry counseled schizophrenics and manic-depressives in self-help groups of their own.

A college student in the class wanted to know about a street person she passed every day on the way to school. "He's obviously mentally ill," she said, "and every time I see him he has on just layers and layers of clothes. It doesn't matter if it's a hundred degrees out. Why do they do that?"

"Well, there's a practical reason," Jerry said. "He doesn't have a closet to store his stuff; it's easier just to carry everything he owns with him. But the other reason is that people suffering from schizophrenia are detached from feelings of heat and cold. In some ways, they're detached from their physical selves."

"My son has delusions about the FBI, the CIA," a woman commented. "He thinks they're in the TV and that they're coming after him. What is that all about?"

"Those paranoid delusions are real as far as he's concerned," Jerry said. "Whether it's the FBI, the CIA, terrorists, someone controlling their thoughts—paranoid schizophrenics have no doubt that people are out to get them. Maybe someone's trying to implant a device in their body. Maybe that person sitting across the room and laughing is laughing at them. Most of the delusions are logical outgrowths of what the person's brain is experiencing. It has to do with an overacuteness of the senses. The brain can't interpret. It can't respond to the flood of stimuli the way a normal brain does."

I could see heads nodding, smiles of recognition. We may not have heard the voices, but we certainly knew how our family members responded to those voices, and how frustrating it was to try to discuss what they believed.

"But what do I do when he comes out with these things?" the woman wanted to know.

"Well, there's no use arguing with him," Jerry said. "You can't talk your son out of his symptoms. What you can do is disagree without arguing. Simply state your view of things and drop it. If you can respond to the emotion that may be fueling the hallucination, that can be helpful, too. You can tell him that he has nothing to fear. Or you can let him know you'll be there to make sure he's all right."

Sometimes we could only laugh. What else can you do when you hear about a patient who collected the souls of departed spirits in a plastic bag, letting them out once a day to exercise? At least, he had them under control.

"We're built to respond to crisis in short-term situations," Jerry said. "Schizophrenia goes on and on. No weekends, no holidays, no time off, ever." Tara and most others in the group knew exactly what he was talking about.

We learned about resources and family support services I never knew existed, and I don't think Tara did, either. They probably didn't exist a decade earlier. In a program called family-respite care, the state's mental health–mental retardation agency sends trained providers to give families two- to six-hour breaks, up to three times a week. We learned about one patient who had not been out of the house for five years but was now going out regularly with the family-respite provider.

We heard about men and women suffering from schizophrenia who were managing to function on their own. One group of four in Austin was living together in a leased house and had organized their own business, a janitorial service. They cleaned office buildings at night. One of them had told Jerry about how one of his cleaning partners began hallucinating on the job one night. "You don't have time to talk to those voices," his partners told him. "You've got work to do," they told him. "You tell those voices to leave you alone." As every schizophrenic knows, the voices are indefatigable and overpowering, but through a tremendous act of will, this young man managed to tune them out.

Much has changed in the years since a young, gifted woman in Hollywood began to wage her lonely, desperate battle with the voices causing havoc in her mind. Effective treatments—treatments that are continually being improved through ongoing research—now make it possible for many mentally ill people to lead satisfying and productive lives at home, at work, and in the community. Although community-based care is usually spotty and inadequate, establishing a comprehensive network of community mental health centers, psychosocial rehabilitation programs, and assisted-living arrangements remains the goal. One day, every person learning to live with severe mental illness will be able to find services and treatment in the community. And some day, researchers will find the key to either prevent or cure schizophrenia and other diseases of the brain. No one will have to experience what Dawn has experienced.

Meanwhile, we bow to fate. For Tara and her aunts, for all those who care deeply about Dawn, that doesn't mean giving up or turning away. It doesn't mean losing hope. I know Tara. I know she'll never give up searching for the most promising medication, the most effective therapy for her mother, but at the same time she acknowledges the rock-hard fact that many of Dawn's difficulties will not be solved, ever. It means accepting the human condition. We will not know the golden Dawn her sisters and her childhood friends remember with such affection; we will not know the accomplished person she would have been except for the illness.

We accept the experience and all it entails. We accept Dawn as she is. We love her for who she is at this moment, not who she was or who she could have been. It's a delicate balance between hoping for the richest, fullest life possible for the person we love and accepting what is.

Perhaps it's easier to describe than explain:

I have come to understand that even when a person is psychotic, a part of the brain is not psychotic. The person with schizophrenia sees, hears, knows, and feels—perhaps even more acutely at times than the rest of us do. Every time I'm with Dawn, I sense that she's watching, assessing, taking in what's happening around her, and yet she either isn't able or doesn't choose to share with me, or with anyone else, more than disconnected fragments of what she's experiencing. I can't even say how much she knows, or wants to know, about her illness. Tara and I have longed for her to tell more of this story, her story, but we haven't been able to find the key that would unlock the rich flow of reminiscence. Perhaps it's too painful, or it may be that she's just not able.

I drop by Oakwood one morning and find Dawn on the patio outside. She is sitting, bent over and looking down at the ground,

Tara Elgin Holley with Joe Holley

in a lawn chair apart from the other residents. She is smoking a cigarette. The cigarette butts scattered around her feet suggest she's been sitting in her little patio hideaway a pretty good while. When she sees me, and it registers with her who I am, she smiles. She stands and gives me a hug. We walk inside.

"Can I buy you a Coke?" she asks. We stroll into the clean and sterile, brightly lit dining room, and she pulls two quarters out of her blouse pocket and drops them into the machine. The bright red can clatters down to the mouth of the machine.

We sit at a table, and in her characteristic breathy whisper she asks about Pete, Kate, and Tara. She probably wonders why I have come alone to visit her, but she is too polite to ask. I have so many things I want to know about her life and about what she experiences now, but I'm always careful not to interrogate. I think of the writer Janet Malcolm and her claim that every journalist is a confidence man preying on people's vanity, ignorance, or loneliness, gaining their trust and betraying them. With Dawn, I want to be a son-in-law, nothing more. If she chooses to confide in me, then I'll be happy to listen. I'll feel privileged.

A dozen or so of her fellow residents are lining up at the door that leads to the cafeteria line. It's almost noon, so we join the line. "Is Dawn your girlfriend?" a blond-haired woman apparently in her forties wants to know. She peers intently at me through thick glasses. Dawn and I glance at each other and laugh, and I explain who I am.

Minutes later, over a bland lunch of ground meat slathered in brown gravy, carrots and peas, and Jell-O, she mentions that Betty Lee has been to see her a few days earlier. "She came up with Bob," she says. "You know Bob? We went on a picnic."

I knew Bob. Bob Kuldell had been Betty Lee's special friend and frequent companion for many years. Bob is a saxophone player and big-band veteran who still plays for charity functions around Houston. He remembers hearing Dawn sing in Houston clubs fifty years ago, "with Ted Fiorita's band," he told me not long ago. Ted Fiorita was yet another name in Dawn's musical past, a name I'd never heard.

I called Betty Lee, and she filled in the details for me. She and Bob, she explained, had made the two-hundred-mile drive from Houston in Bob's roomy old Cadillac. On the way to Granger, Bob and Betty Lee had stopped at Elgin, the town named for Dawn's and Betty Lee's grandfather, and bought picnic supplies, including ice cream and the town's famous Elgin Hot Sausage. They picked up Dawn and drove to a small lake nearby where they could find shade and a picnic shelter to ward off the late-summer Texas heat.

"Dawn sang for us as we drove," Betty Lee said. " 'Somewhere there's music, how faint the tune/somewhere there's heaven, how high the moon.' She was perfectly on pitch."

I know the little rural park where they picnicked. I can see Bob's blue Cadillac as it cruises like a big boat down a narrow country road, a road that parts rolling blackland fields bursting with fluffy white cotton. Just past an old, one-lane wooden bridge over a sluggish brown creek, Bob turns into the park area and pulls up beside a picnic shelter at the edge of a small lake. In the middle of the lake, ghostly gray branches of dead trees protrude out of the grayish-brown water. Betty Lee and Dawn carry the picnic basket to the table, and Bob hauls out his electronic keyboard. The parched grass crunches underfoot.

While Betty Lee makes sandwiches, Bob flips a switch on the keyboard. The tinny programmed sounds of Mitch Miller quiet the droning whir of cicadas in the scrub oaks along the shore. Tall, silver-haired and distinguished, Bob ambles over to Dawn, bows low, and holds out his hand. She smiles shyly and steps into his arms.

I can see the two of them as they swing and twirl and sway across a concrete slab. They are smiling, and so is Betty Lee as she watches her baby sister and her old friend. Behind them, the water shimmers. For a little while, for the three of them, there is no illness, no nagging insistent voices inside Dawn's head. The years lost, the wells of longing and regret—for a while they are forgotten. There is music on this hot summer day, music and affection and acceptance of what is. For a little while, Dawn is dancing.